A Reader's Companion to *The Prince, Leviathan*, and the *Second Treatise*

John T. Bookman

A Reader's Companion to *The Prince*, *Leviathan*, and the *Second Treatise*

palgrave
macmillan

John T. Bookman
Department of Political Science
University of Northern Colorado
Greeley, CO, USA

ISBN 978-3-030-02879-4   ISBN 978-3-030-02880-0   (eBook)
https://doi.org/10.1007/978-3-030-02880-0

Library of Congress Control Number: 2018962972

© The Editor(s) (if applicable) and The Author(s), under exclusive licence to Springer Nature Switzerland AG 2019
This work is subject to copyright. All rights are solely and exclusively licensed by the Publisher, whether the whole or part of the material is concerned, specifically the rights of translation, reprinting, reuse of illustrations, recitation, broadcasting, reproduction on microfilms or in any other physical way, and transmission or information storage and retrieval, electronic adaptation, computer software, or by similar or dissimilar methodology now known or hereafter developed.
The use of general descriptive names, registered names, trademarks, service marks, etc. in this publication does not imply, even in the absence of a specific statement, that such names are exempt from the relevant protective laws and regulations and therefore free for general use.
The publisher, the authors, and the editors are safe to assume that the advice and information in this book are believed to be true and accurate at the date of publication. Neither the publisher nor the authors or the editors give a warranty, express or implied, with respect to the material contained herein or for any errors or omissions that may have been made. The publisher remains neutral with regard to jurisdictional claims in published maps and institutional affiliations.

Cover illustration: iStock / Getty Images Plus
Cover design: Fatima Jamadar

This Palgrave Macmillan imprint is published by the registered company Springer Nature Switzerland AG
The registered company address is: Gewerbestrasse 11, 6330 Cham, Switzerland

To Andra, Leah, Jessica, and Rachel and in memory of Barbara A. Colgan

PREFACE

The Prince, *Leviathan*, and the *Second Treatise* mark a significant turning point in the history of political philosophy. Unlike their ancient and medieval predecessors, Machiavelli, Hobbes, and Locke are not concerned with human excellence. They do not make the best way of life a part of their philosophical enterprise. For them, the preservation of life itself is the more pressing problem. If life is to be preserved, people need strong, stable government. And there can be no strong, stable government without the obedience of those subject to it. Thus, the problem of political obligation displaced the quest for human excellence.

The problem raises a perennial question or set of questions: Why are we obligated to obey a government? Are there limits on that obligation? To whom or what is obedience due? These are questions about which political philosophers and ordinary citizens have argued ever since the ancient Greeks. Machiavelli, Hobbes, and Locke made them the central concern of political philosophy. Over recent decades, the politics of identity has acquired prominence in theory and practice. Identity now commands the attention and elicits the passion reserved for political obligation in the 1960s and 1970s. Heightened recognition of the importance of identity has inspired the deconstruction of canonical texts like *The Prince*, *Leviathan*, and the *Second Treatise*. Such deconstruction aims at unmasking philosophers like Machiavelli, Hobbes, and Locke as apologists for the domination of society by white, affluent, educated males. They certainly shared many of the prejudices of their age with regard to gender, race, class, and status.

vii

viii PREFACE

This book does not ignore difference. Whenever they assume exclusion or prescribe disabilities based on gender, race, class, or status, I bring that to the attention of the reader. This book is not, however, a project in deconstruction. It proceeds from the assumption that Machiavelli, Hobbes, and Locke may have something to teach us about the problem with which they were principally concerned and which remains a significant problem to the present day—the problem of political obligation.

This companion seeks to bring the reader to a fuller understanding of *The Prince*, *Leviathan*, and the *Second Treatise*. The reader who undertakes a serious study of these works will find especially helpful the commentaries which begin where he or she begins—on page one. Every step of the way arguments are unpacked, concepts analyzed, references identified, archaic words defined, and questions asked. Those questions encourage the reader to do a little political philosophy on her own: Is it necessary to acquire "dirty hands," as Machiavelli contends, in order to govern? Is Hobbes's state of nature more revelatory of human nature than civil society? Do we consent, and in what sense, to the institution of civil society? The commentaries aim at a systematic, informed, and sensitive explication of *The Prince*, *Leviathan*, and the *Second Treatise*. The final chapter engages Machiavelli, Hobbes, and Locke in a critical way. How successful are they in solving the problem of political obligation? I suggest an alternative solution to that they propose.

Many others have labored in the fields turned over once again in this book. The bibliographic essays are testimony to the efforts of those earlier scholars. My debt to them is great indeed. I am indebted as well to my colleagues at the University of Northern Colorado, Bill Agan and John Loftis, who helped to clarify my thinking about textual interpretation and who read with a critical eye one or another chapter; to Michelle Chen, my editor at Palgrave Macmillan, for her support of the book; and to Denise Connell for getting the manuscript ready for publication. I thank, too, the anonymous readers at Palgrave Macmillan for their comments. Any obscurity and error that remain are my responsibility alone.

Greeley, CO, USA   John T. Bookman

CONTENTS

1   Introduction: Historical Context and Textual
Interpretation   1

2   *The Prince*   19
    Machiavelli (1469–1527): A Brief Sketch of His Life   19
    The Prince: *A Commentary*   27
    A Bibliographical Essay   45
    A Select Bibliography of Works in English   53

3   *Leviathan*   65
    Hobbes (1588–1679): A Brief Sketch of His Life   65
    Leviathan: *A Commentary*   77
    A Bibliographical Essay   111
    A Select Bibliography of Works in English   125

4   The *Second Treatise*   139
    Locke (1632–1704): A Brief Sketch of His Life   139
    Second Treatise: *A Commentary*   156
    A Bibliographical Essay   182
    A Select Bibliography of Works in English   192

5   A Critique   205

CHAPTER 1

Introduction: Historical Context and Textual Interpretation

The ancient and medieval understanding of politics came out of a concern for human excellence. The basic questions addressed were: What is human excellence (alternatively, what is the best way of life for humankind) and does the state contribute to the realization of human excellence? Plato and Aristotle believe that human excellence can be discerned by reason—by reflection on the kind of creatures that we are and in conversation with others who also seek to know.[1] In the course of his inquiry, Plato likens the human psyche to a charioteer driving two horses.[2] A black horse on the left represents the appetitive, the part that desires physical satisfaction and bodily ease but also love and friendship. The desires are not to be ignored. The psyche inhabits a body (the chariot). The desires have a place, indeed cannot be denied a place, in a life of *human* excellence. A white horse on the right represents spirit, the part that feels indignation in the face of moral wrong when it obeys the charioteer and anger at the thwarting of desire when it sides with the black horse. The charioteer represents reason, the part that seeks to guide the horses and chariot to truth, beauty, and justice.[3] There is constant struggle between the charioteer and the horses

[1] Plato, *The Republic*, Bk. VII: 532a-534e and Aristotle, *Nicomachean Ethics*, I. 12: 1102a13-26.

[2] *Phaedrus*, 246a-254e.

[3] Cf. Aristotle, *Nicomachean Ethics*, III, 12: 1119b3-16 and *The Politics*, I, 7: 1254b2-16; and VII, 14:1333a16-23.

© The Author(s) 2019
J. T. Bookman, *A Reader's Companion to* The Prince, Leviathan, *and the* Second Treatise,
https://doi.org/10.1007/978-3-030-02880-0_1

2   J. T. BOOKMAN

for control. There is constant struggle in the psyche as reason seeks to impose constraint on the desires and emotions. Which part acquires control and for how long depends upon the state into which one is born and raised and the decisions that one makes.

The ancients conceived the human condition as ineluctably political. Aristotle characterizes man as the "political animal." Only a beast or a god can exist outside the *polis*. The *polis* is the association that comprehends all that we today would call "social." Supreme over all the component parts of the *polis*—family, neighbors, religious cults, schools, business associations, and so on—is the state giving direction to the whole.[4] It is within the *polis* that human beings must realize their humanity, their specifically human ends—reason manifest in the practical sphere as morality and in the intellectual sphere as wisdom. Although the *polis* is the setting for moral and intellectual development, it also circumscribes the possibilities of such development. This is so because most people cannot acquire a point of view outside the ethos of their own society. They may or may not live up to the standards of that ethos and those standards may be higher or lower, but the particular ethos defines the measure and most cannot critically reflect upon it. People might as well be chained in a cave and converse about images reflected upon a wall—so Plato proposes in his Allegory of the Cave.[5] Only a few are able to apprehend the true nature of things behind the images and, thereby, acquire a point of view that permits critical evaluation of the prevailing ethos.

The *polis* also circumscribes the possibilities of moral and intellectual development because none gives sufficient authority to reason. Just as reason ought to rule in the individual psyche, so ought it to rule in the state. Only those in whom reason rules know in what human excellence consists and how to foster it, and only they are disposed to take the necessary actions to realize it. The claims to authority, however, are many. The claim of reason is usually lost in the clamor raised by others. Consequently, conflict occurs within the state and between states as people compete for power, glory, and gain.[6]

Medieval thinkers like Augustine and Aquinas also ask after the nature of human excellence and the contribution the state might make to its realization. Despite some differences, they are at one in thinking that human beings

---

[4] *The Politics*, I, 1–2: 1252a1-1253a29.
[5] *The Republic*, Bk. 7: 514a-520a; cf. Aristotle, *N. E.*: X, 9: 1179b1-20 and *Politics*, III, 7: 1279a40-b2.
[6] Plato, *The Republic*, VIII–IX.

INTRODUCTION: HISTORICAL CONTEXT AND TEXTUAL INTERPRETATION   3

have both eternal and temporal ends—the eternal far more important than the temporal. Human excellence for these Christians has its zenith in salvation and beatitude and is realized in the hereafter.[7] The ancient Greeks found human excellence in a temporal achievement—the well-ordered psyche of the just man. In the well-ordered psyche, reason rules over spirit and appetite, and it is by reason that humans can discern their ends.

Augustine and Aquinas do not dismiss reason as a faculty for discerning human ends. It is that quality that distinguishes humankind from all else in God's creation and marks the presence of the divine. It provides access to natural law—God's moral order for all men and women living on earth. Reason, however, provides no knowledge of man's eternal end. Men must have faith. They must believe in God, in the possibility of redemption, and in the life to come. Only then can reason enlarge understanding of the human prospect and of the world in which humans live. And faith is the consequence of God's saving, albeit unmerited, grace. The priority accorded to faith is necessary because humans are fallen and recalcitrant children of God. Reason unassisted cannot withstand the temptations of desire. More significantly, reason, the very faculty that provides access to natural law, also encourages men and women to think that they are not dependent upon God for their salvation. Their pride, the mark of their unwillingness to acknowledge God, is the root of ignorance, disagreement, and conflict.[8]

Like their ancient predecessors, Augustine and Aquinas regard everyone as a member of a complex social web and as subject to authority. Unlike Plato and Aristotle, they assign a distinctly secondary role to the state in the realization of human ends. For Augustine, the state is necessary only because man strayed from the divine path. In a state of innocence, men and women would be social creatures. They need one another to secure the necessaries of life and to provide companionship. They would live as equals, as brothers and sisters without power over one another and without private property. They would not, however, be political. The state, as well as other institutions like private property and slavery, is a consequence of the fall. It is the punitive and remedial agency ordained by God to cope with fallen man. Augustine gives to the state the task of maintaining peace and order.

---

[7] St. Augustine, *City of God*, XIV, 28; St. Thomas Aquinas, *Summa Contra Gentiles*, III, 37, 48 and IV, 54.

[8] St. Augustine, *City of God*, XIX, 21–24; St. Thomas Aquinas, *Summa Contra Gentiles*, III, 53, 64, 81 and IV, 54.

4   J. T. BOOKMAN

This enables the faithful to worship unmolested and the church to save souls. The state restrains the human propensity to sin, to commit injustice, by the threat of punishment. It does not make men better men.[9]

Aquinas nods in Aristotle's direction when he declares that the state is natural. Even had there been no fall the state would have existed. It is a manifestation of man's social nature and a necessary condition for the realization of man's temporal ends, practical and intellectual. Aquinas follows Augustine in denying to the state any significant educative role. By the exercise of reason, men and women can know natural law. They are not dependent upon the particular society to which they belong to define, and thereby circumscribe, human excellence. To be sure, human reason, owing to the fall, is an impaired faculty and, therefore, only dimly apprehends natural law, and humans often fail to obey natural law. The state can mitigate these problems by giving more specific expression to the prescriptions and prohibitions of natural law, and it can exact obedience to the law. Nevertheless, by their common possession of reason, humans are members of a universal society ruled by eternal law (natural law is part of eternal law) and whose justice is far superior to any human regime. The gulf between even Aristotle's best regime and the perfect society is made broader still in the Christian, and Thomistic, understanding that the entire natural order is subject to divine law. By God's grace, men and women learn that they have an eternal end. The perfect society is the kingdom of God which unites the good angels, the elect who have departed earthly life, and those who are still on their pilgrimage through the world. Against this understanding, Aristotle's political theory is an expression of unassisted reason that wholly neglects the realization of man's eternal end. While the state can help men and women to realize their temporal ends, another institution, the church, is necessary to minister to man's eternal end. And, since the ends that the state promotes are subordinate to everlasting blessedness, the state must defer to the church where the temporal and spiritual overlap as they do in man's heart and mind. The state, of course, does have an interest in the development of citizens who observe rules of right conduct, who obey the strictures of natural law. In its efforts to develop such a citizenry, however, the state is confined to the regulation of conduct. The church assumes the educative role that Plato and Aristotle assign to the state.[10]

[9] St. Augustine, *City of God*, XIX, 12–17.
[10] St. Thomas Aquinas, *Summa Contra Gentiles*, I, 8, III, 48, 53, IV, 54; *Summa Theologiae*, I–II, Qu. 90–97; and On Kingship, Ch. 14.

The sixteenth and seventeenth centuries marked a significant turn in thinking about politics. Europeans during that period experienced profound intellectual disorientation and social disruption. The Copernican theory and the astronomical observations of Galileo cast doubt on long-held views of the cosmos and the centrality of human beings in God's creation. The voyages of discovery revealed a new world unknown to the geography of earlier generations and made more widely known the existence of peoples with beliefs and practices quite different from those of Europeans. The Protestant reformers attacked the theoretical foundations of the medieval church. They criticized the church for its worldly splendor, its hierarchical structure, and its claim to a monopoly on the means of salvation, and the theology for its implication that faith is the giving of assent to correct doctrine. In its place, they offered a Christianity that stressed justification by faith alone, the authority of the Word, the priesthood of all believers, vocation in the service of one's fellows, and a faith involving feeling and personal devotion. Questions about what to believe and how to live no longer had settled answers.

For some there were no answers to be had. Skepticism, of course, has a long history beginning with the ancient Greeks.[11] In all its manifestations, it raises questions about the reliability of claims to knowledge. At its most extreme, it doubts even those claims about which we have the most confidence—those based on immediate experience. In the sixteenth and seventeenth centuries, skeptical doubt seemed a reasonable response to the many competing philosophical and theological claims. The French publisher Stephanus had, in 1562, a ready audience for a Latin translation of a recently discovered manuscript of Sextus Empiricus, the leading exponent of skeptical ideas developed in the ancient Pyrrhonian school. Montaigne in his *Essays*, published 1580–1595, gave increased currency to the skeptical position. So compelling did Montaigne find the arguments for the fallibility of the senses in discerning the real nature of things and for the relativism of belief and conduct that he urged suspension of judgment and the living of a quiet life under local law and custom.[12]

---

[11] See Allan Hazlett, *A Critical Introduction to Skepticism* (London: Bloomsbury Academic, 2014); and John Greco, *The Oxford Handbook of Skepticism* (Oxford: Oxford University Press, 2011).

[12] The central essay is *An Apology for Raymond Sebond*, M. A. Screech, trans. and ed. (New York: Penguin, 1987). Screech produced a complete edition of *The Essays of Michel de Montaigne* for Penguin in 1991.

6   J. T. BOOKMAN

The skeptic's lack of confidence in human faculties and his prescription of withdrawal from the world ran counter to other intellectual currents that encouraged a different attitude. The nascent natural science as exemplified by the physiology of Vesalius and Harvey and the chemistry of Boyle as well as by the astronomers and physicists held out the hope that by understanding nature human beings might control it to the improvement of life. Such a prospect complemented humanist ideas about the temporal life. This literary and philosophical movement flourished in the fourteenth and fifteenth centuries in Italy. Machiavelli was a contemporary or near-contemporary of some of the leading humanists. By the time of Hobbes and Locke, their ideas had spread across Europe. The humanists regarded this life, not as a vale of tears to be endured while preparing for life in the hereafter, but as one of possibility, of accomplishment, of beauty. They rejected asceticism in all its forms and, in particular, the medieval ideal of monastic life. Instead of quiescence and withdrawal, they urged engagement. Marsilio Ficino, Pico della Mirandola, and Leonardo Bruni, among others, claimed for the individual a freedom to develop his or her own interests and capacities and to shape the world in which he or she lived. They criticized the medieval hierarchies, including the Roman Curia, that denied that freedom. The humanists were neither anti-religious nor anti-Christian, but they did give an emphasis to the cultivation of human personality and to the joy in the exercise of all man's faculties that placed a value on temporal life unknown since the ancient Greeks and Romans.[13]

Spiritual and intellectual crises coincided with the dissolution of the old social order. The Roman Catholic Church, the feudal nobility, the guilds, and the manorial system had long dominated medieval society. During the sixteenth and seventeenth centuries that social order underwent great change. The growth of cities encouraged production in the countryside of foodstuffs and fibers for sale rather than home consumption. Innovations in agriculture realized efficiencies that both increased production and permitted landlords to dispossess some of their tenants. The opening of new sea routes to Asia and the discovery of the Americas also quickened the pace of

---

[13] The classic study is Jacob Burckhardt, *The Civilization of the Renaissance in Italy*, S. G. C. Middlemore, trans. (Old Saybrook, CT: Konecky & Konecky, 2003 [1890]), especially Part II: Chs. 1–3, Part IV: Chs. 5–8, and Part VI: Chs. 2–3. Cf. Paul O. Kristeller, *Renaissance Concepts of Man, and Other Essays* (New York: Harper & Row, 1972), and Roberto Weiss, *The Spread of Italian Humanism* (London: Hutchinson, 1964).

INTRODUCTION: HISTORICAL CONTEXT AND TEXTUAL INTERPRETATION   7

commerce by reducing prices and enlarging the market. The development of the market spurred growth in an urban merchant class eager to secure recognition of rights to freedom and property. The national monarchies also played a part in the development of the market by constructing an infra-structure of roads, canals, and bridges over which trade could occur. They also funded scientific and technological research and eliminated local restrictions on trade. These several forces eroded the manorial system and the guilds.

Increased national feeling but, above all, the provision of greater peace and security than that afforded under feudalism allowed national monarchs in Britain, France, Spain, and Sweden to wrest power and authority from the nobility. The invention of firearms contributed to their success by destroying the dominance of the mounted, armored knight on the battlefield. In the effort to extend their authority throughout their realms, the new monarchies required lawyers, clerks, and agents for the administration of the law. Commerce was no less in need of educated people to organize workers, direct production, keep the books, and negotiate deals. With its emphasis on the Word and individual conscience, Protestantism, too, fostered increased literacy and made necessary an educated clergy. In response to these demands, universities and secondary schools multiplied throughout Europe in Protestant and Catholic countries alike. The needs of commercial enterprise and governmental administration were felt everywhere. And, in its prosecution of the Counter-Reformation, the Catholic Church sought a more effective priesthood. These developments, joined with the invention of the printing press about 1450, broke the dominance of the medieval church over learning and widened the intellectual horizons of many.

This description generalizes about events that occurred in Western and Central Europe in the sixteenth and seventeenth centuries. Certainly the pace of change and the particular form that it took varied from country to country and region to region. Nevertheless, throughout Europe medieval institutions were crumbling, and their theoretical foundations were under vigorous attack. It was out of this ferment that Machiavelli, Hobbes, and Locke sought to fashion a new order. *The Prince, Leviathan,* and the *Second Treatise* are their responses to the impulse given to political philosophy at its most ambitious by the dissolution of the medieval order. Their responses have been subjected to a variety of interpretations. It is to questions of interpretation that we now turn.

8 J. T. BOOKMAN

"Contextualist" and "textualist" name basic orientations in the interpretation of texts. The issue between them is the attention, if any, that should be given to the historical context in which a political philosopher wrote in trying to understand what he or she did write. The textualist position has no proponent in the study of political theory who thinks that the text is all and that context can be ignored altogether. Perhaps Gordon Schochet comes closest. He allows that the historical context of a text, including the author's intention in writing it, "tell us why a book was written. It does not tell us *what* it says, what its meaning is or was." He concedes that the context "may contribute to our working out that meaning."[14] John Plamenatz also denies that "to understand what a man is saying, we must know why he is saying it. ... We need understand only the sense in which he is using words." And, he contends that we can often learn more about a writer's arguments "by weighing them over and over again than by extending our knowledge of the circumstances in which ... [he] wrote."[15] Textualists like Schochet and Plamenatz would agree with the leading exponent of contextualism among students of political philosophy, Quentin Skinner, that "'good critical practice depends above all on close and sensitive reading' of the text itself."[16]

Skinner insists, however, that such a reading "can never be sufficient in itself ... to supply even the most plausible and coherent internal analysis of ... [the] arguments of any of the classic texts."[17] In addition, the "grasp of force [the intention of the writer in saying what he or she said] as well as meaning [propositional] is essential to the understanding of texts."[18] For example, he adduces Machiavelli's assertion in Chapter 15 of *The Prince* that "a prince must learn how to be not good" to show that the neglect of context would leave unknown "the fact that *The Prince* was in part intended as a deliberate attack on the moral convictions of advice-books to princes. ... No one can be said fully to understand Machiavelli's text who

---

[14] Gordon J. Schochet, "Radical Politics and Ashcraft's Treatise on Locke," *Journal of the History of Ideas*, 50 (July, 1989), 509.

[15] John P. Plamenatz, Man and Society: *Political and Social Theory: Machiavelli through Marx*, 2 vs. (New York: McGraw-Hill, 1963), V. 1: ix–x.

[16] He quotes David Lodge with approval in "Motives, Intentions and the Interpretation of Texts" in James Tully, ed., *Meaning and Context: Quentin Skinner and His Critics* (Princeton: Princeton University Press, 1988), 69.

[17] "Some Problems in the Analysis of Political Thought and Action" in Tully, 99.

[18] "Meaning and Understanding" in Tully, 61.

INTRODUCTION: HISTORICAL CONTEXT AND TEXTUAL INTERPRETATION   9

does not understand this fact about it."[19] Attending to the historical context might also have discouraged what Skinner calls the "exegetically plausible but historically incredible interpretations" of Hobbes by Warrender, Hood, Macpherson, and Strauss.[20] The relevant context to be considered in the determination of intention he identifies in two interpretive rules. First, "focus not just on the text … but on the prevailing [linguistic] conventions governing the treatment of the issues or themes with which the text is concerned." Second, "focus on the writer's mental world, the world of his empirical beliefs."[21] Those conventions and empirical beliefs can be discovered by examination of contemporaneous texts. This historical context defines a domain of meaning that should inform our understanding of a philosopher's work. That domain includes far more than the contemporary meaning of the words used. It also includes the questions to which he responded and the assumptions that he made. It limits the very things that he could think about. Machiavelli, Hobbes, and Locke all announce their intentions in writing their works. Whether these statements should be taken at face value is another matter. Locke, for example, in the preface to the *Two Treatises* says that he intends "to establish the throne of our Great Restorer, Our Present King William; to make good his Title, in the Consent of the People." Historical research has established that the preface was added well after the composition of the body of the work. Locke wrote the *Two Treatises* in the circumstances of the Exclusion Crisis of 1679–1681 and its immediate aftermath. It would seem, then, in light of what he says there, that he intended to justify a revolution in prospect against Charles II (which never occurred) and not, as so long thought, the revolution accomplished in 1688 that put William on the throne. Machiavelli says in Chapter 15 of *The Prince* that "my intent is to write a thing that is useful for whoever understands it." This is sufficiently obscure to have inspired a wide variety of interpretations of what he is doing. Perhaps his intention was manifold. The statement of his intention occurs in the same paragraph of the same chapter as his most shocking observation, namely, a prince must learn how not to be good—a contention upon which he elaborates in the next four chapters. If Machiavelli's analysis of the conflict between conventional morality and the responsibilities of rule is not his principal intention, it must be among his main intentions.

[19] "Social Meaning and the Explanation of Social Action" in Tully, 95.
[20] "Some Problems" in Tully, 99.
[21] "Motives, Intentions and Interpretation" in Tully, 77–78.

10   J. T. BOOKMAN

Hobbes explicitly states in "A Review, and Conclusion" to *Leviathan:* "my Discourse ... occasioned by the disorders of the present time, ... and without other design, than to set before mens eyes the mutual Relation between Protection and Obedience" and to ground the "Civil Right of Sovereigns and both the Duty and Liberty of Subjects ... upon the known natural Inclinations of Mankind." Since his express intention is entirely consistent with what he does, I take Hobbes at his word.

Several things are worth noticing. Firstly, the ascription of intentions made above would have the assent of many scholars but certainly not all. Most prominently, Leo Strauss and his followers would have us ignore any overt expressions of intention and instead discover the presumed covert intentions of writers. Contrary to Skinner, they urge looking for clues of a writer's real intention in the text rather than in the historical circumstances of its composition. Secondly, the expressions of intention cited earlier pertain to the whole work. Particular statements and arguments might be informed by other, albeit subordinate, intentions. Thirdly, if the intentions ascribed above to Machiavelli, Hobbes, and Locke are correct, only that ascribed to Locke required going beyond the text to uncover it. Even in Locke's case, Skinner's interpretive rules scarcely apply. Fourthly, learning the intention of a writer leaves the text unchanged; no word, no statement, no argument is altered.

Skinner distinguishes between those often conflated concepts of motive and intention. Let us do the same. Consider these hypothetical, if homely, examples. My intention, say, is to help an elderly lady to safely cross a busy intersection. My motive might be to impress my wife with my thoughtfulness. And, a member of Congress claims that a government contract for a transport plane ought to be awarded to Boeing because the company can better satisfy the contract requirements at lower cost. The intention of the congressman in saying what he said is, at least in part, to win the support of his fellow members for the Boeing application. His motive might well be to increase his chances for re-election to his Seattle-area seat. In the world of political philosophy, Skinner cites as an example of intention Hobbes's statement of his intention in *Leviathan* quoted above. He does not identify Hobbes's motives. Hobbes may have been inspired to write in order to burnish his reputation, to advance science, to make money or still other reasons. In any event, Skinner regards motives as "irrelevant to the determination of meaning." Motives are reasons "*for* writing (though not ... [an] intention in writing)."[22]

---

[22] "Motives, Intentions and Interpretation" in Tully, 74.

INTRODUCTION: HISTORICAL CONTEXT AND TEXTUAL INTERPRETATION   11

A few examples may make clearer something of what is at issue here. The first is drawn from Locke's *A Letter Concerning Toleration* and concerns the range of governmental authority. Locke responds to an imagined critic of his exclusion of government from religious matters.

> You will say: What if he neglects the care of his soul? I answer: What if he neglects the care of his health or of his estate, things which more nearly concern the government of the magistrate? Shall the magistrate provide an express law against such a man becoming poor or sick? Laws endeavour, as far as possible, to protect the goods and health of subjects from violence of others, or from fraud, not from the negligence or prodigality of the owners themselves. No man against his will can be forced to be healthy or rich.[23]

It did not occur to Locke that a government might adopt a program like the National Health Service (NHS) as the British government did in 1948. Such a possibility did not fall within his domain of meaning. No state in his day had the administrative reach, the political authority, and the financial resources to implement such a program. And, of course, it would be several centuries before medicine could do much good for very many people. For Skinner, such observations count decisively against any interpretation of Locke that countenances health care as an appropriate subject for governmental policy.

The textualist, on the other hand, while acknowledging that Locke did not contemplate the NHS, might point out that the passage from the *Letter* does not prohibit the government from providing health care. Locke asserts that "no man against his will can be forced to be healthy." True. One might also agree that no man ought to be forced to be healthy against his will. The NHS is consistent in most of its provisions with both these affirmations. Furthermore, does Locke not enjoin us to preserve all humankind? If, he says, we allow another to die of starvation when it is within our means to save him, we commit murder.[24] It came to be within the means of the British government to save, or attempt to save, its citizens from terminal disease and trauma. Locke's principles do not forbid, may even require, some provision of health care.

---

[23] *Epistola de Tolerantia: A Letter on Toleration*, Raymond Klibansky and J. W. Gough, eds. (Oxford: Clarendon Press, 1968), 91.

[24] *First Treatise*, §42; "Venditio," 342; "Essays on the Law of Nature," 123; and "An Essay On the Poor Law," 198 in Mark Goldie, ed., *Locke: Political Essays* (Cambridge: Cambridge University Press, 1997).

12   J. T. BOOKMAN

The second example is drawn from the *Second Treatise* and concerns Locke's servant—he who digs turfs at §28. That servant figures in the controversy over Locke's role in preparing the moral ground for capitalism. Contextualists argue that capitalism, neither in word nor concept, was part of Locke's domain of meaning. They point out that, unlike Marx's proletarian, his servant does not labor alongside many others in the performance of repetitious operations, his days are bounded by the rising and setting of the sun—not by the stroke of the clock, and he is not free to move in the search for better opportunities. Furthermore, Locke's proposed revision of the poor law aims at keeping the unemployed in their parishes, not at the creation of a mobile workforce. Such a workforce is a prerequisite for a capitalist labor market. For Skinner, such observations count decisively against an interpretation of §28 that calls his servant as witness to Locke's alleged capitalist sympathies.

The textualist, while he might acknowledge all the above, could argue that there are some important similarities between Locke's servant and Marx's proletarian. They both work at the direction of another, they are dependent on another for the opportunity to work, and the product of their labor belongs to their employers. More tellingly, Locke claims for everyone a right to dispose of himself and his possessions as he sees fit within the bounds of the law of nature. A mobile workforce was not part of Locke's domain of meaning, but such a force may well be implied by his political philosophy. The textualist interpretations of Locke set out above would count among those that Skinner regards as "exegetically plausible but historically incredible interpretations."

There are other contextualists who share Skinner's conviction that it is necessary to go beyond the text to the historical context of the text if we are truly to understand it. They seek to find relationships between ideas and political, social, economic, and psychological circumstances in order to reveal the *real* meaning of those ideas, namely, as serving the interests of one group or another or as providing solace or encouragement to troubled men and women. This is to treat ideas as ideology—an expression of self-deception or calculated deceit and all the permutations in between. The presumption is that once the real meaning is revealed, human beings will be able to think more clearly about their situation and to devise more satisfactory solutions to human problems, free of the distorting effects of interest and neurosis. There is nothing illegitimate about such inquiry, but it does raise hard questions—to be identified shortly.[25]

---

[25] As J. G. A. Pocock points out in "The Myth of John Locke and the Obsession with Liberalism" in Pocock and Ashcraft, *John Locke.*

INTRODUCTION: HISTORICAL CONTEXT AND TEXTUAL INTERPRETATION   13

Religion was early on made the subject of such scrutiny.[26] Hobbes, for example, argues that religion, a belief in powers invisible, is an expression of ignorance for most people. Human beings discern a world of cause and effect, but only a few pursue the natural science that allows identification of the true causes of things. Anxious to explain their own fortune or misfortune, most imagine a god or gods onto whom are projected human qualities—in the case of the Christian God, the best human qualities magnified. Men and women seek to propitiate God by prayer, sacrifice, humble behavior, gifts, and so on.[27] Furthermore, pagan priests, the papacy, and Presbyterian ministers have exploited the religious beliefs of the credulous to aggrandize themselves.[28] The advance of science and understanding will produce, in Hobbes's view, not the demise of religion altogether, but a conception of God as first mover and the practice of religion as civil undertaking.

Religion persists, of course, down to the present day as a target of ideological criticism. It has been joined by others. Marx brought to the fore connections between economic interests and ideas.[29] Several prominent interpreters of Locke follow his lead. Macpherson argues that Locke in his theory of property "has done what he set out to do. ... He has erased the moral disability with which unlimited capitalist appropriation had hitherto been handicapped" and thereby "provides a positive moral basis for capitalist society."[30] Macpherson, here, regards the relationship between an idea, unlimited capitalist appropriation, and historical circumstances, a nascent capitalist society, as functional, that is, Locke's principles legitimize capitalism—presumably as Locke intended. Richard Ashcraft maintains that "we need to think of political theory in terms of its relationship to a political movement" and that "the interest—primarily socioeconomic—of the participants structure the kind of theoretical arguments to be made." Locke as the ideologue of a political movement defends the "widely shared and easily recognizable religious, economic, and historical

---

[26] Mark Goldie shows just how central religion has been for ideological analysis in "Ideology" in Terence Ball, James Farr, and Russell L. Hanson, eds., *Political Innovation and Conceptual Change* (Cambridge: Cambridge University Press, 1989), Ch. 13.

[27] *Leviathan*, see particularly Ch. 12.

[28] Ibid., see particularly, Ch. 47.

[29] His ideas on the matter are most fully set out in Part I of *The German Ideology* in Robert C. Tucker, ed., *The Marx-Engels Reader*, 2nd. ed. (New York: Norton, 1978), 146–200.

[30] C. B. Macpherson, *The Political Theory of Possessive Individualism: Hobbes to Locke* (Oxford: Clarendon Press, 1962), 221.

14   J. T. BOOKMAN

beliefs of the Whigs."[31] Ashcraft sees the relationship in a different light. Locke's ideas, the beliefs of the Whigs, he regards as "structured" in some way by his socioeconomic circumstances. It would be remarkable indeed were that not true. Whether those circumstances were the only, or even the decisive, circumstances that shaped Locke's intentions is another matter.

Questions about intention aside, the contemporary reader in trying to understand some classic text in political philosophy has interests, a vocabulary, conceptual distinctions, and experiences unknown to the writer of that text. The writer has one worldview, the reader another. Both are informed by the political, social, and economic circumstances of the time and by the psychological state of the individual. Political philosophy is not an autonomous enterprise that exists in a world of its own; there is no standpoint unshaped by circumstance. This is in part the contextualist's point. However true it may be that a text is informed by the circumstances of the time in which it was written, it is also true that a political philosophy is not determined by those circumstances. Certainly no one has demonstrated such a relationship.

Such a demonstration will forever be hindered by the fact that those circumstances are mediated by the mind of the individual philosopher. No one experiences similar, or even the same, circumstances in quite the same way. This is evident in the differences, sometimes large, among writers of the same time and place. Skinner himself regards the classic texts as poor expressions of the conventional understandings of an age.[32] This is so, he explains, because, while a writer "must be limited by the prevailing conventions of discourse," he may "aim ... to extend, to subvert or ... alter a prevailing set of accepted conventions and attitudes."[33] The classic texts are classic because they develop more fully their arguments, take better account of the facts, and are more mindful of the assumptions they make. More significantly for the textualist, their authors, in the course of responding to contemporary problems, elaborate a conception of humankind and of the world in which such beings live that transcends the historical particularities of their times whatever their intentions might have been.

---

[31] "The Two Treatises and the Exclusion Crisis: The Problem of Lockean Political Theory as Bourgeois Ideology" in J. G. A. Pocock and Richard Ashcraft, *John Locke: Papers Read at Clark Library Seminar* (Los Angeles, CA: William Andrew Clark Memorial Library, 1980), 36, 37, and 67.

[32] "Some Problems" in Tully, 99–100.

[33] "Some Problems" in Tully, 105.

INTRODUCTION: HISTORICAL CONTEXT AND TEXTUAL INTERPRETATION   15

The differences in worldview between the contemporary reader and the writer of a classic text create a hazard in trying to understand that text—the attribution to a philosopher of positions that he or she never took. Whether the reader is so blinkered by a worldview that misinterpretation occurs can only be settled by consulting the relevant evidence. While recognizing that a worldview can obscure vision, it is worth appreciating that a worldview also permits vision. Would, for example, Locke's ideas about women have been so clarified had not Butler, Clark, and the contributors to Hirschmann and McClure brought to bear a feminist perspective?[34] Would Locke's position on property have been so clarified had not Macpherson and Cohen brought to bear a Marxist perspective?[35] These scholars have required us to read and think again about Locke's political philosophy from a new vantage point.

There is no one correct way to interpret a text. This is not to say that one interpretation is as good as another. Both textualist and contextualist approaches have been used well and badly. For textualists, the significant context of a work is not constituted by the historical particularities with which the contextualists are concerned but by the shared circumstances of human life. Men and women have physical, emotional, and intellectual needs. They experience fear. They are rational and self-conscious—capable of thought and speech. They must work together to satisfy their needs. They create social institutions including government in order to secure food, shelter, security, companionship, and so on. Human beings also create myth, religion, science, and philosophy to provide explanation and justification. It is out of these circumstances that the perennial questions of political philosophy arise. What does government contribute to the realization of human ends? What is the proper range of governmental authority? Why and to what extent are people obligated to obey the law? Who should be entrusted with power? The textualist is interested in the cogency of a text as an answer to perennial questions such as these. Are the claims made to knowledge true? Are the arguments made valid? What vision of the human condition is disclosed? Examination of the text alone

---

[34] Melissa A. Butler, "Early Liberal Roots of Feminism," *American Political Science Review*, 72 (Mar., 1978), 135–150; Lorene M. G. Clark, "Women and John Locke; or Who Owns the Apples in the Garden of Eden?" *Canadian Journal of Philosophy*, 7 (Dec., 1977), 699–724; and Nancy J. Hirschmann and Kristie M. McClure, eds., *Feminist Interpretations of John Locke* (University Park, PA: Pennsylvania State University Press, 2007).

[35] Macpherson, *Possessive Individualism*, Ch. 5; and G. A. Cohen, "Marx and Locke on Land and Labour," *Proceedings of the British Academy*, 71 (1985), 357–388.

16   J. T. BOOKMAN

is relevant to an answer to these questions. To be sure, we must first determine the propositional meaning of the text and that requires consultation of the philosopher's domain of meaning to determine how words are being used. The textualist approach is philosophical, not historical.

For a contextualist like Skinner, the textualist approach is badly misconceived for that reason. According to him,

> Any statement ... is inescapably the embodiment of a particular intention, on a particular occasion, addressed to the solution of a particular problem, and thus specific to its situation in a way that it can only be naive to try to transcend. The vital implication here is not merely that the classic texts cannot be concerned with our questions and answers, but only with their own. There is also the further implication ... that there simply are no perennial questions in philosophy.[36]

Instead, contextualists seek to answer questions about the relations among texts written about the same time, about the relations between those texts and the political, social, economic, and psychological circumstances in which they were written and how those relations change. What is the nature of the relationship asserted? What are the circumstances asserted to influence belief? In what way, for example, do socioeconomic circumstances influence what a writer has to say? As cause? As condition? Or, is the relationship a functional one? Whatever Locke intended, his words, Macpherson asserts, had as a consequence the promotion of possessive individualism. Does the asserted relationship obtain universally or is the relationship culturally specific? These are hard questions and difficult to answer. The asserted relationships and descriptions of circumstances may be true or false. In determining their truth or falsity, evidence well beyond the text must be weighed. Furthermore, the truth or falsity of any such assertions is irrelevant to the truth of propositions or to the logical validity of arguments advanced in a text. Let us return to the congressman from Seattle. His advocacy may well express his interest in re-election, but that has no bearing on the truth of his contention that Boeing is the best candidate for the contract. And, even as it were shown that Locke advocated a right to private property because the Whigs feared that a ruthless monarch would seize property, this is irrelevant to a consideration of Locke's argument for

[36] "Meaning and Understanding" in Tully, 65.

a right to private property. One must be clear, then, about what one is doing. Why does Locke contend that people have a right to private property? The contextualist understands the question to ask: How did Locke come to hold this position? He looks for *causes* in contemporary historical circumstances and finds those causes in the Whig political program and the king's ambitions. The textualist understands the question to ask: Why should anyone think that people have a right to private property? He looks for *reasons* in the text and finds the reasons that Locke adduced in his labor theory of value. Textualists and contextualists ask different questions and the evidence relevant to answer the questions posed is different.

In describing the historical context in which Machiavelli, Hobbes, and Locke wrote, I have assumed that contemporary political, social, and economic circumstances, as well as their psychological make-up, had great influence in the development of their ideas. I leave to others, however, the task of sorting out how and in what ways those circumstances were related to their ideas. In reading *The Prince, Leviathan,* and the *Second Treatise,* we will adopt the textualist approach. The commentaries on the texts and the bibliographical essays that follow will focus on the ideas themselves and not on the question of how Machiavelli, Hobbes, or Locke came to hold them. I have also taken notice of their intellectual predecessors. They were not the first philosophers to consider questions about, say, government authority or political obligation. Machiavelli, Hobbes, and Locke often comment on the positions taken by earlier philosophers, sometimes named, often not. Such allusions and references can help us better understand similarities and differences.

CHAPTER 2

The Prince

MACHIAVELLI (1469–1527): A BRIEF SKETCH OF HIS LIFE

Machiavelli regarded the loss of his post as second chancellor in the Florentine Republic as the greatest misfortune of his life. For 14 years he had labored in the service of a city which, he would say later, he loved more than his own soul.[1] With the armies of Pope Julius II (r(uled) 1503–1513) nearly in the shadow of the city's walls, the Medici returned to Florence, and Piero Soderini, head of the republican government and Machiavelli's patron, fled. The Medici, a family of wool-traders turned bankers dominated Florentine politics for centuries and supplied popes, queens, and grand dukes until the last of the dynasty died in 1737. Upon their resumption of power in September 1512, they dissolved the republic, and on 7 November dismissed Machiavelli as too republican in his sympathies and too closely tied to the Soderini, their political rivals in Rome as well as in Florence. His arrogance and candor may have offended the Medici as well.[2] On 10 November 1512,

[1] James B. Atkinson and David Sices, eds. and trans., *Machiavelli and His Friends: Their Personal Correspondence* (DeKalb, IL: Northern Illinois University Press, 1996), 416 (Letter 331). See also *A Discourse on Remodeling the Government of Florence* in Allan Gilbert, trans., *Machiavelli: The Chief Works and Others*, 3 vs. (Durham, NC: Duke University Press, 1965), v. 1, 113–114 for the expression of similar sentiments.

[2] John M. Najemy, "The Controversy Surrounding Machiavelli's Service to the Republic" in Gisela Bock, Quentin Skinner, and Maurizio Viroli, eds., *Machiavelli and Republicanism* (Cambridge: Cambridge University Press, 1990), 101–117.

© The Author(s) 2019
J. T. Bookman, *A Reader's Companion*
to The Prince, Leviathan, *and the* Second Treatise,
https://doi.org/10.1007/978-3-030-02880-0_2

Machiavelli was ordered to remain within Florentine territory for a year and to pay surety of 1000 gold florins—a substantial sum which had to be made good by friends. On 17 November, he was forbidden to enter the *Palazzo*, the seat of government, for a year. Things were to take on a still more threatening aspect. Implicated, wrongly, in a suspected plot, he was arrested, imprisoned, and tortured. In March 1513, Machiavelli was released as part of the general amnesty declared by the Florentine government upon the election of Cardinal Giovanni de' Medici as Pope Leo X (r.1513–1521). This was the pope who provoked Martin Luther into posting his 95 theses in 1517.

The torture broke Machiavelli in neither body nor spirit. Indeed, he bore it so well that he thought the better of himself for it.[3] The physical aches and pains soon went away. The loss of his salary as chancellor, although not large, had more lasting effect. Never a wealthy man, Machiavelli was forced to quit the city and take up residence at the family's country house, Sant'Andrea, in Percussina, six miles south of Florence, where he lived with wife and children a life of shabby gentility. Most disabling of all was the denial of the opportunity to influence Florentine and Italian politics. Although Machiavelli came from a family that had in years past supplied minor government officials, it had lately experienced a decline in status. His father, Bernardo, was a lawyer who enjoyed only modest success in Florence. This did not, however, prevent a close friendship between Bernardo and Bartolomeo Scala, the humanist historian and first chancellor, when Niccolò was a youth. Nevertheless, the Machiavelli were not among the great houses of the city. Niccolò, then, did not have elevated social status or wealth or arms. His influence depended upon his occupying a position in government or upon his pen. It is to the pen that Machiavelli turned. He enjoyed his scholarship and his writing. They brought him into contact, vicariously, with great men and large events, and provided a respite from the tedium of his country days.[4]

From this period, after his dismissal in 1512 down to his death in 1527, came all the works so much praised and condemned in later years. But, for all the attention paid him posthumously, in several instances at least, he wrote not for the ages but out of his ardent desire to secure a place in the Florentine government from which he could have an influence on policy. And thus we find Machiavelli importuning the Medici in poems and essays

---

[3] Atkinson and Sices, *Machiavelli and His Friends*, 222 (Letter 206).
[4] *Ibid.*, 262–265 (Letter 224); see also (Letter 236).

until his death. His best known work, *The Prince*, he dedicated initially to Giuliano de' Medici and then to Lorenzo de' Medici (nephew of Giuliano and Pope Leo X) after Giuliano's death in 1516. Machiavelli wrote to his friend Francesco Vettori, Florentine envoy to the court of the Medici pope: "And through this study of mine, were it to be read, it would be evident that during the fifteen years I have been studying the art of the state I have neither slept nor fooled around, and anybody ought to be happy to utilize someone who has had so much experience at the expense of others."[5] Alas, it was not to be. Machiavelli's gift of a copy of *The Prince* went unacknowledged because Lorenzo was more interested in a gift of two hunting dogs that he received the same day.[6] So Machiavelli got no job. For him a great personal setback, but, he believed, also a loss for the cause of Italy. Machiavelli hoped for an Italy under stable and secure governments free from foreign domination, and he thought, however unrealistically, that the Medici had a rare opportunity to create out of Rome and Florence a center of resistance to invasion. And who better to advise them in this task than Machiavelli, who had learned well the lessons taught by the Romans and by such contemporaries as Cesare Borgia?

Machiavelli had learned those lessons, he says, "through long experience of modern things and constant reading about ancient things."[7] The study of antiquity began early on. The modest circumstances of the family left little beyond necessities. What little was left *papa* Bernardo spent on books and tutors for his two sons, Niccolò and Totto. Machiavelli learned Latin, but probably not Greek, and read the histories, among them Livy, that his father collected.[8] There was much to be learned, too, in the piazzas and caffes—largely about the darker side of politics. In the course of the fifteenth century, Florence had undergone pronounced corruption of political and social life. At the connivance of the Medici, power had been progressively confined to fewer and fewer hands, even though many of the old republican forms were preserved. Coincident with this development

---

[5] *Ibid.*, 265 (Letter 224).

[6] Ricardo Riccardi, "Machiavelli's Presentation of *The Prince* to Lorenzo de' Medici" in William J. Connell, trans. and ed., *The Prince by Niccolo Machiavelli with Related Documents* (Boston: Bedford/St. Martin's, 2005), 142.

[7] Niccolo Machiavelli, *The Prince*, Dedication.

[8] Much of what is known, and that is not very much, about Machiavelli's life before 1498 must be gleaned from the diary of his father. See Catherine Atkinson, *Debts, Dowries, Donkeys: The Diary of Niccolo Machiavelli's Father, Messer Bernardo, in Quattrocento Florence* (New York: Peter Lang, 2002).

was the loss of civic-mindedness by the Florentines. Each looked out for himself and his family in the cultivation of a life of ease and easy virtue. The Florentines grew cynical about government and about any behavior that was not self-serving. In the background lurked the danger from abroad.

The French and Spanish monarchies were busy and successful in consolidating their realms at this time, while the Italians remained hopelessly divided. The Holy Roman Emperor Maximilian I (r.1485–1519) collected armies and asserted territorial aims in Italy. Beginning with the invasion by the French king Charles VIII (r.1483–1498) in 1494 and culminating in the sack of Rome in 1527, foreign powers, often at the invitation of an Italian state that wished to gain at the expense of another, much affected politics in Italy. The invasion by Charles VIII induced Piero de' Medici to turn over Pisa and to promise a large tribute to the French. Outraged by this treachery and inspired by the fiery sermons of the Dominican friar Girolamo Savonarola, the Florentines forced Piero de' Medici into exile and restored the republic. Savonarola as prior of San Marco had undertaken a moral crusade against corruption in places public and private, within and without the church, and a campaign on behalf of republican government, including the writing of a *Treatise on the Organization and Government of Florence*. The friar's exhortations on behalf of a simple, morally upright life culminated in February 1497 in the Bonfire of the Vanities, in which many manuscripts, paintings, and sculpture went up in flames. Soon thereafter Savonarola's fortunes declined rapidly. His attacks on the papacy for its worldliness and venality brought excommunication. His attacks on the citizenry for its corruption led to a fall from popular favor. With the support of Pope Alexander VI (r.1492–1502), and in the face of his threats to seize the city's goods and merchants in the Papal States if the friar were not dealt with, the Florentines put Savonarola to death. They did keep the republic however and the enlarged popular assembly instituted by Savonarola. Machiavelli's opportunity to get involved came shortly after Savonarola's death and the defeat of his supporters in the elections of June 1498. New officers were needed for the executive agencies of the republic.

These, then, were the conditions of Machiavelli's youth and of his selection as Chancellor of the Second Chancery. He came to the post at the age of 29. Why he was chosen is a matter of speculation. While we know little of him before 1498, his family had lived in Florence for generations and been members of its guilds and religious groups. He was known to be unfriendly to Savonarola's puritanism. He was acceptable to the branch of the Medici family that favored a greater sharing of political power. Furthermore, his father's best friend, Bartolomeo Scala, had served as first chancellor for 33 years (1464–1497) mostly under Lorenzo the Magnificent. Perhaps Scala had arranged small commissions in the chancery for his friend's son. Marcello Virgilio Adriani, professor of classical studies at the university and first chancellor after the June 1498 elections, may have had Machiavelli as a student and been sufficiently impressed by his intelligence and diligence to nominate him. In any event, Machiavelli was able to win the approval of the Council of Eighty and election by the Great Council.

The principal decision-making body of the Florentine government during the Renaissance was the *Signoria*. This body was made up of two members from each of the four quarters of the city and a ninth member, the standard-bearer of justice (*gonfaloniere*), who was the head of government. It was to them that Machiavelli addressed his diplomatic correspondence. Their term of office was just two months, although Piero Soderini was given a lifetime appointment as *gonfaloniere* in 1502. Under Savonarola's reforms the members of the *Signoria* were elected by the Great Council, as were the first and second chancellors. The latter had to be re-elected every year with an initial appointment for two years. Major decisions of the *Signoria* had to secure the approval of other councils, including the Great Council, the most popular legislative body which, at the end of the fifteenth century, numbered about 3000. Even in principle, the reformed republic was not very democratic. The total population of Florence at the time has been estimated at between 50,000 and 100,000. Only tax-paying male resident citizens over 30 were eligible to hold office. These and other restrictions produced a political class that constituted a small fraction of those subject to Florentine rule: citizens who did not satisfy the requirements for political eligibility, non-citizens resident in Florence, all those who lived in the surrounding countryside, and the citizens of her subject cities.

Both the First and Second Chanceries were responsible to the *Signoria*. The primary responsibility of the Second Chancery was the administration of Florence's subject territories, including the cities of Arezzo, Pistoia, and Volterra. In addition, Machiavelli's appointment as secretary to the Ten of War brought foreign relations to his portfolio.[9] Within a month of his assuming office, he was off on the first of many diplomatic missions. There

---

[9] H. C. Butters, *Governors and Government in Early Sixteenth-Century Florence*, 1502–1519 (New York: Oxford University Press, 1986).

were foreign missions to the French court of Louis XII (r.1498–1515) and to the Holy Roman Emperor Maximilian I and many more to the Italian states.

Notable among the latter were several missions to Cesare Borgia (1475–1507), Duke of Valentino. These permitted Machiavelli to observe at first hand a political leader whose aims were large and who was prepared to do what was necessary to realize them. When Machiavelli first saw him in October 1502, the Duke was at the height of his power. Machiavelli was impressed. "The power of his Excellency the Duke," he wrote, "was not to be measured in the same way as that of the other lords ... who had nothing to show but simply their carriages, whilst the Duke must be looked upon as a new power in Italy with which it was better to conclude a friendship and alliance rather than a military engagement."[10] Machiavelli also recognized the conditions of the Duke's power: "So long as the present Pope lives, and so long as the Duke preserves the friendship of the king of France, he will not be abandoned by that good fortune which until now has steadily increased."[11] When the Duke's fortunes sank upon the death of his father Rodrigo, Pope Alexander VI, Machiavelli observed that "we now see that the Duke's sins have little by little brought him to expiation,"[12] and "the Duke is little by little slipping into his grave."[13]

As emissary for Florence, Machiavelli showed himself to be a faithful and competent representative of his city. This is not to say that Florentine interests were always advanced. Indeed, they often were not—much to Machiavelli's chagrin. He wrote during his first mission to France that the French "have consideration only for those who are either well armed, or who are prepared to pay."[14] The same considerations, Machiavelli would learn, counted most heavily with all those whom he entreated, and Florence was neither well-armed nor willing to give money. The city was riven by internal factions—one great family against another, supporters of Savonarola against his opponents, those who wanted more authoritarian government against the proponents of greater participation. Machiavelli in the preface to his *History of Florence* observed: "Not content with one faction, Florence has produced a number of them." The city was also reluctant to raise taxes

---

[10] Christian E. Detmold, ed. and trans., *The Historical, Political and Diplomatic Works of Niccolo Machiavelli*, 4 vs. (Boston: James R. Osgood, 1882), v. 3, 202.

[11] *Ibid.*, 169.

[12] *Ibid.*, 354.

[13] *Ibid.*, 369.

[14] *Ibid.*, 83.

THE PRINCE   25

to support armies, and it was enervated by the restiveness of its subject cities. Cautious and short-sighted, his superiors often found Machiavelli's proposals too ambitious and unrealistic. His advocacy of a citizen army was seen in such a light. In his first known political work *Report on the Pisan War* (1498), Machiavelli expressed his disdain for mercenaries. From that time forward he repeatedly urged the acquisition of Florence's own arms. His recommendations were long ignored.

Many within the government also expressed skepticism of a project to divert the Arno at Pisa to deny her supplies from Lucca and Genoa and to deny water to the city. This would be the first phase of a far larger plan conceived by Leonardo da Vinci to make Florence into a seaport and to tame the unruly river in the interest of irrigation and flood control. Machiavelli probably met Leonardo while on his mission to Cesare Borgia in the fall of 1502. Da Vinci was in Borgia's service at the time as cartographer and military engineer. Both were back in Florence by the summer of 1503 and began at that time their collaboration to implement Leonardo's idea. Machiavelli praised the project as a way to retake Pisa. Unsuccessful in previous attempts to take the city by assault and siege, the *Signoria* voted approval the next summer. Work began on 20 August 1504. Before the fall was out, the Florentine military commander on the outskirts of Pisa pronounced the effort a failure.[15] This did not discourage Machiavelli from renewing his campaign to raise a citizen army. After mercenaries in the pay of Florence were unable to break through Pisan defenses in 1505–1506, he persuaded the *Signoria* to give the idea a try. Machiavelli was given the job of organizing this force, although he did not get the troops he wanted; his superiors excluded Florentine citizens from the draft. Nevertheless, his influence increased with the success of his forces and reached its zenith with the capture of Pisa in 1509.

Elsewhere there were developments that in a few years would bring down the republic and the Chancellor of the Second Chancery. Pope Julius II with much determination and duplicity was seeking to extend his dominion in Italy. An alliance with Spain in 1511 encouraged him to lay plans for proceeding against the French and against Florence if she would not cooperate in the campaign. Soderini rode the fence between the papacy and France with a tilt in the direction of the latter. Machiavelli traveled to Pisa

---

[15] This tale is well told in Roger D. Masters, *Fortune is a River: Leonardo da Vinci and Niccolo Machiavelli's Magnificent Dream to Change the Course of Florentine History* (New York: Penguin, 1998).

26   J. T. BOOKMAN

to see to the defenses. The second night after his departure, 4 November 1511, a lightning bolt struck the tower of the *Palazzo* and passed through the chancery, where it destroyed three lilies over the door. The event was immediately interpreted as a bad omen for the French and the Florentine government. Machiavelli made out his first will on the 22nd. Within a year the Medici were back in the *Palazzo* and Machiavelli was on the outside.

In 1513, after his retirement to Sant'Andrea, he wrote: "Fortune has seen to it that since I do not know how to talk about either the silk or wool trade, or profits or losses, I have to talk about politics. I need either to take a vow of silence or to discuss this."[16] Machiavelli took no vow of silence. By early fall, 1513, he was hard at work on *The Prince* and, in the space of a few months, had largely completed it.[17] The *Discourses* took rather longer. Begun in 1515, he worked on them for several years. As he wrote, he read the *Discourses* to a group of friends, the Oricellari Circle, which got its name from the Oricellari Gardens in Florence, where it met. This group of literati and political notables provided the stimulation of learned conversation to Machiavelli down to 1522 when the Medici broke up the Circle.

Machiavelli's long-standing efforts to secure employment from the Medici finally issued in a commission from Cardinal Giulio de' Medici, later Pope Clement VII (r.1523–1534), in 1520 to write a history of Florence. At this time he was also commissioned to write a discourse on Florentine affairs for presentation to Pope Leo X (Giovanni de' Medici) who sought advice on a way to reorganize the Florentine government. In these discourses Machiavelli aimed at the city's good far more than the Pope's approval. He urged the Pope to restore the republic after his lifetime and that of the Cardinal de' Medici.[18] While at work on the *History of Florence*, Machiavelli was offered a job as secretary by Prospero Colonna, the Roman prince and *condottiere*, at 200 gold ducats a year—twice the salary of the first chancellor of Florence and nearly five times what he had made as Chancellor of the Second Chancery. He declined.

In the last year of his life, 1527, he was again in the service of the Medici. To them, the Pope and the Cardinal, rulers of the church and of Florence, fell the task of defending Italy against the impending imperial invasion. Irresolution and faithlessness, however, plagued the efforts of Machiavelli and others to erect defenses. Rome fell in May 1527 and the

---

[16] Atkinson and Sices, 225 (Letter 208).

[17] See his letter of 10 December 1513 to F. Vettori in Atkinson and Sices, 262–265.

[18] *A Discourse on Remodeling the Government of Florence* in Allan Gilbert, v. 1, 101–115.

THE PRINCE 27

Medici fled from Florence soon after. The republic was reinstituted, which created an opening in Machiavelli's old position. It was given to another; Machiavelli tainted by association with the Medici was passed over. He died on 21 June 1527 and was buried in Santa Croce Church in Florence.

Five years after Machiavelli's death and with the permission of the Medici pope Clement VI, Antonio Blado, a Florentine printer, published the first edition of *The Prince*. Manuscripts had earlier circulated. Blado gave the work its present title in place of the *On Principalities* used by Machiavelli in his letter to Vettori on 10 December 1513 and as it appears on early manuscripts.[19] Seven copies dating before the first publication in 1532 have survived: three done by Machiavelli's former chancery colleague Biagio Buonaccorsi. Although it is not known how widely these handwritten copies circulated, the other four copies seem to have their origins in Siena, Rome, and Venice.[20] This suggests that *The Prince* had acquired some currency even before its publication. In 1550, the first collected works (the Testina edition) appeared. Shortly thereafter Pope Paul IV placed all of Machiavelli's works on the Index of Forbidden Books in 1559. Nevertheless, by the end of the century, *The Prince* had been translated into French in 1553 and into Latin in 1560. The earliest edition in English appeared in 1636. The absence of an English translation did not impede Elizabethan dramatists from making Machiavelli's name a synonym for all that is evil.

THE PRINCE: A COMMENTARY

Machiavelli The Prince with Related Documents. William J. Connell, trans. and ed. Boston: Bedford/St. Martin's, 2005.

Dedication When he had, at least largely, completed *The Prince* late in 1513, Machiavelli dedicated his book to Giuliano de' Medici who was in Rome with his brother Pope Leo X. In a letter to his friend Francesco Vettori, Florentine ambassador to the Vatican, he says that the book should be welcome to a prince, especially a new prince, and that is why he dedicates it to Giuliano. The pope was thought to be planning a campaign to acquire a state for his brother in which he would be a new prince.

---

[19] Connell, 149n4. See also the early prefaces to *The Prince* in the same place, 145–152.

[20] Brian Richardson, "*The Prince* and Its Early Italian Readers" in Martin Coyle, ed., *Niccolo Machiavelli's Prince: New Interdisciplinary Essays* (Manchester: Manchester University Press, 1995), 18–39.

28 J. T. BOOKMAN

Lorenzo de' Medici, nephew of the pope and Giuliano, ruled Florence on behalf of the family. It was to him that Machiavelli dedicated the book upon Giuliano's death in 1516.

The metaphor concerning perspective does not express Machiavelli's real conviction. He does not think that the people are well placed to understand princes or governing. In Chapter XVIII, for example, he says that "the masses are always captivated by appearances, and by the outcome of the thing." He, on the other hand, is well placed "to discourse on and give rules for the conduct of princes" because he has "long experience of modern things and constant reading about ancient things." Machiavelli is the authoritative observer.

He says that I wish "to offer myself to Your Magnificence with some evidence of my devotion to you." Machiavelli wanted a job. Nevertheless, it is a mistake to think that he wrote *The Prince* simply to get a job and, therefore, wrote what he thought a prince would want to hear. To be sure, the writing of *The Prince* was occasioned by his personal circumstances and informed by the current political situation in Italy, but what he has to say is directed at persuading a much larger audience than Medici princes. In Chapter 15, he announces that "my intent is to write a thing that is useful for whoever understands it." Furthermore, the *Discourses*, which had no such ulterior motive and which he dedicates to two friends, contains nothing that contradicts *The Prince* in any significant way. His audience is the politically ambitious.

Ch. 1 States are classified as either "republics" or "principalities" which he nowhere explicitly defines. We may infer that "republics" are states in which power is dispersed (among how many is unspecified) and that "principalities" are states in which power is concentrated in one, the prince. The initial classification is elaborated by distinguishing principalities that are hereditary from those that are new. The significance of this distinction is explained in Chapters II and III.

- Are these distinctions informed by a principle of classification based upon the ends for which power is exercised?

Ch. 2 The Prince concerns principalities only. The reference to a discussion of republics may refer to the *Discourses*. If that is the case, then the sentence was added after the work was completed late in 1513. Machiavelli did not

THE PRINCE   29

begin work on the *Discourses* until 1515. David Wootten in the introduction to his translation suggests an alternative understanding: Machiavelli's discussion occurred with his interrogators while in prison on a charge of complicity in a plot against the Medici. Both Giuliano and Lorenzo would know about that discussion.

"The orders of one's ancestors" means the settled ways of doing things, the institutions of the society.

Ch. 3 A number of empirical generalizations are asserted here and in later chapters which have inspired some to characterize Machiavelli as a realist, a scientist, or a technical writer. Many, even all, of those generalizations might prove false without affecting the appropriateness of the characterization. Scientists after all have often been wrong about even strongly held beliefs. On this understanding, Machiavelli is ethically neutral, indifferent as to what people do or want. The rules that he propounds for princely conduct should be understood as hypothetical imperatives: if you want this, then do that.

- Is Machiavelli ethically neutral, indifferent about the ends to be pursued?

Ch. 4 Machiavelli further refines his classification scheme by distinguishing principalities in which power is centralized from those in which it is decentralized.

Ch. 5 Machiavelli describes a city living at liberty and under its own laws. Florence was such a city before the Medici, on the heels of the papal armies of Julius II, reinstituted princely rule. In the centuries preceding Machiavelli's day, the Italian city-states had found it necessary to increase their resources and to extend their territories in order to preserve their independence. Florence governed the citizens of tributary states like Pisa, Arezzo, and Pistoia as subjects. As Florence grew, direct popular government became increasingly unmanageable. Eligibility to participate was, therefore, greatly restricted. No system of representative government based on a broad franchise was ever devised. When the republic, as Machiavelli knew it, was restored in 1494, only a small fraction of those subject to Florentine rule were politically eligible.

30   J. T. BOOKMAN

Ch. 6 Machiavelli proposes to take his bearings from the founding of new states and from their founders. Plato and Aristotle, on the other hand, took their bearings from what they regarded as the end of man and the political community. For them, understanding is only possible in light of the end, because the end provides the measure of individuals and of particular states. For Machiavelli, beginnings, the actions of founding princes, are significant because they inform the actions of their successors.

- Have there ever been states that are "wholly new," that is, groups of people without customs of their own upon whom founders could impose "whatever form they chose?"
- Is this what the founders of the United States did in creating the so-called first new nation?

Any prince who undertakes to introduce "new orders" faces formidable obstacles, namely, "those who are doing well under the old orders" and those "who do not truly believe in new things."

- Is this an answer to the first question above?

In the face of these obstacles, innovators must have force of their own that they can use to compel obedience. "Armed prophets were victorious and the unarmed ones were ruined." However dispositive this may sound of the issue between force and ideas, it did not discourage Machiavelli from taking up the role of unarmed prophet. He accounts Savonarola a failure, but Christ, too, was an unarmed prophet, and he was victorious in the sense that Christianity won many adherents and eventually became the official religion of the Roman Empire.

Machiavelli's emphasis on armed prophets who introduce new orders and methods may have horrific resonance for the reader. The armed prophets of the twentieth century, like Lenin, Hitler, and Mussolini, brought catastrophe. As you read more in *The Prince*, ask yourself if Machiavelli proposes their new orders.

- Does he glorify the use of violence for its own sake?
- Does he praise irrationalism?
- Does he advocate the elimination of whole classes of people?
- Does he demand adherence by all to some ideology?
- Does he advocate the elimination of all associations not closely controlled by the state?

THE PRINCE   31

Before you leave this chapter, notice that Moses is included among the most notable of founders. He is distinguished from the others as "a mere executor of the things that were ordered of him by God" and whose actions, therefore, should not be considered. Presumably his actions should not be considered because his authority rested on revelation, and reason is incapable of evaluating that claim. But Machiavelli observes that if the "particular actions and orders [of the other founders] are considered they will appear no different from those of Moses."

Virtù is a frequently used word in all of Machiavelli's works, and its use has posed problems for both translators and readers. It occurs 59 times in *The Prince* and nowhere more frequently than in this chapter. The word has broad meaning. Depending on the context, it may be translated as "ability," "skill," "strength," "courage," "determination," "energy," or "talent" among other things. We shall return to Machiavelli's understanding of *virtù* in Chapter 16, where he discusses princely *virtù*. Suffice it to say for the moment that he does not usually mean by *virtù* what Christians or the ancient Greeks meant by virtue. Usually he means to refer to nonmoral qualities, as when he speaks of the virtue of the archer's bow. We do the same when we refer to a good plumber or a good apple, say, without intending any moral evaluation. Nor do we intend to convey any ethical connotations when using the phrase "by virtue of."

Ch. 7 This chapter and other passages throughout *The Prince* suggest another understanding of Machiavelli's teaching. Instead of the hypothetical imperative mentioned in the comments on Chapter 3, these passages may be read as implying that the imperative is egoistic: Do whatever is necessary to increase one's power and reputation as a prince. Although Cesare Borgia is not given as an example in Chapter 8 as one of those who acquired power "through some wicked and nefarious way," he did commit wicked acts, a good many of them, as the account here testifies. Nevertheless, Machiavelli asserts that "I would not know what better precepts to give to a new prince than the example of his actions."

- How candid is Machiavelli in describing the acts that may be necessary to acquire power?
- Does he gloss over wrong acts by using euphemisms?

Ch. 8 Machiavelli denies Agathocles a place "among the most excellent men." And yet he is described as one who used cruelty well. Cruel deeds are well used when "they are done all at once, out of the necessity of securing

32   J. T. BOOKMAN

oneself, and when afterward they do not persist, but are converted into as much utility for the subjects as possible." Agathocles, and presumably Cesare Borgia, "can have remedy for their state with God and with men." This suggests that the wrong of cruelties committed to acquire power is mitigated by the exercise of power to serve the common good. Machiavelli departs from the humanists in rejecting Seneca's censure of cruelty (*On Clemency*. I. xiii. iv; and II. ii. iii) and that of Cicero who held that "there are some acts ... so wicked, that a wise man would not commit them, even to save his country" (*De officiis*. I. xlv. 159).

In this chapter, and in Chapters 15, 17, and 18, Cicero's *De officiis* serves as foil for *The Prince*. The second-century Roman statesman and orator was well known to Machiavelli and his humanist contemporaries. The humanists often invoked Cicero as a moral authority and his *De officiis* (Of Duties) as a leading text setting out the rules of right conduct. Machiavelli could depend on his educated readers to compare his teaching with that of Cicero. Devoted Christians, of course, looked to the church for guidance about such things.

- Must a prince intend that the common good be advanced by his cruelties?
- Or, is it sufficient to mitigate his cruelties that law and order, for example, are coincidentally realized when the prince solidifies his rule?
- Do you suppose that wearing the cloak of law and order a prince would suppress any challenge to his power and by whatever means necessary?

Machiavelli gives something of an answer to these questions in the *Discourses*. I. 18: "It happens only very rarely that a good man wishes to become prince through evil means, even though his goal may be a good one; while, on the other hand, we discover that it is equally rare for an evil man who has become prince to act correctly, for it would never enter his mind to employ that authority for a good which he has acquired by evil means."

Even if the blame of cruelty may be mitigated, "one cannot call it virtue to kill one's fellow-citizens, to betray one's friends, to be without faith, without compassion, without religion. These modes may be used to acquire rule, but not glory."

- Do we have here a distinction between legitimate and illegitimate principalities based upon the means whereby power was acquired?
- If all princes, that is, political leaders, were to follow the egoistic imperative, what would be the result?
- Is this consistent with what Machiavelli wants? What does he want?
- Are all political leaders interested solely in increasing their own power and reputation?
- Even if all political leaders want power and reputation, does Machiavelli make moral distinctions among the means they employ and the ends they pursue?

Ch. 9 Machiavelli's popular sympathies receive expression in his description of the two "humors" to be found "in every city." He says much the same thing in the *Discourses* I. 5,40. From these two humors come one of three effects. Only principality is analyzed in *The Prince*. Machiavelli treats liberty and license at length in the *Discourses*, the *History of Florence*, and elsewhere.

Ch. 10 Machiavelli frequently refers the reader to other chapters. The referents in this chapter are as follows: "As to the first case, it had been discussed [Chapter 6], and in what is coming we shall say about it what is needed [Chapters 19–20]. ... Whoever has fortified his town well, and managed himself concerning the other affairs of his subjects, as stated above [Chapter 9] and as will be said below" [Chapter 19].

Ch. 11 Machiavelli concludes his examination of the different types of principalities by taking up the ecclesiastical. He has the same reservations about discussing them as he had about discussing Moses as a founder in Chapter 6. "Since they are ruled by superior causes that the human mind is unable to reach, I shall leave out speaking about them." The ecclesiastical principality is the invisible church ruled by God. In this spiritual realm, ecclesiastical princes are kept in power "however they proceed and live." Their subjects, those who have received God's grace, although they are not governed [by ecclesiastical princes], they "do not care."

He has no such reservation about discussing the church in its visible (temporal) manifestation. In the *Discourses*. I. 12, he goes so far as to say that because of "the wicked examples of that court [of Rome] this province has lost all devotion and all religion." However wicked the court of

34   J. T. BOOKMAN

Rome may have been, and it was often quite wicked, the influence of its example could not have been so great as Machiavelli asserts. Many continued to believe in a salvation to be secured only under the auspices of the church, and to disdain worldly things in favor of the spiritual. It was those beliefs that contributed to the acquisition of temporal power by the church during the papacy of Alexander VI. This pope, father of Cesare Borgia, "showed how far a pope with money and armies could prevail." Thus, ecclesiastical princes acquire temporal power by the same means as other princes. Piety and humility will not do, but money and arms may come from the pious and humble.

- In Machiavelli's view, does the authority of temporal princes come from God?
- Is the obedience of subjects to temporal princes a divine command?

Chs. 12 and 13 Machiavelli states that "the principal foundations that all states must have … are good laws and good arms." And "because good laws cannot exist where there are not good arms, and where there are good arms there should be good laws, … I shall speak of arms."

- What are good laws?
- Is a law that is not enforced, cannot be enforced, nevertheless, a good law?
- Are all laws that are enforced good laws?
- Do good arms indicate the presence of some other qualities, for example, civic-mindedness, that make the adoption of good laws more likely?

"Good arms" are composed of "your subjects, your citizens, or your dependents," not mercenaries whose services are for hire and only for campaigns without "labor and fear," not auxiliaries whose first loyalty is to another ruler, and not mixed troops. Machiavelli does not tell us here whether troops of one's own, if they are to provide good arms, ought to be raised as volunteers or by conscription, to be paid or unpaid, or whether it is necessary that they be of the same nationality or speak the same language. They must, he says, be ready to die for you.

The use of mercenary and auxiliary troops by Italian states brought, he contends, the loss of autonomy, the loss of freedom from foreign domination. In language that anticipates that of Chapter 26, Machiavelli describes the

THE PRINCE   35

result: "Italy was overrun by Charles, plundered by Louis, forced by Ferdinand, and insulted by the Swiss" and "conducted … into slavery and shame."

Ch. 14 Machiavelli repeats in somewhat different language a maxim earlier expressed in Chapter 6: "[A]rmed prophets were victorious and the unarmed ones were ruined." For princes, the value of arms is clear: "[I]t not only maintains those who are born princes, but many times it makes men of private fortune rise to that rank." For everyone else, it can be inferred from Chapter 13 that an army has value as defense against foreign domination and from Chapters 7 and 8 that arms have value in the preservation of domestic order. Aristotle acknowledged (*The Politics*. 1291a7–8) that the military is a necessary part of the state and necessary for the same reasons as advanced by Machiavelli. For Aristotle, however, neither defense against foreign invasion nor the preservation of domestic order is the only end of the state or even its principal end.

Machiavelli's emphasis on arms in the acquisition and maintenance of power and in the preservation of political autonomy no doubt reflects the unsettled conditions of Italian politics. All around him the Italian city-states constantly fought for territorial gain. And foreign states, with and without alliance with some Italian state, pursued conquest. Domestic politics too was marked by armed struggle as this or that faction sought supremacy. The same unsettled condition of Greek politics made a lesser impression on Aristotle.

- Is a state free from foreign domination and ruled by a prince who knows nothing but war worth having?
- What are the alternatives?
- What is in it for the prince? For everyone else?
- Does Machiavelli really mean to suggest that war is the principal end of the state?
- For Machiavelli, is war simply the necessary means to external security and domestic order?
- In addition to external security and domestic order, are there other components of the common good?

Machiavelli elaborates his position on these matters in *The Art of War* (see particularly Book I) and in the *Discourses*. As for his contention that the prince should know nothing but war, see the close of Chapter XXI.

36   J. T. BOOKMAN

Ch. 15 Machiavelli announces that "I shall depart from the orders of the others" in order to go after "the effectual truth of the thing." The ancients like Plato and Aristotle and medieval thinkers like Augustine and Aquinas asked: What is human excellence and what form of community best promotes the achievement of human excellence? Machiavelli seems to dismiss the attempt to discover the community best suited to promote the achieve ment of human excellence—"republics and principalities that have never been seen or known to exist in truth." He does not identify those unseen republics and principalities, but Plato's republic and Augustine's city of God immediately suggest themselves.

Machiavelli abandons the project undertaken by Plato and Aristotle, Augustine and Aquinas, not out of a conviction that excellence in either people or states cannot be discovered. He may be contending that the good life as conceived by them is beyond reach: "There is such a difference from how one lives to how one ought to live" and "human conditions do not allow it." But he also says that "a man who would wish to make a career of being good in every detail must come to ruin among so many who are not good." This leaves open the possibility of living the morally good life but at the cost of worldly success. He is not interested in people who disdain worldly things like power, wealth, and glory. In the dedication of his *A Discourse on Remodeling the Government of Florence*, he says that "no man is so much exalted by any act of his as are those men who have with laws and institutions remodeled republics and kingdoms; these are, after those who have been gods, the first to be praised. ... And so much has this glory been esteemed by men seeking for nothing other than glory that when unable to form a republic in reality, they have done it in writing, as Aristotle, Plato, and many others."

In any event, the good life is not open to a prince "who wants to keep his authority" because he might have to practice vices "without which he would find it hard to save his state." Compare this observation with that of Chapter 18: "to preserve the state, he often has to do things against his word, against charity, against humanity, against religion" and with that of Chapter 19: "a prince who wants to keep his state is often bound to do what is not good." As a consequence, a prince must "learn to be able to be not good." Machiavelli, then, adopts what Cicero calls a "pernicious doctrine": "a thing may be morally right without being expedient" (*De officiis*. II. iii. 9–10).

THE PRINCE   37

In these passages, Machiavelli employs the conventional understanding of what constitutes a good person. It is the moral good with which he is concerned here. To be sure, there is ambiguity about what are the desirable qualities in the list given in this chapter, but no such ambiguity exists in Chapter 18, where he says that "it is useful to seem compassionate, faithful, humane, honest, honest, and religious—and to be so." Nevertheless, he advises the prince that "he needs to have a spirit disposed to change as the winds of fortune and the variation of things command him, and ... not to depart from the good if he is able, but to know how to enter into evil when he needs to."

- Is it possible to govern without getting "dirty hands"?
- Do the ends justify the means? What ends? What means?
- Who is to judge what ends are to be pursued and by what means?
- If we hold that the ends never justify the means when the means are wrong, does this turn the field of effective political action over to the unscrupulous?
- How can we know if political leaders have any scruples?

In *The Prince*, Machiavelli is concerned with princely virtue. Most of what he says about the ordinary citizenry is disparaging. The nobility he regards in an even worse light. Ordinary citizens are not always in the dissolute condition that makes necessary a prince if they are to be governed at all. They may possess virtue. In the *Discourses*, he defines virtue in the citizenry as civic-mindedness, that is, devotion to the state and community.

Ch. 16 In this chapter and those that immediately follow—Chapters 17, 18, and 19—Machiavelli elaborates on the observation expressed at the end of Chapter 15: "For, if everything be well considered, something will be found that will appear a virtue, but will lead to his ruin if adopted; and something else that will appear a vice, if adopted, will result in his security and well-being." He argues that the nature of politics is such that its successful practice requires adherence to the paradoxical principle: it is right to do wrong. Generosity, mercy, and honesty, all accounted virtues on the conventional understanding, have undesirable consequences under some circumstances. Stinginess, cruelty, and dishonesty, on the other hand, may have desirable consequences. Desirable for whom? There are passages in *The Prince* that suggest the egoistic imperative: Do whatever is necessary to acquire the throne and to maintain one's position as prince.

Ch. 17 Machiavelli here, indeed throughout *The Prince*, reminds us that politics is informed (in part? in large part?) by coercion—either force or the threat of force. He dismisses love as a "bond of obligation" between government and those subject to its laws, contrary to Cicero's admonition (*De officiis.* II. vii. 24–25). He would seem to have little more regard for the efficacy of persuasion (or education?) as a way to secure voluntary obedience to the law—witness the fate of unarmed prophets. Given the bleak view of human nature set out in this chapter and elsewhere in *The Prince*, the reader might wonder if people are governable at all. Machiavelli insists, however, that people can be governed and that the prince must rely on fear, the dread of punishment.

Since coercion must be employed in the governing of men and women, the question for Machiavelli is "how much force is necessary?" In Chapter 8 and again here he advocates "cruelty well-used." Cruelty can be minimized if the prince avoids the hatred and contempt of his subjects. If the prince avoids those things, he says in Chapter 19, most men will "live content," and the prince will "have only to contend with the ambition of the few."

- Does Machiavelli concede then that fear alone provides an insufficient foundation for government?

Ch. 18 No state can preserve itself without the capacity and the will to use force, because, Machiavelli argues, the law "many times … is not enough" and neither persuasion nor love can be relied upon. He acknowledges that force is the way of beasts, but, unlike Cicero (*De officiis.* I. xiii. 41), he does not on that account find force unworthy of man. Indeed, he appropriates Cicero's own metaphor in recommending a stance for the prudent prince: depending on the circumstances, be a lion (forceful) or a fox (cunning). These qualities are required because people are usually greedy, self-interested, and recalcitrant.

The ruled do not know what their rulers really are. In part, this is so because the ruled are inattentive and unperceptive—"the masses are always captivated by appearances, and by the outcome of the thing" and, in part, because princes, or rather prudent princes, deceive their subjects about what they really are. Machiavelli advises princes to appear to be what they cannot always be. Because the ruled do not know what their rulers really are, a ruler's acts must be judged according to their consequences: "one looks to the end." Machiavelli's Italian is "*si guarda al fin*"—sometimes

THE PRINCE   39

interpreted as the end justifies the means. In the *Discourses*. I. 9, he says about Romulus's fratricide: "It is fitting, indeed, that while the action accuses him, the result excuses him; and when this result is good ... it will always excuse him." Did the prince's acts bring victory against the enemy, preserve law and order, or promote prosperity?

Ch. 19 The prince must find support for his rule among the ruled—"whether the people or the army or the nobility." More particularly, princes "must first try not to be hated by collectivities, and when they cannot achieve this, they must contrive with all industry to avoid the hatred of those collectivities that are more powerful." In Machiavelli's judgment, the people have become a powerful group (see also Chapter 9) upon whom a prince can base his regime. In order to win popular support, he must not only avoid hatred and contempt, but he "ought to keep them friendly to him" (Chapter 9) and "satisfy the people and keep them content." Machiavelli says this can be done by not oppressing them (Chapter 9) and by not taking their property or violating their women (Chapter 17). To these prohibitions, Machiavelli adds the recommendations at the end of Chapter 21.

Ch. 20 Machiavelli invokes the idea of fortune (*fortuna*, i.e., luck) to explain the acquisition of greatness by a prince. For example, when fortune "makes enemies arise for him," the prince has an opportunity to demonstrate his *virtù* and, should he prevail, to acquire greatness. In this chapter, fortune is invested with intentions of her own—in Machiavelli's example, "when she wants to make a new prince great."

- What implications does this conception of fortune have for political leaders, indeed for any person, acting in the world of secular affairs?

In this regard, it is worth remembering that Machiavelli complains at the close of the Dedication "how undeservedly I endure a great and continuous malignity of fortune." Cesare Borgia lost his kingdom, we are told in Chapter 7, not through any fault of his own but "from an extraordinary and extreme malignity of fortune." And, at the beginning of that chapter, our author says that even a private person, in the absence of any demonstration of virtue, might "through fortune alone" become a prince.

In Chapter 6, fortune is not personified but designates the circumstances in which action might or might not be taken. The existing circumstances created an opportunity for the great founders to demonstrate *virtù*. Those circumstances were daunting. Nevertheless, Moses, Romulus, and

40   J. T. BOOKMAN

the others were so virtuous that they needed only an opportunity, "and without that opportunity the virtue of their spirit would have been wasted; and without that virtue, the opportunity would have come in vain."

- Does the possession of virtue ensure success and the acquisition of glory?
- Even by leaders who are not mythical founders?
- Are there limits to what even the virtuous can do in contending against the circumstances of their time?
- Is a leader wholly dependent upon fortune for the provision of opportunity to demonstrate virtue and thereby to acquire glory?

Machiavelli observes that no definite rule about the defensive measures the prince ought to adopt can be formulated "without knowing the particular circumstances of the state to be managed." We were told earlier in Chapter 19 that "a prince must have two fears: one inside, on account of his subjects, the other outside, on account of external powers." The critical circumstance would not seem to be the military prowess of foreign states but the identity of the prince's domestic adversaries. In that same chapter, he says that "it is … necessary to contend … with the ambition of the great and the insolence of the people." If he uses force to curb the people and thereby incurs their hatred, he ought to build fortresses which, however, afford an uncertain refuge. If, on the other hand, he wins the support of the people by avoiding their hatred and contempt, he can eschew fortresses. What is more, by arming his subjects the prince acquires the arms he needs to counter the ambition of the nobles.

Ch. 21 Machiavelli's attitude toward the Roman Church is hostile. In the *Discourses.* I. 2, he blames the papacy for its "wicked examples" that have caused Italians to abandon their religion, "which brings with it infinite inconveniences and infinite disorders." And, the church has kept Italy divided— too weak to unite Italy herself but strong enough to prevent any other Italian state from doing so. His attitude toward religion, and Christianity in particular, is more complicated than it appears in this and earlier chapters of *The Prince.* One aspect of that attitude receives expression in his remarks about the king of Spain, Ferdinand the Catholic, as he was often called. Ferdinand, he says, was "ever making use of religion." In Chapter 18, he advises the prince to appear "all religion—and there is nothing more necessary to appear to have than this … quality." Religion, for him, is, in part, a form of political control under whose guise secular purposes can be advanced.

Machiavelli again expresses his disdain for the irresolute, the indecisive. In Chapter 19, he characterized these qualities as "effeminate" and sure to evoke contempt for a prince.

Chs. 22 and 23 It is easy to see these chapters as an advertisement for himself, but, whatever his motives, Machiavelli's observations have some force. He sought also in Chapter 20 to supply assurances to his Medici dedicatee that "princes, and especially those who are new, have found more faith and more usefulness in those men who were held suspect at the beginning of their states than in those of whom they were confident at the beginning." Self-assertion came easily to Renaissance men. Machiavelli's self-promotion is restrained by the standards of the day.

Ch. 24 Italian princes, Machiavelli asserts, have wrongly blamed fortune for the loss of their states. In fact, it was their own "laziness" and lack of foresight—their failure to "think of storms during a calm." Some of those princes, including the King of Naples and the Duke of Milan both of whom he cites, lost their states as a result of foreign invasion. Italian princes, he says, should have been raising troops of their own (see Chapters 12 and 13), making their peoples happy, and mollifying the nobility (see Chapters 9, 19, and 20).

- How satisfactory an explanation is this for the loss of states by Italian princes?

In the *Discourses*. II. 2, he advances another consideration: "Our religion has glorified humble and contemplative rather than active men. It has then placed the highest good in humility, abjectness, and contempt for things human; the other [pagan religion] placed it in greatness of spirit, strength of body, and all other things capable of making men very strong."

- How satisfactory an explanation is this for the loss of states by Italian princes?

At the end of the chapter, Machiavelli asserts that "the only defenses that are good, certain, and enduring are those that depend upon yourself and your own virtue." Perhaps no other passage in *The Prince* expresses so baldly his remove from Christian thought in particular and medieval thought generally. By these words, he commits the sin of pride. Like so

42   J. T. BOOKMAN

many Renaissance thinkers, he has a heightened confidence in human ability and a desire for autonomy—a desire to live according to one's own laws or principles. And he may well believe that there is nothing else to rely on but one's own virtue. According to Christian thought, humans, flawed by original sin, must rely on God. Only by the bestowal of God's grace can we attain salvation and everlasting blessedness. Machiavelli, of course, is interested only in the attainment of earthly ends.

Ch. 25 What can people do to change their institutions in desired directions and to preserve what they find desirable? Machiavelli addresses this question directly in this chapter, but it is never far out of his thoughts throughout *The Prince*. In Chapter 3, he speaks of the difficulty rulers have in recognizing threats to the state until they have grown so great that counter-measures are unavailing. In Chapter 6, he mentions the opposition to change offered by those who are advantaged by the status quo and by those who fear anything new.

For his medieval predecessors, educated and uneducated alike, government and law, indeed all social institutions, are founded on custom and divine providence. As a consequence of the Fall, humankind has instituted government, entered into private property relations, and cast some into slavery. These institutions serve to constrain the wicked impulses of fallen men and women. Until the final Day of Judgment the human condition will remain the same—created in the image of the divine but fallen and dependent on divine grace for redemption. No change that humans might make can significantly affect the human condition. Any changes that might be attempted are jeopardized by the fallibility of human reason and by the unintended consequences of human action. Moreover, in relying on unassisted reason to identify human ends and to effect change directed at their realization, men and women fall prey to pride. Rather than attempt to make changes, it is far better to rely on God and to look after one's soul in preparation for the life to come.

Machiavelli takes a different view. He does not ask after God's purposes. He is interested only in what people want for themselves in this life. He regards political institutions as human contrivances for secular ends, rather than as ordained by God to constrain fallen men and women from falling further into sin. Existing institutions do not serve Italians well. They do not provide external security or domestic order. He is well aware that to work change intentionally is difficult: "Nothing is more difficult to

THE PRINCE   43

treat, nor more doubtful to succeed, nor more dangerous to manage than to make oneself a leader who introduces new orders" (Chapter 6). Custom and interest bind people to the familiar (Chapters 2, 5, and 6).

Nevertheless, Machiavelli dissents from the view "that many persons have held, and hold, ... that the things of the world are governed by fortune and by God, that men, with their prudence, cannot correct them, and that instead they have no remedy whatsoever." This was the prevailing Christian view as set out by Boethius (c.480–c.524) in *The Consolation of Philosophy* (2: 1–4 and 3: 9–10). That Roman statesman and philosopher sought to dispel the idea that fortune's favor might be won by prayer or sacrifice. Not even the virtuous as described by the ancients can depend on the award of fortune's gifts. The Christian conception renders fortune blind and undiscriminating. God has placed the distribution of all earthly goods in fortune's capricious hands to teach humankind to look beyond earthly things.

Although he acknowledges that "sometimes" he is inclined to that view, Machiavelli claims some efficacy for human effort in the control of events: "It may be true that fortune is the arbiter of half of our actions, but that she indeed allows us to govern the other half of them, or almost that much."

- What are we to make of this?

"It may be true," he says, but, one supposes, it might not be true. "She ... allows us." Is this an allowance that might be withdrawn? "The other half ... or almost that much"? Is this a maximum?

Machiavelli has another go at gauging fortune's power by means of two metaphors. In the first, fortune is likened to a river in flood sweeping all before it, and, in the second, to a woman waiting to be won. Dikes and embankments can be built to confine the torrent and, thereby, to make it "neither so boundless nor so harmful."

- In erecting dikes and embankments, have political leaders exercised at least half the control over events?
- What qualities constitute that virtue that resisted fortune in this case?
- Is there a beast with whom these qualities are associated?

"Fortune is a lady," and, if she is to be won, it is necessary "to beat her and to dash her."

44   J. T. BOOKMAN

- In winning the lady has one exercised half the control over events?
- What qualities constitute that virtue that overcame fortune in this case?
- Is there a beast with whom these qualities are associated?

Notice that in both these cases Machiavelli rejects passivity. Something can be done. Do it. In Chapter 18, he argues that leaders must be able to act as either a fox or a lion depending upon the circumstances.

- Does Machiavelli think that a leader can act in both these ways?
- What are the implications of this for effecting change?

In any attempt to effect change, no person or group can anticipate all eventualities or control all the forces in play. Human affairs are just too complicated. Furthermore, things that could have been foreseen are sometimes ignored and things that could have been controlled are left unrestrained.

- Does Machiavelli think that Cesare Borgia could have foreseen the enmity of Pope Julius II?
- Does Machiavelli think that Italian princes could have better controlled those forces that brought their downfall?

Fortune is the unforeseen and the uncontrolled. The less that political leaders depend on things breaking their way, the more success they will have. Machiavelli put it this way in Chapter 6: "He who has relied less on fortune has kept more of what he has acquired."

- Upon what should political leaders depend?

Ch. 26 Machiavelli suggests that circumstances are favorable for the introduction of a form to Italy by a new prince that "would do honor to him and good to the collectivity of its inhabitants."

- Why does Machiavelli think so? What "things are coming together"?

What form he has in mind is unspecified. He does say that he wants an Italy free from foreign domination and, before that can be accomplished, a prince must invent new laws and new orders. In the *Discourses*. I. 12, he expresses a decided preference for national government: "And truly

THE PRINCE 45

no province has ever been united or happy unless it has all come under obedience to one republic or to one prince, as happened to France and to Spain." Unification would be "Italy's redemption" and the leader in this effort her "redeemer." Italians, however, were too divided in their loyalties to support any new form that comprehended them all. The word "Italy" would remain for more than three centuries a "geographical expression" as Count Metternich put in the mid-nineteenth century.

- Is *The Prince* well-calculated to gain the favor of a prince?
- What portrait of a prince is depicted in its pages?
- Do you think that leaders see themselves as Machiavelli does?
- Would a prince who follows Machiavelli's advice hire him?

A BIBLIOGRAPHICAL ESSAY

The quincentenary of Machiavelli's birth in 1969 occasioned a flowering of scholarship about this enigmatic political theorist. The outpouring of biographies, books of commentary, and editions of his writings, particularly *The Prince*, continues unabated to the present day. Our understanding of Machiavelli has been deepened thereby, but few of even the hoariest questions about his teaching have been laid to rest. For all the attention devoted to him, the nature of his contribution to political philosophy remains very much a controverted matter. In what follows I identify and describe works by and about Machiavelli that have appeared in English. The numbers in parentheses refer to the appended list.

The most complete recent collection of Machiavelli's works is A. Gilbert's three-volume translation (33). It contains in their entirety all the works of first importance to the student of political philosophy, namely, *The Prince*, the *Discourses, The Art of War*, and the *History of Florence*, as well as others including all the letters Gilbert had published earlier under separate cover. Germino called A. Gilbert "unquestionably the most accurate and reliable translator of Machiavelli into English" and characterized *Chief Works* as a "reliable and stylistically felicitous translation." F. Gilbert also found the translation "excellent." A. Gilbert displaced Detmold (32) as the standard translation. The latter, however, must be consulted for the legations (Machiavelli's diplomatic correspondence) which are largely omitted by A. Gilbert. Atkinson and Sices (52) have brought out a superb and large collection of Machiavelli's personal correspondence that includes all the letters to be found in A. Gilbert (33), Hale (35), Bondanella and Musa (31), and many more.

A few of the many other translations of *The Prince* and several of the *Discourses* bear mention for their distinguishing characteristics. Musa's edition of *The Prince* (59) is bilingual, and his introduction lists every instance in which the word *virtù* appears and how he has translated it. This list is helpful in following the ongoing dispute over the explication of Machiavellian *virtù*. Adams (55) contains a number of critical essays written by the editor and others and a brief publishing history of *The Prince*. The Modern Library edition by Max Lerner (36) brings *The Prince* and the *Discourses* under one cover and includes an introductory essay by the editor. Wootten (39) provides *The Prince* entire and somewhat less than half the *Discourses*. His introduction warrants attention for the light it throws on several puzzles in *The Prince*, for example, the reference to a discussion of republics in Chapter 2. Bondanella and Musa (63) have revised their translation originally published in *The Portable Machiavelli*. An appended set of notes identifies people, events, and places to which Machiavelli refers or alludes. An even more extensive glossary of proper names is attached to the editions by Skinner and Price (57) and by Viroli and Bondanella (62). Both these editions and those by Connell (56) and Adams (55) address the difficulties of translating Machiavelli's Italian. Connell's comments are the most extensive, and he refers to other translations. Skinner and Price also have a useful set of notes, running to some 13 pages, on the vocabulary of *The Prince*.

As for Machiavelli's other works, Bondanella and Musa (31) is a compilation of many works both political and literary including *The Prince*, the *Life of Castruccio Castracani*, and abridged versions of the *Discourses*, *The Art of War*, and the *History of Florence*. Walker's translation (44) of the *Discourses* is preceded by an analytical table of contents and succeeded by lengthy notes cited by number in the text; there is also an introductory essay. In dissent from the high praise accorded Walker by several scholars—notables to be sure, but not in Italian studies— Whitfield found "abundant evidence throughout the text that this translation is the work of an amateur with an insufficient command both of standard Italian, and of the special Florentine of Machiavelli's time and use." This evaluation did not discourage Crick (45) from bringing out a new edition of Walker's translation revised by Richardson. Whitfield found the repairs incomplete and inexpert, and lamented that "like Niccolo da Uzzano, I thought that while I lived nobody could make the mistake of reprinting Father Walker's mistranslation of Machiavelli." Fortunately, recent and highly praised translations are available by Mansfield and Tarcov (46) and the Bondanellas (47).

THE PRINCE   47

There is no exhaustive bibliography of work on Machiavelli. Norsa's bibliography (4), which includes work in English as well as in other languages, is lengthy, some 2000 entries, but it is quite dated. He lists works, mostly books, that appeared from 1740 to 1935. There are no annotations. Ruffo-Fiore (5) picks up where Norsa leaves off and moves forward to 1986. Most of the more than 2000 entries are annotated. She organizes the bibliography chronologically and provides a thorough index. The essays of Clark (1) and Cochrane (2) cover some of the same ground as Ruffo-Fiore, but in a much more selective and critical fashion. While the opinions of Clark and Cochrane can be faulted, they have surveyed widely and at length in the literature. The same can be said of Eccleshall and Kenny (3), whose more recent and ambitious effort includes nearly 100 entries on Machiavelli with, in most instances, brief, critical annotations.

The standard biography remains Ridolfi (24), which displaced the rambling work of Villari (28). Ridolfi does try credulity in seeking to show that Machiavelli lived a life of "substantial Christianity." Prezzolini (23) takes the opposite line in condemning Machiavelli as anti-Christian. Hale (16) treats both his life and thought in a more nuanced way than either of the preceding. C. Atkinson (6) has made available the principal source of information about Machiavelli before his election as second chancellor: his father's diary. Black (126) describes the circumstances of that election. Black and Najemy evaluate Machiavelli's career in government in Coyle's collection of articles (66), as does Chiappelli (13). Mattingly (21) permits us to see Machiavelli's diplomatic experience in broader context. Among more recent biographies, Capponi (11) is quite engaging. He finds that Machiavelli had "all the traits typical of the Florentines of his day (and even of today): love of contradiction, provocation, and *bella figura*, with a pronounced jocular streak of seasoning." Oppenheimer (22) is overwrought and full of exaggerated claims. Viroli (29) incorporates recent scholarship and advances an understanding of Machiavelli as a rhetorician.

To learn more about three important men who figured prominently in Machiavelli's political experience, see Martines (19) and Weinstein (30) on Savonarola, Bradford (8) on Cesare Borgia, and Shaw (26) on Julius II. Butters examines Machiavelli's relations with the Medici in Najemy's collection (74). Baron (7) identifies the crisis of the early Italian Renaissance as the clash between the supporters of the republican communes and the proponents of more authoritarian government. Florence, the last bastion of republicanism, succumbed finally to the Medici in 1532 with the establishment of a hereditary monarchy. Hale (17) and Rubinstein (25) describe how the Medici were able to subvert republican institutions. Butters (10) analyzes the Florentine government during Machiavelli's tenure as second chancellor, and Stephens (27) describes the last years of the republic. Brucker (9) and Goldthwaite (15) fill in the social and economic background.

Dunn and Harris (67) has no rival as the most comprehensive compila tion of articles on Machiavelli. The two volumes comprise more than 1000 pages and have a chronological arrangement, beginning with a piece published in 1827 by T. B. Macaulay. Dunn and Harris is available only in large research libraries, however, so one may have to turn to Gilmore (70), Jensen (72), and Parel (75). There are important essays in the last three collections, but far fewer of them than appear in Dunn and Harris. Gilbert (69), Mansfield (73), and Whitfield (79) have contributed much to Machiavelli scholarship. Each has brought out a selection of their previously published articles, including some published in Italian. Najemy (74) and Vilches and Seaman (78) include in their compilations essays written since the publication of Dunn and Harris. Bock, Skinner, and Viroli (65) and Rahe (76) focus on Machiavelli's republicanism. Sullivan (77) is concerned with his literary works, and Ascoli and Kahn (64) with the literary dimensions of his works, including the political.

Although Machiavelli is often candid and plain-spoken, ambiguity and inconsistency abound in his writing. He is not a systematic thinker. He uses terms imprecisely, and he speaks in several voices, here matter-of-factly, there impassioned, and he often emphasizes something to make a point without indicating its relative importance. These qualities give plausibility to a variety of interpretations.

The "contextualist" approach closely associated with Skinner (113 and 114) is also followed by Chabod (89). Skinner's examination of the historical context in which Machiavelli wrote leads him to conclude that Machiavelli is not entirely *sui generis.* On the contrary, *The Prince* is "a recognizable contribution to a well-established tradition of later quattrocento political thought," namely, the mirror-of-princes literature as contended by A. Gilbert (96), and the *Discourses* "a relatively orthodox contribution to a well-established tradition of Republican political thought." Skinner concedes some originality to Machiavelli. Unlike so many of his contemporaries, Machiavelli denies any necessary connection between *virtù* and the Christian virtues for either the prince or the republican citizen. "For all the many differences between *The Prince* and the *Discourses,* the underlying political morality of the two works is thus the same." Skinner also finds in the *Discourses*, as does Ingersoll (143), a strong dissent from the belief, prevalent at the time, that civic discord must be suppressed if society is to flourish. Machiavelli maintains that class conflict bounded by the right institutions forces a compromise among sectional interests that benefits all.

Pocock (109) places Machiavelli at the center of the Renaissance revival of republican ideas that can be traced back to Aristotle. On his reading, Machiavelli's advocacy of popular participation and institutions that create a balance between the few and the many had great influence on the development of republican thought down to the American Revolution. The Machiavellian moment is that in which a republic has achieved the necessary internal balance of forces and built up sufficient military might to ensure its security against its neighbors. That moment cannot be sustained; the life of a republic is finite, although innovation might postpone the inevitable. In a more recent piece in Najemy (74), Pocock allows that "there is a narrative, continuing into a present, in which he [Machiavelli] is still at least quotable." McCormick (104) accuses Pocock of a "preoccupation ... with the question of the 'temporal finitude' of republics" and thereby "conceals the oligarchic character of modern republicanism." McCormick finds in the *Discourses* measures that would allow popular government "to surveil and control political and economic elites." He "accentuates the fundamentally populist—that is, citizen-empowering— and anti-elitist foundations of Machiavelli's political thought." Like Pocock, McCormick fails to address inclusion as a problem for the contention that Machiavelli is a populist.

The relationship of *The Prince* and the *Discourses* has been much controverted. The controversy has concerned in part the question of just when the two works were written. Chabod (89), F. Gilbert in Dunn and Harris (67, v. 1:280) and also in F. Gilbert (68: 115), Hexter in Dunn and Harris (67, v. 1: 396), Richardson (157), and Whitfield in Dunn and Harris (67, v. 1: 554) and also in Whitfield (79, Ch. 10) have all proposed an answer or found fault with that of another. Hans Baron has given the matter the most attention—see his articles in Dunn and Harris (67, v. 1:372 and v. 2: 1 and 539). In the most recent he concluded that Machiavelli all but completed *The Prince* in the fall of 1513, added Chapter 26 in early 1515, and only then began the *Discourses*. Cochrane (2) urges that "the question of dating is not just another empty academic quarrel. If Baron's chronology is correct, indeed, it casts a completely new light on the meaning of all Machiavelli's work, both major and minor."

Whether or not a chronology, Baron's or that of another, does have large implications for understanding Machiavelli turns on the existence of significant differences between the works. Thus those interpretations that find continuity and similarity between the works make dating a less important matter than those that find discontinuity and dissimilarity. Baron places himself among the latter: "We can now grasp, unconcerned, the pragmatic character of *The Prince* and appraise it realistically; we are at liberty to draw the picture of Machiavelli's evolution from the Machiavellianism of *The Prince* to the new historical vision and the republican and moral values of the *Discourses*." F. Gilbert in Dunn and Harris (67, v. 1:280) holds a similar view. Among others, Mansfield (73, Intro.), Plamenatz (108), and Skinner (113) find no such disjunction. They find the basic principles in both works to be the same. Many scholars have sought to dispel some of the uncertainty about Machiavelli by paying close attention to his use of such terms as *virtù, stato, ordini, fortuna, necessità,* and *libertà*. Most of these studies by Colish (v. 2: 559), Flanagan (v. 2:109), F. Gilbert (v. 1: 248), Kahn (v. 2: 380), Mansfield (v. 2: 355), Plamenatz (v. 2: 139), Price (v. 2: 161), and Whitfield (v. 1:340) are reprinted in Dunn and Harris (67). In each of these articles, the writer has undertaken a conceptual analysis that ranges across the whole Machiavellian corpus. Other contributions along these lines that escaped the net of Dunn and Harris are Hannaford (139), Hexter (140), Price (154, 155, 157), and Wood (168). Pitkin's chapter on fortune (107) also deserves attention. Indeed Pitkin's whole book is worth reading. She argues that the tensions and ambiguities in Machiavelli "arise neither from ineptitude nor from manipulative cleverness but from ambivalence ... [about] manhood: anxiety about being sufficiently masculine and concern over what it means to be a man."

Although there has been modulation from time to time in the volume and tone of criticism visited upon him, seldom has Machiavelli escaped condemnation from at least several quarters. Pole, Gentillet, Bodin, Campanella, Frederick the Great, Fichte, Maritain, Russell, and Strauss span the life of Machiavelli interpretation and all are joined in outrage, more or less acute, at Machiavelli's alleged immorality. Strauss (117) deserves attention as the most thought-provoking and influential attack. He announces early on that he is "inclined to the old-fashioned and simple opinion according to which Machiavelli was a teacher of evil." He reaches that conclusion, however, by a path decidedly different from that traveled by earlier critics. The latter found evidence for Machiavelli's immorality in his exoteric teaching. Strauss

THE PRINCE   51

adopts that point of view and analytical apparatus set out in his *Persecution and the Art of Writing* to reveal an immoral esoteric teaching. For Strauss, Machiavelli came to displace Hobbes as the founder of the modern age. Hobbes rejected natural right (the truth discerned by the morally excellent) on the grounds that it could not be known; Machiavelli rejected natural right on the grounds that it is unobtainable. The significance of this for Strauss lies in his claim that the rejection of natural right "leads to nihilism— nay, it is identical with nihilism."

Strauss's *Thoughts* were the subject of an exchange between Mansfield (148 and 73, 219) and Pocock (152) to which Vaughn (164) also contributed. Bloom (127) defended Strauss in the face of criticism from McShea (147) and Germino (136). Mansfield renews the Straussian indictment in his book on the *Discourses* (101). His commentary is informed by Strauss's ideas about textual interpretation. J. A. Gunn observed about Mansfield's contribution in Fleisher (68): "Esoteric interpretation requires some basis in exoteric statement elsewhere, but if this statement is too obvious the need for reading between the lines may vanish. It is in this sense that I wonder if perhaps Mansfield has employed engines of exquisite refinement to force an open door." Mansfield defends his approach in the preface to his study of the *Discourses* (101).

Machiavelli advocates the use of violence and deception. But to what end, if any? Strauss (117), Mansfield (73), and De Alvarez (91) charge that Machiavelli is an apologist for princely egoism, and, they suggest, the subject-ego is Machiavelli's own. Lerner (36), Chabod (89), Whitfield (79), and McCormick (104) respond that he is a republican. Ingersoll (143) maintains that Machiavelli is a supporter of both authoritarian and republican rule—which is more desirable depends on the circumstances. Tsurutani (162) believes Machiavelli to be aware of the dangers of authoritarian rule. Machiavelli thinks, however, that when the conditions for popular government do not obtain, when the state is in decay, the risks must be run and power seized by a prince for there is no other alternative. If the prince does not bring order and does not institutionalize the rule of law, then, according to Tsurutani, "society must start all over again." Others have argued that, for Machiavelli, the end that justifies violence and deception is the national unification of Italy. This thesis has been advanced most vigorously by De Sanctis (92), Villari (28), and other Italian scholars, although it is not peculiar to them—Lodge in Dunn and Harris (67, v. 1: 153), for example, takes the same line. F. Gilbert in Dunn and Harris (67, v.1: 329) takes issue with this thesis as Machiavelli is cast

52   J. T. BOOKMAN

as a latter-day Cavour. Still others maintain that the singling out of Machiavelli for reprobation is unwarranted. According to Adams (55), Villari (28), and A. Gilbert (96), Machiavelli recommends the means used at the time, and Adams adds that "we are less inclined to blame Machiavelli … for being tarred with a brush which seems to have left its sticky touches on our hands and on practically everyone else's."

One may of course insist that, even as Machiavelli is a republican or a nationalist or a man of his time, the means that he countenances are morally repugnant and ought not to be used—the end does not justify the means. It is to this position that Plamenatz (108), Wolin (122), and Walzer (166) respond. Plamenatz argues that the principle, the end justifies the means, is in itself undeserving of the scorn heaped upon it. The utilitarians maintain much the same principle. But, while many find the greatest happiness of the greatest number an acceptable end, the might and greatness of the state as the end that justifies the means is unacceptable. For a consequentialist ethics like utilitarianism, and Machiavelli comes closer to espousing such an ethics than the principles of his predecessors, the end *justifies* the means. Wolin and Walzer take a different approach. They argue that Machiavelli regards violence and deception as essential parts of the nature of politics—one cannot govern without "dirty hands." Now, hands can be dirtied only by committing wrong acts. Does Machiavelli acknowledge the wrong in doing murder, telling lies, taking what does not belong to you, and so on? They find that he does. But, for Machiavelli, under some circumstances it is necessary to do those things to secure the internal order or the external security of the state. Therefore, rulers must learn how not to be good. In committing wrong acts that aim at realizing the internal order or external security of the state, rulers are not justified but they ought to be excused.

The question of Machiavelli's morality or immorality is wrongly answered, according to some, both by those who find an ethics in his works and those who find evil. He is a scientist. Thus, for Cassirer (88), "*The Prince* is neither a moral nor an immoral book: it is simply a technical book. In a technical book we do not seek for rules of ethical conduct, of good and evil. It is enough if we are told what is useful or useless." Machiavelli's science, then, consists of the suspension of ethical judgment in the study of political behavior. His recommendations are instrumental valuations. Olschki (106) sees Machiavelli's science as an empirical investigation of history for universal laws. Chabod (89) and Plamenatz (108) criticize this position. The view of Machiavelli's originality and his contribution to political philosophy—as the

THE PRINCE   53

progenitor of a value-free social science—directs attention to important differences that separate him from his ancient and medieval predecessors. He is secular and empirical to a degree to which they were not. He sees the state as neither the punitive nor the beneficent provision of God. Nor does he regard it as natural in the sense in which Plato and Aristotle intended. And he abjures any attempt to order state and society according to the strictures of natural or divine law.

Meinecke (105) observed years ago that "Machiavelli's theory was a sword plunged into the flank of the body politic of Western humanity, causing it to shriek and rear up." Machiavelli's theory, that is, is discontinuous with the political theories that preceded it and perhaps also with those that succeeded it, and is morally repugnant in that it gives respectability to practices theretofore condemned. With this many are in accord. Strauss, as earlier noted, marks the end of classical political philosophy and the beginning of modernity in the fifteenth chapter of *The Prince*. For Croce (90), the conception of an autonomous political order severed Machiavelli from the tradition of political philosophy: His politics are "beyond or, rather, below moral good and evil." Cassirer (88) agrees that "with Machiavelli we stand at the gateway of the modern world. ... The sharp knife of Machiavelli's thought has cut off all the threads by which in former generations the state was fastened to the organic whole of human existence." In counterpoint may be placed the views of Berlin in Dunn and Harris (67, v.2: 235) and Foucault (94). Berlin finds in Machiavelli a return to antiquity and to a "time-honored ethics, that of the Greek *polis.*" Foucault, "far from thinking that Machiavelli opens up the field of political thought to modernity," says that "he marks instead the end of an age ... in which the problem was actually that of the safety of the Prince and his territory."

A Select Bibliography of Works in English

1. Clark, Richard C. "Machiavelli: Bibliographical Spectrum." *Review of National Literatures,* 1/1 (1970) 93–135.
2. Cochrane, Eric W. "Machiavelli: 1940–1969." *Journal of Modern History,* 33 (June, 1961) 113–36.
3. Eccleshall, Robert and Michael Kenny, comp. *Western Political Thought: A Bibliographical Guide to Post-War Research.* New York: Manchester University Press, 1995.

54 J. T. BOOKMAN

4. Norsa, Achille. *Il principio della forza nel pensiero politico di Niccolo Machiavelli, seguito da un contributo bibliografico.* Milan: Hoepli, 1936.
5. Ruffo-Fiore, Silvia R. *Niccolo Machiavelli: An Annotated Bibliography of Modern Criticism and Scholarship.* New York: Greenwood, 1990.

His Life and Times

6. Atkinson, Catherine. *Debts, Dowries, Donkeys: The Diary of Niccolo Machiavelli's Father, Messer Bernardo, in Quattrocento Florence.* New York: Peter Lang, 2002.
7. Baron, Hans. *Crisis of the Early Italian Renaissance.* 3 vs. Princeton: Princeton University Press, 1955.
8. Bradford, Sarah. *Cesare Borgia: His Life and Times.* New York: Macmillan, 1976.
9. Brucker, Gene A., ed. *The Society of Renaissance Florence: A Documentary Study.* New York: Harper & Row, 1971.
10. Butters, H. C. *Governors and Government in Early Sixteenth-Century Florence,* 1502–1519. New York: Oxford University Press, 1985.
11. Capponi, Niccolo. *An Unlikely Prince: The Life and Times of Machiavelli.* Cambridge, MA: Da Capo, 2010.
12. Chiappelli, Fredi. "Machiavelli as Secretary." *Italian Quarterly,* 14 (1970) 27–44.
13. Cicero, Marcus Tullius. *De Officiis.* Walter Miller, trans. Cambridge, MA: Harvard University Press, 1961.
14. Gilbert, Felix. *Machiavelli and Guicciardini: Politics and History in Sixteenth-Century Florence.* Princeton: Princeton University Press, 1965.
15. Goldthwaite, Richard A. *The Building of Renaissance Florence: An Economic and Social History.* Baltimore: Johns Hopkins University Press, 1980.
16. Hale, John R. *Machiavelli and Renaissance Italy.* New York: Crowell-Collier-Macmillan, 1960.
17. ———. *Florence and the Medici: The Pattern of Control.* London: Thames and Hudson, 1977.
18. Livius [Livy], Titus. *The History of Rome.* B. O. Foster, trans. 14 vs. Cambridge, MA: Harvard University Press, 1967.

THE PRINCE   55

19. Martines, Lauro. *Fire in the City: Savonarola and the Struggle for Renaissance Florence*. New York: Oxford University Press, 2006.
20. ———. *The Social World of the Florentine Humanists*, 1390–1460. Princeton: Princeton University Press, 1963.
21. Mattingly, Garrett. *Renaissance Diplomacy*. Boston: Houghton Mifflin, 1955.
22. Oppenheimer, Paul. *Machiavelli: A Life Beyond Ideology*. London: Continuum, 2011.
23. Prezzolini, Giuseppe. *Niccolo Machiavelli the Florentine*. Ralph Roeder, trans. London: G. P. Putnam's, 1928.
24. Ridolfi, Roberto. *Life of Niccolo Machiavelli*. Cecil Grayson, trans. Rev. ed. Chicago: University of Chicago Press, 1963.
25. Rubinstein, Nicolai. *The Government of Florence under the Medici* (1434–1494). Rev. Ed. Oxford: Clarendon Press, 1997.
26. Shaw, Christine. *Julius II: The Warrior Pope*. Oxford: Blackwell, 1993.
27. Stephens, J. N. *The Fall of the Florentine Republic, 1502–1530*. New York: Oxford University Press, 1983.
28. Villari, Pasquale. *The Life and Times of Niccolo Machiavelli*. Linda Villari, trans. 2 vs. London: Ernest Benn, 1929 [1877–82].
29. Viroli, Maurizio. *Niccolo's Smile: A Biography of Machiavelli*. Antony Shugaar, trans. New York: Farrar, Straus and Giroux, 2000.
30. Weinstein, Donald. *Savonarola and Florence: Prophecy and Patriotism in the Renaissance*. Princeton: Princeton University Press, 1970.

COLLECTED WORKS

31. Bondanella, Peter and Mark Musa, eds. and trans. *The Portable Machiavelli*. New York: Penguin, 1979.
32. Detmold, Christian E., ed. and trans. *The Historical, Political and Diplomatic Works of Niccolo Machiavelli*. 4 vs. Boston: James R. Osgood, 1882. Rpt: New York: Gordon, 1980.
33. Gilbert, Allan, trans. *Machiavelli: The Chief Works and Others*. 3 vs. Durham, NC: Duke University Press, 1965.
34. Gilmore, Myron P., ed. and Judith A. Rawson, trans. *Machiavelli: The History of Florence, and Other Selections*. New York: Twayne, 1970.

56   J. T. BOOKMAN

35. Hale, John R., ed. and trans. *The Literary Works of Machiavelli.* London: Oxford University Press, 1961.
36. Lerner, Max, ed. *The Prince and the Discourses.* Luigi Ricci, trans. of The Prince, and Christian Detmold, trans. of *The Discourses.* New York: Random House, 1950.
37. Sices, David and James B. Atkinson, eds. and trans. *The Comedies of Machiavelli.* Hanover, NH: University Press of New England, 1985.
38. Tusiani, Joseph, ed. and trans. *Lust and Liberty: The Poems of Machiavelli.* New York: Obolensky, 1963.
39. Wootten, David, ed. and trans. *Niccolo Machiavelli: Selected Political Writings.* Indianapolis: Hackett, 1994.

INDIVIDUAL WORKS

40. *The Art of War.* Christopher Lynch, trans. Chicago: University of Chicago Press, 2003.
41. *The Art of War.* Christopher Lynch, Neal Wood, ed. Rev. version of 1775 trans. by Ellis Farneworth. Indianapolis: Bobbs-Merrill, 1965.
42. *Belphagor* [or, The Marriage of the Devil]. London: Rodale Press, 1954.
43. *Clizia.* Daniel T. Gallagher, trans. Prospect Heights, IL: Waveland Press, 1996.
44. *The Discourses on Livy.* Leslie J. Walker, ed. and trans. 2 vs. New Haven, CT: Yale University Press, 1950.
45. ———. Brian Richardson's rev. of Walker's trans. Bernard Crick, ed. Baltimore: Penguin, 1970.
46. ———. Harvey C. Mansfield, Jr. and Nathan Tarcov, trans. Chicago: University of Chicago Press, 1996.
47. ———. Julia Conway Bondanella and Peter Bondanella, trans. New York: Oxford University Press, 1997.
48. ———. Trans. under the title *The Sweetness of Power* by James B. Atkinson and David Sices. DeKalb, IL: Northern Illinois University Press, 2002.
49. *The History of Florence and of the Affairs of Italy.* Felix Gilbert, ed. New York: Harper, 1960.
50. ———. Laura F. Banfield and Harvey C. Mansfield, Jr., trans. Princeton: Princeton University Press, 1988.

THE PRINCE   57

51. *The Life of Castruccio Ca*stracani. Andrew Brown, trans. London: Hesperus, 2003.
52. *Machiavelli and His Friends: Their Personal Correspondence.* James B. Atkinson and David Sices, eds. DeKalb, IL: Northern Illinois University Press, 1996.
53. *Mandragola.* Mera J. Flaumenhaft, trans. Prospect Heights, IL: Waveland Press, 1996.
54. ———. Anne and Henry Paolucci, eds. and trans. Indianapolis: Bobbs-Merrill, 1957.
55. *The Prince.* Robert M. Adams, ed. and trans. 2d ed. New York: Norton, 1992.
56. ———. William J. Connell, ed. and trans. Boston: Bedford/St. Martin's, 2005.
57. ———. Quentin Skinner, ed. and Russell Price, trans. New York: Cambridge University Press, 1988.
58. ———. Harvey C. Mansfield, Jr., trans. 2d ed. Chicago: University of Chicago Press, 1998.
59. ———. Mark Musa, ed. and trans. New York: St. Martin's Press, 1964.
60. ———. James B. Atkinson, ed. and trans. Indianapolis: Bobbs-Merrill, 1976.
61. ———. Peter Constantine, trans. and Albert Russell Ascoli, ed. New York: Modern Library, 2008.
62. ———. Peter Bondanella, trans. and Maurizio Viroli, ed. Oxford: Oxford University Press, 2008.
63. ———. Peter Bondanella and Mark Musa, trans. and eds. Oxford: Oxford University Press, 1984.

COMMENTARY: COLLECTIONS

64. Ascoli, Albert Russell and Victoria Khan, eds. *Machiavelli and the Discourse of Literature.* Ithaca, NY: Cornell University Press, 1993.
65. Bock, Gisela, Quentin Skinner, and Maurizio Viroli, eds. *Machiavelli and Republicanism.* Cambridge: Cambridge University Press, 1990.
66. Coyle, Martin, ed. *Niccolo Machiavelli's Prince: New Interdisciplinary Essays.* Manchester: Manchester University Press, 1995.
67. Dunn, John and Ian Harris, eds. *Machiavelli.* 2 vs. Lyme, NH: Edward Elgar, 1997.

68. Fleisher, Martin, ed. *Machiavelli and the Nature of Political Thought*. New York: Atheneum, 1972.
69. Gilbert, Felix. *History: Choice and Commitment*. Cambridge, MA: Belknap Press, 1977.
70. Gilmore, Myron P., ed. *Studies on Machiavelli*. Florence: Sansoni, 1972.
71. *Italy: Machiavelli "500."* Jamaica, NY: St. John's University Press, 1970.
72. Jensen, DeLamar, ed. *Machiavelli: Cynic, Patriot, or Political Scientist?* Boston: D. C. Heath, 1960.
73. Mansfield, Harvey C., Jr. *Machiavelli's Virtue*. Chicago: University of Chicago Press, 1996.
74. Najemy, John M., ed. *The Cambridge Companion to Machiavelli*. Cambridge: Cambridge University Press, 2010.
75. Parel, Anthony, ed. *The Political Calculus: Essays on Machiavelli's Philosophy*. Toronto: University of Toronto Press, 1972.
76. Rahe, Paul A., ed. *Machiavelli's Liberal Republican Legacy*. New York: Cambridge University Press, 2006.
77. Sullivan, Vickie B., ed. *The Comedy and Tragedy of Machiavelli: Essays on the Literary Works*. New Haven, CT: Yale University Press, 2000.
78. Vilches, Patricia and Gerald Seaman, eds. *Seeking Real Truths: Multidisciplinary Perspectives on Machiavelli*. Boston: Brill, 2007.
79. Whitfield, J. H. *Discourses on Machiavelli*. Cambridge: W. Heffer, 1969.

COMMENTARY: BOOKS

80. Althusser, Louis. *Machiavelli and Us*. Gregory Elliott, trans. 2d ed. London: Verso, 1999.
81. Baron, Hans. *In Search of Florentine Civic Humanism*. 2 vs. Princeton: Princeton University Press, 1988.
82. Belliotti, Raymond A. *Niccolo Machiavelli: The Laughing Lion and the Strutting Fox*. Lanham, MD: Lexington Books, 2009.
83. Benner, Erica. *Machiavelli's Ethics*. Princeton: Princeton University Press, 2009.
84. Bonadeo, Alfredo. *Corruption, Conflict and Power in the Works and Times of Niccolo Machiavelli*. Berkeley: University of California Press, 1973.

THE PRINCE   59

85. Bondanella, Peter E. *Machiavelli and the Art of Renaissance History.* Detroit: Wayne State University Press, 1974.
86. Burns, J. H., ed. *The Cambridge History of Political Thought 1450–1700.* Cambridge: Cambridge University Press, 1991.
87. Butterfield, Herbert. *The Statecraft of Machiavelli.* New York: Crowell-Collier-Macmillan, 1962 [1955].
88. Cassirer, Ernst. *The Myth of the State.* Garden City, NY: Doubleday Anchor, 1955 [1946]. Chs. 10–12.
89. Chabod, Federico. *Machiavelli and the Renaissance.* David Moore, trans. Cambridge, MA: Harvard University Press, 1958.
90. Croce, Benedetto. *Politics and Morals.* Salvatore J. Castiglione, trans. New York: Philosophical Library, 1945.
91. De Alvarez, Leo Paul S. *The Machiavellian Enterprise: A Commentary on The Prince.* DeKalb, IL: Northern Illinois University Press, 1999.
92. De Sanctis, Francesco. *The History of Italian Literature.* Joan Redfern, trans. New York: Basic Books, 1959 [1931; in Ital.: 1870–71]. Ch. 15.
93. Fischer, Markus. *Well-Ordered License: On the Unity of Machiavelli's Thought.* Lanham, Md: Lexington Books, 2000.
94. Foucault, Michel. *Security, Territory, Population: Lectures at the Collège de Paris, 1977–78.* Graham Burchett, trans. New York: Palgrave Macmillan, 2007.
95. Frederick II (the Great) king of Prussia. *The Refutation of Machiavelli's Prince or Anti-Machiavel.* Paul Sonnino, ed. and trans. Athens, OH: Ohio University Press, 1980 [in Fr.: 1740].
96. Gilbert, Allan H. *Machiavelli's Prince and Its Forerunners.* Durham, NC: Duke University Press, 1938.
97. Gramsci, Antonio. *The Modern Prince and Other Writings.* Louis Marks, trans. New York: International Publishers, 1957 [in Ital.: 1929]. Pp. 135–88.
98. Hexter, J. H. *The Vision of Politics on the Eve of the Reformation: More, Machiavelli, and Seyssel.* New York: Basic Books, 1972.
99. Hulliung, Mark. *Citizen Machiavelli.* Princeton: Princeton University Press, 1983.
100. Landon, William J. *Politics, Patriotism, and Language: Niccolo Machiavelli's "Secular Patria" and the Creation of an Italian National Identity.* New York; Peter Lang, 2005.

60 J. T. BOOKMAN

101. Mansfield, Harvey C., Jr. *Machiavelli's New Modes and Orders: A Study of the Discourses on Livy.* Ithaca: Cornell University Press, 1979.
102. Masters, Roger D. *Fortune is a River: Leonardo da Vinci and Niccolo Machiavelli's Magnificent Dream to Change the Course of Florentine History.* New York: Free Press, 1998.
103. ———. *Machiavelli, Leonardo, and the Science of Power.* South Bend, IN: Notre Dame University Press, 1998.
104. McCormick, John P. *Machiavellian Democracy.* Cambridge: Cambridge University Press, 2011.
105. Meinecke, Friedrich. *Machiavellism: The Doctrine of Raison d'Etat and Its Place in Modern History.* Douglas Scott, trans. New Haven: Yale University Press, 1957 [1924].
106. Olshki, Leonardo. *Machiavelli: The Scientist.* Berkeley, CA: Gillick Press, 1945.
107. Pitkin, Hanna Fenichel. *Fortune is a Woman: Gender and Politics in the Thought of Niccolo Machiavelli.* Berkeley, CA: University of California Press, 1999 [1984].
108. Plamenatz, John P. *Man and Society.* 2 vs. New York: McGraw-Hill, 1963. Vol. I, 1–44.
109. Pocock, J. G. A. *The Machiavellian Moment: Florentine Political Thought and the Atlantic Republican Tradition.* Princeton; Princeton University Press, 2003 [1975].
110. Parel, Anthony J. *The Machiavellian Cosmos.* New Haven: Yale University Press, 1992.
111. Prezzolini, Giuseppe. *Machiavelli.* Gioconda Savini, trans. New York: Farrar, Straus and Giroux, 1967 [1954].
112. Ruffo-Fiore, Silvia R. *Niccolo Machiavelli.* Boston: Twayne, 1982.
113. Skinner, Quentin F. *The Foundations of Modern Political Thought.* 2 vs. Cambridge: Cambridge: Cambridge University Press, 1978. Vol. I, Chs. 4–6.
114. ———. *Machiavelli: A Very Short Introduction.* New York: Oxford University Press, 2000.
115. ———. *Machiavelli and Republicanism.* Cambridge: Cambridge University Press, 1990.
116. Sorensen, Kim A. *Discourses on Strauss: Revelation and Reason in Leo Strauss and His Critical Study of Machiavelli.* Notre Dame, IN: Notre Dame University Press, 2006.

THE PRINCE 61

117. Strauss, Leo. *Thoughts on Machiavelli*. Glencoe, IL: The Free Press, 1958.
118. Sullivan, Vickie B. *Machiavelli's Three Romes: Religion, Human Liberty, and Politics Reformed*. DeKalb, IL: Northern Illinois University Press, 1996.
119. Viroli, Maurizio. Machiavelli. Oxford: Oxford University Press, 1998.
120. ———. *Machiavelli's God*. Antony Skugaar, trans. Princeton: Princeton University Press, 2010.
121. Whitfield, J. H. *Machiavelli*. Oxford: Blackwell and Mott, 1947.
122. Wolin, Sheldon S. *Politics and Vision: Continuity and Innovation in Western Political Thought*. Rev. ed. Princeton: Princeton University Press, 2004. Ch. 7.

COMMENTARY: ARTICLES

123. Ball, Terence. "The Picaresque Prince: Reflections on Machiavelli and Moral Change." *Political Theory*, 12 (Nov., 1984), 521–36.
124. Barlow, Jackson. "The Fox and the Lion: Machiavelli Replies to Cicero." *History of Political Thought*, 20 (1999), 627–45.
125. Berki, R. N. "Machiavellism: A Philosophical Defense." *Ethics*, 81 (Jan., 1971), 107–27.
126. Black, Robert. "Florentine Political Traditions and Machiavelli's Election to the Chancery." *Italian Studies*, 40 (1985), 1–16.
127. Bloom, Allan. "Leo Strauss on Machiavelli." *Political Theory*, 2 (Nov., 1974), 372–92.
128. Bonadeo, Alfredo. "The Role of the 'Grandi' in the Political World of Machiavelli." *Studies in the Renaissance*, 16 (1969), 12–30.
129. Bondanella, Peter. "Castruccio Castracani: Machiavelli's Archetypal Prince." *Italica*, 49 (1972), 302–14.
130. Colish, Marcia L. "Machiavelli's *Art of War*: A Reconsideration." *Renaissance Quarterly*, 51 (Dec., 1998), 1151–68.
131. Dietz, Mary. "Trapping the Prince: Machiavelli and the Politics of Deception." *American Political Science* Review, 80 (1986), 777–99.
132. Flaumenhaft, Mera J. "The Comic Remedy: Machiavelli's 'Mandragola'." *Interpretation*. 7 (May, 1978), 33–74.

62 J. T. BOOKMAN

133. Fleisher, Martin. "Trust and Deceit in Machiavelli's Comedies." *Journal of the History of Ideas*, 27 (July, 1966), 365–80.
134. Geerken, J. H. "Homer's Image of the Hero in Machiavelli: A Comparison of *Arete* and *Virtu*." *Italian Quarterly*, 14 (1970), 45–90.
135. ———. "Pocock and Machiavelli: Structuralist Explanation in History." *Journal of the History of Philosophy*, 17 (July, 1979), 309–18.
136. Germino, Dante. "Second Thought on Leo Strauss's Machiavelli." *Journal of Politics*, 28 (Nov., 1966), 794–817.
137. Gilbert, Felix. "Florentine Political Assumptions in the Age of Savonarola and Soderini." *Journal of the Warburg and Courtauld Institutes*, 20 (1957), 187–214.
138. ———. "Machiavelli and the Renaissance of the Art of War" in *Makers of Modern Strategy*, E. M. Earle, ed. Princeton: Princeton University Press, 1944, 3–25.
139. Hannaford, I. "Machiavelli's Concept of *Virtu* in *The Prince* and *The Discourses* Reconsidered." *Political Studies*, 20 (1972), 185–89.
140. Hexter, J. H. "The Predatory Vision: Niccolo Machiavelli, *Il Principe and lo stato*." *Studies in the Renaissance*, 4 (1957), 113–38.
141. ———. "Machiavellian Moment." *History and Theory*, 16 (1977), 306–37.
142. Hulliung, Mark. "Machiavelli's Mandragola: A Day and a Night in the Life of a Citizen." *Review of Politics*, 40 (Jan., 1978), 32–57.
143. Ingersoll, David E. "The Constant Prince: Private Interests and Public Goals in Machiavelli." *Western Political Quarterly*, 21 (Dec., 1968), 588–96.
144. Langton, William J. "Machiavelli's Paradox– Trapping or Teaching *The Prince*." *American Political Science Review*, 81 (1987), 1277–88.
145. Lukes, T. J. "Marshalling Machiavelli: Reassessing the Military Reflections." *Journal of Politics*, 66 (2004), 1089–1108.
146. McIntosh, Donald. "The Modernity of Machiavelli." *Political Theory*, 12 (May, 1984), 184–203.
147. McShea, Robert J. "Leo Strauss on Machiavelli." *Western Political Quarterly*, 16 (Dec., 1963), 782–97.

148. Mansfield, Harvey C., Jr. "Reply to Pocock's 'Prophet and Inquisitor: Or, A Church Built upon Bayonets Cannot Stand'." *Political Theory*, 3 (Nov., 1975), 402–405.
149. Najemy, John M. "Machiavelli and the Medici: The Lessons of Florentine History". *Renaissance Quarterly*, 35 (1982), 551–76.
150. Newell, W. R. "How Original is Machiavelli? – A Consideration of Skinner's Interpretation of Virtue and Fortune." *Political Theory*, 15 (1987), 612–34.
151. Orwin, C. "Machiavelli's UnChristian Charity." *American Political Science Review*, 72 (Dec., 1978), 1217–28.
152. Pocock, J. G. A. "Prophet and Inquisitor: or, A Church Built upon Bayonets Cannot Stand: A Comment on Mansfield's 'Strauss's Machiavelli'." *Political Theory*, 3 1975), 385–401.
153. Preus, J. S. "Machiavelli's Functional Analysis of Religion: Context and Object." *Journal of the History of Ideas*, 40 (Apr., 1979), 171–90.
154. Price, Russell. "Self Love, 'Egoism' and Ambizione in Machiavelli's Thought." *History of Political Thought*, 9 (1988), 237–61.
155. ———. "*Virtu* in Machiavelli's *Il Principe and Discorsi.*" *Political Science*, 22 (Dec., 1970), 43–49.
156. ———. "Machiavelli Quincentenary Studies." *European Studies Review*, 5 (July, 1975), 313–35.
157. ———. "The Senses of *Virtu* in Machiavelli." *European Studies Review*, 3 (1975), 315–45.
158. Richardson, Brian. "The Structure of Machiavelli's *Discorsi.*" *Italica*, 49 (1972), 46–71.
159. Shumer, S.M. "Machiavelli: Republican Politics and Its Corruption." *Political Theory*, 7 (Feb., 1979), 5–34.
160. Strauss, Leo. "Machiavelli and Classical Literature." *Review of National Literatures*, 1 (Spr., 1970), 7–25.
161. Tarlton, C. D. "The Symbolism of Redemption and the Exorcism of Fortune in Machiavelli's Prince." *Review of Politics*, 30 (July, 1968), 332–48.
162. Tsurutani, Taketsugu. "Machiavelli and the Problem of Political Development." *Review of Politics*, 30 (July, 1968), 316–31.
163. Vasoli, C. "Machiavellian Moment: A Grand Ideological Synthesis." *Journal of Modern History*, 49 (Dec., 1977), 661–70.

164. Vaughn, Frederick. "On 'An Exchange on Strauss's Machiavelli'." *Political Theory*, 4 (Aug., 1976), 371–72.
165. Waley, Daniel P. "The Primitivist Element in Machiavelli's Thought." *Journal of the History of Ideas*, 31 (Jan., 1970), 91–98.
166. Walzer, Michael. "Political Action: The Problem of Dirty Hands." *Philosophy and Public Affairs*, 2 (Wint., 1973), 160 80.
167. Whitfield, J. H. "Machiavellian Moment." *European Studies Review*, 8 (July, 1978), 365–72.
168. Wood, Neal. "Machiavelli's Concept of *Virtu* Reconsidered." *Political Studies*, 15 (June, 1967), 159–72.

CHAPTER 3

Leviathan

HOBBES (1588–1679): A BRIEF SKETCH OF HIS LIFE

Hobbes was among the few in seventeenth-century England who lived to a ripe old age—91 to be precise.[1] The average life-span at the time was about 40. He somehow for all those years managed to avoid the violence and disease that brought low so many. This was not wholly a matter of luck and a robust genetic endowment. His contemporary and biographer John Aubrey reports that he exercised restraint, at least in his later years, in what he ate and drank. In Hobbes's own recollection he was drunk fewer than a 100 times, hardly witness to the abstemious life, but by the standards of the day pretty moderate. He gave up drinking wine altogether at the age of 60 and at about the same time declined meat in favor of fish. In the morning he walked for two hours or so, thinking as he went. In addition to his daily walks, he from time to time played tennis and was still at it at the age of 75. In the afternoon he took a short nap. Persuaded that respiratory vigor declined with age, he sang popular songs before bed in an effort to prolong his life. A minor complaint was to "keep-off the

[1] In the writing of this sketch, I have drawn upon A. P. Martinich, *Hobbes: A Biography* (Cambridge: Cambridge University Press, 1999); Miriam Reik, *The Golden Lands of Thomas Hobbes* (Detroit: Wayne State University Press, 1977); and Arnold Rogow, *Thomas Hobbes: Radical in the Service of Reaction* (New York: Norton, 1986).

© The Author(s) 2019
J. T. Bookman, *A Reader's Companion*
to The Prince, Leviathan, *and the* Second Treatise,
https://doi.org/10.1007/978-3-030-02880-0_3

66   J. T. BOOKMAN

flies from pitching on the baldness."[2] His thick, black hair had earned him the nickname "Crow" as a youth, but, with advancing years, he became quite bald.

Concerned as he became about living a healthy life, Hobbes was preoccupied with living a secure life. He placed the origins of this preoccupation in the circumstances of his birth. He was born in 1588, the year of the Spanish Armada, in a village outside Malmesbury, Wiltshire. We now know that the weather and the Royal Navy routed the invading fleet and put an end to Spain's imperial pretensions in the British Isles. In prospect, the fortunes of the English appeared black. As Hobbes wrote in his verse autobiography:

> For Fame had rumor'd, that a Fleet at Sea,
> Wou'd cause our Nations catastrophe;
> And hereupon it was my Mother Dear
> Did bring forth Twins at once, both Me and Fear.[3]

Fear of violent death informs all that he wrote about politics. The recurrent theme in *The Elements of Law* (1640), *De Cive* (1642), and *Leviathan* (1651) is that, in the absence of strong government, men and women would be in constant fear of their lives. In that belief, he argued for the establishment of absolute sovereignty, preferably in the form of absolute monarchy, and he defended such authority against any claims to impose limits upon it. The seeds of civil war, he thought, are sown by such claims, and civil war is the greatest misfortune that can befall a people.[4] Hobbes did not write about that misfortune until he was in his 50s.

Not much is known about Hobbes's early life. We do know that his father, also called Thomas, was a clergyman who served a small parish near Malmesbury, Wiltshire, although not very well judging from the many complaints lodged against him. The young Thomas attended local schools, where he learned Greek and Latin. Under the instruction of Robert Latimer he prepared for college at Oxford. Many years later, on a visit to his old teacher, Hobbes met his future biographer John Aubrey (then

[2] John Aubrey, *Aubrey's Brief Lives*, Oliver Lawson Dick, ed. (London: Secker and Warburg, 1960), 154.

[3] "Verse Life" in J. C. A. Gaskin, ed. *The Elements of Law Natural and Politic* (Oxford: Oxford University Press, 1994), 254.

[4] "Preface to the Reader" of *De Cive* in Bernard Gert, ed. *Man and Citizen* (Garden City, NY: Doubleday, 1972).

LEVIATHAN 67

eight), who was also briefly a student of Latimer. Aubrey's notes describe the meeting.[5] Coincident with Hobbes's departure for Oxford in the fall of 1603, his father was brought up before an episcopal court on a charge of slandering a fellow cleric. The jury convicted him and this in turn led to his excommunication. Months later Hobbes senior confronted his accuser and assaulted him. Faced with possible corporeal punishment at the hands of the civil authorities, he abandoned his wife and children (Hobbes had a brother and a sister) and fled to London. Hobbes never recorded his feelings about these events. Whether he ever saw his father again is unknown.

Supported by his Uncle Francis, a successful glover who had married late and had no children of his own, Hobbes entered Magdalen Hall, Oxford, from which he graduated with a B.A. in 1608. Magdalen Hall grew out of a grammar school that had been attached to Magdalen College, among the most prestigious at Oxford. Magdalen Hall in 1602, when it separated from the college, could claim among its alumni William Tyndale, the translator of the Bible, John Donne, poet and dean of St. Paul's, and John Selden, the jurist and historian of English law. The Hall later became Hertford College from which Jonathan Swift, satirist and dean of Christ Church, Dublin, Charles James Fox, the Whig politician, and, more recently, Evelyn Waugh, all graduated.[6] As to the education he received, Hobbes had in later years mostly critical things to say. He was put off by the domination of the curriculum by the Schoolmen and the ancients, particularly Aristotle. He was critical, too, in *Leviathan* and *Behemoth* of university professors, whether Puritan or papist in their leanings, for teaching that subjects may on religious grounds oppose their rulers. And, he had little regard for his fellow students, whom he accused of debauchery. For his own part, he allowed that he was a slow but diligent student. However, bored he might have been with the curriculum, he sufficiently impressed the principal of the college to secure his recommendation as tutor to William Cavendish, who would become the second Earl of Devonshire in 1626.

Thus began Hobbes's lifelong association with the Cavendish family. His employer, William's father, was Baron Hardwick (the barony had cost him £2900 in 1605) until 1618, when, upon payment of £10,000 to King James I, he became Earl of Devonshire.[7] Hobbes was just two years older

[5] *Aubrey's Brief Lives*, Dick, ed. 150.

[6] Arnold Rogou, *Thomas Hobbes: Radical in the Service of Reaction* (New York: Norton, 1986), 47 and 259n5.

[7] Lawrence Stone, *The Crisis of the Aristocracy*, 1558–1641 (Oxford: Oxford University Press, 1965), 101 and 106.

68 J. T. BOOKMAN

than his student and served more as companion than as a tutor. In those first years, they spent much time in country pursuits like hunting and riding, and, while at the Cavendish house in London, William liked to go gambling, drinking, and wenching. Hobbes's failure to restrain his young charge might explain why he was not retained by the Cavendishes after William's death in 1628. The latter's wife was saddled with her husband's substantial debts accumulated during his forays into the dens of pleasure. William's sybaritic adventures did not, as scion of one of the wealthiest families in England, reduce his social prominence. He was Member of Parliament (MP) for Derbyshire in the Parliaments of 1621 and 1624 and a stockholder in the Virginia Company. Hobbes's association with William, as secretary from 1621 to 1628, provided him with the opportunity to meet the wealthy and powerful. Among these people was Francis Bacon, author of the *Essays* and former Lord Chancellor, for whom Hobbes served as sometime secretary and translator of several of the *Essays* into Latin.

Hobbes did not long remain unemployed. He was soon off to the Continent for two years, 1629–1630, on the grand tour as tutor to the son of another wealthy landowner. It was the second such trip. The first he had made in the company of William Cavendish probably in 1614–1615. A third occurred with William's son, the third Earl of Devonshire, in 1634–1636. The second tour was marked by Hobbes's enthusiastic embrace of geometry. Aubrey reports that Hobbes in a Genevan "gentleman's library" came upon a copy of Euclid's *Elements* open to proposition 47, the Pythagorean theorem. He traced out the steps and "at last was demonstratively convinced of that truth. This made him in love with Geometry."[8] It also encouraged him to regard himself as a mathematician, which inspired in later years a fruitless effort to solve several mathematical puzzles and blemished his reputation as a philosopher.

Upon his return from the Continent in 1630, Hobbes once again took up the education of a young Devonshire Earl. Whatever reservations the family matriarch may have had about Hobbes, she put them aside. Save for his exile in France in the 1640s, Hobbes spent the rest of his life under a Cavendish roof and in the family's pay. His duties were not time-consuming. He attended, at least sporadically, meetings of the Welbeck Academy, a group of intellectuals who gathered around the Earl of Newcastle, Hobbes's sometime patron, at his Welbeck estate and whose principal interest was natural philosophy. He also sometimes joined the

---

[8] *Aubrey's Brief Lives*, Dick, ed. 150.

Great Tew Circle at the house of Lucius Cary, Viscount Falkland, where the cultivation of a moderate Anglicanism dominated conversation. Neither group survived the beginning of the civil war. Perhaps the most significant consequence of these associations for Hobbes was letters of introduction to scientists and philosophers on the Continent. On his third grand tour, Hobbes, in the company of the third Earl of Devonshire, was able to meet Marin Mersenne and Pierre Gassendi, two of the leading French intellectuals of the day, and Galileo with whom he spoke of a scientifically conceived universe. With patrons as generous as the Cavendishes, Hobbes had time to write *The Elements of Law*, which first expressed most of the doctrines to be found in *De Cive* and *Leviathan*, and to lay out a three-part project, "The Elements of Philosophy," that would address all that exists: *De Corpore* (1655), concerned with metaphysics and physics; *De Homine* (1658), concerned with psychology and perception; and *De Cive* (1642), concerned with politics.

Disposition and experience led Hobbes to support the powers that be. In 1629, he published a translation of Thucydides's *History of the Peloponnesian War*. He wrote in the preface that Thucydides taught him "how stupid democracy is and by how much one man is wiser than an assembly." He stated that "I made it my business that this author should speak to the English in their own tongue and warn them against the temptation to listen to rhetoric." What democracy and whose rhetoric he does not make clear. Parliament was far from democratic, but it was an assembly that had increasingly sought a larger voice in taxing and spending decisions and in the determination of policy with regard to religious matters. And, Hobbes may well have regarded the speeches championing Parliament's claims and challenging royal authority as rhetorical.

Throughout the reigns of James I (1603–1625) and Charles I (1625–1649) relations between crown and Parliament were contentious. Both monarchs were particularly insensitive to the great religious differences among their subjects. Charles's attempt to impose Anglicanism on the Presbyterian Scots marked the beginning of civil war. In order to put down the rebellion, Charles called a Parliament to grant money. It refused and, after three weeks, the king dissolved the "Short Parliament" in early May 1640. Hobbes left no doubt in his *The Elements of Law*, manuscript copies of which were circulating at the time, where his sentiments lay. "When a man covenanteth to subject his will to the command of another ... he resign his strength and means to him ... he that is to command may by the use of all their means and strength, be able by the terror thereof, to

70   J. T. BOOKMAN

frame the will of them all to unity and concord."[9] Parliament was not, he thought, justified in denying Charles the money. Pressed by his advisors to renew his request, the king convened another Parliament in the fall of 1640. This, the "Long," Parliament remained in being for the next 20 years. During its tenure, Britains carried on a bloody civil war, executed Charles I in 1649, abolished the monarchy in favor of a Commonwealth, and saw the defeat in 1651 of an army organized on behalf of Charles's son.

In *The Elements of Law* Hobbes was no less an advocate of absolute monarchy than he became in *De Cive* and *Leviathan*. That doctrine provoked complaints by several members of the Long Parliament. As he reports in his "Prose Life," "having consulted with some of those who were of the Parliament during the first three or four days of the session, that civil war was unavoidable," and fearing his own prosecution, he fled to France.[10] He would later claim "for every man … a right to preserve himself … [and] *to use all the means, and do all the actions, without which he cannot preserve himself*"[11] that not even the covenant creating the sovereign overrides. At the time, however, Hobbes made no such provision in *The Elements of Law*. Just as the sovereign required the means of his subjects, he also required, and was due, their strength to secure "unity and concord." In Hobbes's case, fear overcame obligation. His friend, Sidney Godolphin, for whom he expressed great admiration in "A Review and Conclusion" to *Leviathan*, chose another course. He left Parliament in 1642, joined the king's army, and died at the age of 32 on the battlefield. Honor overcame fear.

Civil war was a calamity for the British. Although in exile for most of the hostilities, Hobbes was a keen student of the civil war and well aware of its ferocity. Over the period 1638–1660, many parties entered into shifting alliances in response to emerging issues. Presbyterian Scots, Irish Catholics, English Puritans and Catholics, Anglicans, royalists, supporters of parliamentary authority, and advocates for a more democratic politics fought over independence for Scotland in religion, the authority of Parliament vis-à-vis the king, toleration for Catholics and dissenting Protestants, the inclusion of dissenting Protestants in the Anglican Church, landholding in Ireland, and the bases of parliamentary representation, among other things. The antagonists applied themselves to the contest with deadly effect. The number of deaths suffered is a matter of some

[9] *Elements of Law*, XX. 5.
[10] "Prose Life" in Gaskin, *Elements of Law*, 247.
[11] *De Cive*, Gert, ed., 116.

speculation. No one doubts that the numbers were great. Two recent studies rough out the number of deaths to combatants and civilians from battle and the attendant famine and disease (principally plague) as amounting to over 3 percent of the English population, 6 percent of Scots, and 40 percent of the Irish.[12] In comparison, the American Civil War killed about 3 percent of the population. Fearful Hobbes may have been, but experience, if only as an observer, also made a profound impression.

Several years before he left for France Hobbes read *Discourse on the Method* (1637), in which Descartes claims to have arrived at a way that will lead to the discovery of indubitable propositions and thereby provide a secure foundation for all philosophy and science. Skeptical thinkers like Montaigne in his *Essays* (1580–1588) had cast doubt on the idea that any such foundation was possible. For him, human understanding of anything would always be uncertain. He advised that, in the face of uncertainty and the danger of the times, one suspend judgment and live quietly according to law and custom. Only through faith and revelation could real understanding be acquired. For others, skeptical doubt brought into question and inspired opposition to ideas about religion and authority that had propped up the medieval world. What principles might take their place and upon what grounds were they to rest? It was with these questions, among others, that Hobbes was concerned in his political works and that provoked publication of *De Cive*.

Hobbes responded to Descartes's *Discourse* in a letter to Marin Mersenne late in 1640. Mersenne at the time was acting as a go-between for Descartes, who was living in exile in Holland. Descartes saw at least parts of Hobbes's commentary. He did not like it. "I was very surprised by the fact that, although the style in which it is written makes its author look clever and learned, he seems to stray from the truth in every single claim which he advances as his own."[13] The relationship did not improve despite their shared views on some important matters. They both had high regard for the new science as exemplified by Copernicus and Galileo. And, they both sought a more certain foundation for human understanding.

Their intellectual differences were expressed starkly in an exchange over Descartes's Meditations on *First Philosophy*. Mersenne gave Hobbes, now in Paris, a prepublication copy and asked him to comment upon it. In 1641, the *Meditations*, six sets of objections, Hobbes's among them,

---

[12] Charles Carlton, *The Experience of the British Civil Wars* (London: Routledge, 1992), 211–214; and Trevor Royle, *Civil War: The Wars of the Three Kingdoms*, 1638–1660 (London: Abacus, 2006), 602.

[13] As quoted by Martinich, 163–164.

and Descartes's replies came from the press. Hobbes's materialism, his insistence that there are no immaterial substances, runs counter to Descartes's contention that mind and body, spirit and substance, are distinct. Hobbes, like Descartes, argues for the existence of God. The arguments take very different forms. For Hobbes, God is the First Cause. We experience effects the occurrence of events and in reasoning back to their causes, we infer the existence of something that has the power to produce such effects. That something is what people call God. Sense experience, however, tells us nothing of the attributes of such a being. Descartes, on the other hand, begins with the idea of a perfect and infinite being whose existence is attested by the occurrence of such an idea to a doubting and ignorant consciousness (his own). To God, he attributes all the qualities we would associate with a perfect and infinite being, including the creation of an external world. God would not deceive us, he contends, about the existence of an external world because reason teaches that deception is a sign of defect and the perfect being that is God has no defect. The rancor of the exchange between the two men expressed their vanity and desire for recognition and esteem as original thinkers. Neither thought there was room for more than one titan in seventeenth-century philosophy.

During his exile in Paris, Hobbes published, in Latin, *De Cive*, the projected third part of his "Elements of Philosophy." It was, he would say later, the book that made him famous.[14] *De Cive* elaborates and clarifies many of the arguments of *The Elements of Law*. The doctrines remain largely the same. He explains in a preface to the 1647 second edition that questions concerning authority and political obligation, so controverted in the years leading up to the civil war, caused him to defer work on *De Corpore* and *De Homine* and "ripened and plucked from me the third part. Therefore it happens that what was last in order is yet come forth first in time." In that preface he also decries "the mischiefs that had befallen mankind from its counterfeit and babbling form" of political philosophy and asserts that the right political philosophy can contribute to peace. *De Cive* made its first appearance in English in 1651 under the title *Philosophical Rudiments Concerning Government and Society*. The publication of *Leviathan* the same year overshadowed the event.

De Cive found favor among many in the court of the exiled Prince of Wales (the future Charles II). Absent the anti-Catholic and anti-papal invective of *Leviathan*, it also won the support of many French Roman

[14] "Verse Life" in Gaskin, *Elements of Law*, 258.

Catholics. None, however, held the book in higher esteem than Hobbes himself, who regarded it as providing the foundation for a science of politics.[15] The respect that he enjoyed among the Prince's advisors, secular and religious, made easier his appointment in 1646 as tutor in mathematics to the future king. It helped, too, that among those advisors was the Earl of Newcastle, who had spent a fortune and risked his life in support of Charles I and who had been governor to the young prince in the 1630s. The Earl was a friend and patron (Hobbes dedicated *The Elements of Law* to Newcastle), and it may well have been on his recommendation that Hobbes got the job. It lasted just six months, but during that time Hobbes gained the friendship of his pupil.

In August 1647, Hobbes became very ill and remained bedridden for several months. So grave was his condition that Mersenne, himself a priest, sought to convert him to Catholicism and urged him to receive last rites. Hobbes declined. He did accept from an Anglican cleric an offer of communion administered according to the rites of the Church of England. Hobbes recovered to live another 30 years but not unscathed. In the next year, his hands began to shake so much that he could write only with great difficulty. This affliction (probably Parkinson's disease) required that he rely on amanuenses in the production of manuscript. Nevertheless, he soon thereafter began work on his most famous book, *Leviathan*.

Hobbes's ten years of exile came to an end in late 1651. He had always intended to return to England when political conditions permitted. The reception accorded the publication of *Leviathan* that year hastened his decision to return.

> Then home I came, not sure of safety there,
> Though I cou'd not be safer any where.[16]

As he explains in his "Verse Life," *Leviathan* turned many of Charles's advisors against him. *De Cive* had acknowledged an expertise in scriptural interpretation in the bishops of the church and granted the church some independence in determining doctrine and ritual. *Leviathan* invests authority over these matters exclusively in the secular sovereign, who may, if he chooses, even administer the sacraments. This doctrinal reversal much offended Anglican clerics. Furthermore, royalists at the English court-in-exile and at Versailles objected to Hobbes's denial of divine right as the

---

[15] *The English Works of Thomas Hobbes of Malmesbury*, Sir William Molesworth, ed. (11 vs.; London: Bohn, 1839–1845), VII, 471 and I, ix.
[16] "Verse Life" in Gaskin, *Elements of Law*, 260.

74   J. T. BOOKMAN

foundation of monarchical authority. And, Part IV, the "Kingdom of Darkness," is a bitter attack on Catholicism and the papacy, to which the French authorities took exception. No longer welcome at court and fearing prosecution by the French or assassination at the hands of ultraroyalists, Hobbes left for England and an uncertain future. His pro-monarchical and anti rebellion views were, of course, well known.

Once in England he did what he could to smooth his way. He took the oath of "Engagement," acknowledging the legitimacy of the Commonwealth and pledging allegiance to it. He took up residence in London rather than at the country estate of the Earl of Devonshire, his long-time patron, in order to reduce association with out-of-favor royalists. Some of his contemporaries even suggested that *Leviathan's* "A Review and Conclusion" aimed at conciliation of the Commonwealth's rulers, Cromwell and the Rump Parliament. He does say there that "the point of time, wherein a man becomes subject to a Conqueror, is that point, wherein having liberty to submit to him, he consenteth, either by expresse words, or by other sufficient sign, to be his Subject." The charge was misplaced; *De Cive* (8. 1–3), published nine years earlier, takes the same position.

Hobbes's apprehensions about his safety under the Cromwellian regime proved to be misplaced. No threats were made against his person, he associated with whom he pleased, and censors erected no bar to publication of his books. Much that he produced during the period, ranging across a variety of subjects, provoked or responded to criticism. Anglican bishops, Presbyterian divines, and university professors took Hobbes to task for one and another of his positions, political, religious, scientific, and mathematical. His attempt to "square the circle" initiated a years-long quarrel with John Wallis, Oxford professor of geometry. The quarrel had theological implications for them both as evidenced by Wallis's remark that "[o]ur Leviathan is furiously attacking and destroying our universities ... and especially ministers and clergy and all religion ... as though men could not understand religion if they did not understand mathematics. Hence it seemed necessary that some mathematician should show him ... how little he understands the mathematics from which he takes his courage."[17] The tenor of the quarrel is suggested by the title of Hobbes's reply, which included, by the way, a defense of his religious views: *Six Lessons to the Professor of Mathematicks*, etc. *Stigmai* etc.; *or Marks of the Absurd Geometry, Rural Language, Scottish Church Politics and Barbarisms of John Wallis Professor of Geometry and Doctor of Divinity*. John Bramhall, an

[17] Quoted by Reik, *Golden Lands*, 178–179.

LEVIATHAN   75

Anglican cleric, took offense at the appearance in 1654 of a short treatise by Hobbes entitled *Of Liberty and Necessity*. Bramhall and Hobbes, at the urging of Newcastle, had exchanged views on the subject while both had been in exile in Paris in the mid-1640s. They had agreed not to publish. Bramhall believed, wrongly, that Hobbes was guilty of bad faith. Hobbes had not authorized publication; indeed, he had been duped by those responsible. Nevertheless, this caused a long-running, and sometimes acrimonious, exchange between the two on a number of theological and political matters. On the question that initiated their dispute, Hobbes reaffirmed his determinism. People are free, he contended, to do as they will. Their wills, however, have causes in earlier events. Among those earlier events, childhood experiences, but also an immediately preceding period of deliberation, might figure. He agreed with Bramhall that unless a person is free, he ought not to be held responsible for his actions. For Bramhall, freedom and necessity are incompatible. An action is free only if it occurs outside the chain of causation.

The Restoration marked no abatement of the criticism directed Hobbes's way. Throughout the 1660s and 1670s, Anglican clerics assailed him for his purported atheism, his rejection of God and nature as the foundation of morality, his promotion of licentious behavior, and so on. "Hobbism" named this popular view of Hobbes's teaching. His disrepute helps explain his exclusion from the recently chartered Royal Society of London for the Improving of Natural Knowledge.[18] He wanted to be a member. He had friends as well as enemies among the Fellows. And, by the end of 1663, the Society numbered some 137 members—almost everyone in the country of any scientific stature. John Locke was made a Fellow in 1668 on the strength of credentials far less impressive than those of Hobbes. By the early 1660s, Hobbes, then over 70, could count among his accomplishments an English translation of Thucydides's *History of the Peloponnesian War, A Brief of the Art of Rhetoric*, all three parts of his "Elements of Philosophy," and, of course, *Leviathan*. The first part of *De Homine* he devotes to optics. Much of the rest of that work concerns perception. *De Corpore* sets out his views on scientific method. Hobbes's

---

[18] Noel Malcolm, "Hobbes and the Royal Society" in his *Aspects of Hobbes* (Oxford: Clarendon Press, 2002), 317–335; Quentin Skinner, "Thomas Hobbes and the Nature of the Early Royal Society," *Historical Journal*, 12 (1969), 217–239; and Steven Shapin and Simon Schaffer, *Leviathan and the Air-Pump: Hobbes, Boyle and the Experimental Life* (Princeton: Princeton University Press, 1985) all take up the subject.

interests and publications were not confined to political philosophy. No Englishman was better known on the Continent as a philosopher. Nevertheless, he was not invited to join the Royal Society. Why?

The explanation must be speculative. His approach to the study of natural things was at odds with that of the Society. He was systematic and abstract. Science for him was a body of conditional propositions, general in nature. The Society emphasized close observation and experiment. Instead of wasting their time on experiments, Hobbes thought, the Fellows ought to proceed from the foundation he had laid in *De Corpore*. Hobbes had in *Dialogus Physicus* (1661) stated these views in an attack on the scientific establishment in general and Robert Boyle in particular—the experimenter-in-chief and founding member of the Society. Hobbes could be contentious and arrogant, as he was in *Dialogus Physicus*, and this could not have recommended him to those who sought an easier fellowship. Probably more important, however, was Hobbes's reputation in some quarters as an atheist. The Royal Society's purposes aroused suspicion among some, and it may be that "the more disreputable Hobbes became, the more necessary it was for the other scientists to dissociate themselves from him by attacking him, precisely because he was in some ways embarrassingly close to their own position."[19] The Society felt sufficiently threatened by criticism that it published its history just five years after grant of its charter. Part III of that history argues at length that science is not a threat to religion or government.

Hobbes's reputation drew the attention of Parliament in 1666. Many attributed to sin an outbreak of plague in 1665 and the Great Fire of 1666. Both were catastrophic events. The plague killed some 25 percent of London's residents, and the Fire consumed most of the old city including 13,000 houses and St. Paul's Cathedral. In response, the House of Commons established a committee to investigate books that "tend" to atheism, blasphemy, and profanity and in particular *Leviathan*. At the same time, some Anglican clerics wanted to drag Hobbes before an ecclesiastical court on charges of heresy. Neither threat to his well-being advanced beyond the talking stage. He did have friends at court, including the king with whom he had reconciled in 1661 and the secretary of state. Their support dissuaded the more vindictive in the church and Parliament from pressing things through.

[19] Malcolm, *Aspects*, 328.

Hobbes, perhaps out of gratitude for his support on that occasion, dedicated *Behemoth* to the secretary of state Henry Bennet, Lord Arlington. This work, published under several titles, is a history of the civil war. In a wide-ranging analysis, he identifies the causes of the war. Religious difference, constitutional defect, London's self-aggrandizement, and individual failure among the governing elite, all played a part. Not least among the causes was the reading of ancient texts that deceived many about the purpose of the state and the duties of subjects. Hobbes sought the permission of the king to publish. Although sympathetic with the book's treatment of the subject, Charles denied the license in keeping with his general ban on the publication of Hobbes's work on politics and religion.

In his last years he published translations of the *Iliad and Odyssey*, because, he said, "I had nothing else to do." Even in his late 80s there was to be no resting on his laurels. He left London, never to return, in 1675 for the Cavendish country estates. There he lived a quiet life, visiting with members of the family and their guests and pursuing his studies well into the fall of 1679. He suffered a stroke in October and died several weeks later.

Leviathan: A Commentary

Hobbes Leviathan. Richard Tuck, ed. Rev. Student ed. Cambridge: Cambridge University Press, 1996.

References to Hobbes's other works identify the individual book and cite volume and page of the Molesworth edition of *English Works* (E. W.).

Epistle Dedicatory Sidney Godolphin was a royalist M. P. in 1628 and 1640. He lost his life in the service of the king's army at the age of thirty-two. Hobbes is full of praise for him here and in the "Review and Conclusion" (484). Godolphin bequeathed £200, "reall testimonies," to Hobbes whom he counted as a fast friend. Hobbes anticipates a hostile reaction from both the proponents of freedom from governmental control and the proponents of governmental authority. He makes clear that he speaks not of persons but of institutions. He thinks, too, that his observations about Scripture will elicit the most hostile response. He seeks "to advance the Civill Power" and regards Scripture as "the Outworks of the Enemy, from whence they impugne the Civill Power." He proved to be right about the response to *Leviathan*. It was criticized from all quarters.

Intro Hobbes calls into question the distinction between the natural and the artificial. Nature is "the Art whereby God hath made and governes the World" (9). Men imitate God by the exercise of art in the creation of the state. He also questions the attribution of superiority to the natural. As we shall see, the natural state of humankind in Hobbes's view is a terrible condition. It is the commonwealth, the construct of art, that provides peace and order and the possibility for one to live out one's days unmolested and to enjoy life's delights.

- Does this impugn God's creation and his governance of the world?

Hobbes here calls the commonwealth, the state, "that great LEVIATHAN" (9), and on two other occasions he invokes the same image—in Chapters 17 (120) and 28 (221). In the latter chapter, he indicates that he found the image in "the last two verses of the one and fortieth of *Job*, where God having set forth the great power of *Leviathan*, calleth him King of the Proud." The Biblical *Leviathan* (Job 41 and Isaiah 27:1) is described as a kind of sea monster. Hobbes wishes to emphasize the power of the state even going so far as to describe the state as "that *Mortall God*" (120).

He argues that behavior is not a reliable guide to intention: "by men's actions we do discover their designe sometimes" (10), but our experience is limited—confined to our "acquaintance, which are but few" (11). Furthermore, the inferences we make about another's intentions are informed by the objects of our own passions, and these depend on the "constitution individuall, and particular education" (10). Thus a good man (here Hobbes uses the conventional understanding of "good"), in following the imperative to "Read thy self," would presumably impute benevolent intentions to at least some. Hobbes contends that he "that is to govern a whole Nation" must not attempt to discriminate among his subjects by observing their behavior. Instead, he "must read in himself … Man-kind" (11). He urges the same upon us all if we are "truly to read one another" (10). What can be learned in this way, however, is limited. Introspection teaches that others have thoughts and passions. It does not tell us what the objects of the passions are—"the things *desired, feared, hoped,* & c" (10). Some other method will have to be employed to discover the things desired, feared, hoped, and so on.

Ch. 1 In this and the following chapters, Hobbes provides an account of his epistemology and, in particular, his theory of perception. A fuller account, he indicates, can be found elsewhere. He may be referring to *The Elements of Law*, I. ii, which had been circulating in manuscript since 1640, to *Humane Nature* which reproduced the aforementioned section of the Elements and appeared in print in 1650, or to *De Corpore*, Chapter 25.

Hobbes believes that all human beings have reason (19, 23, 35, 36) and, therefore, have the capacity to know. The knowledge acquired by most men is derived from experience (36) and is called "prudence" when there is "*Praesumtion of the Future*" and "history" when there is "Praesumtion of Things Past" (22, 23, 60). Such knowledge is fallible "through the difficulty of observing all circumstances" (22, cf. 458). Those in the universities (14, 19) and the "Councells of the Commonwealth" (37) who pretend a greater understanding of the ways of the world rely on "deceived Philosophers, and deceived, or deceiving Schoolemen" (24, cf. 29–30). He urges people to think for themselves (28, 29, 33, 37). Even if they do not acquire science which requires "study and industry" (23), they "are in better, and nobler condition ... than men [who] fall upon false and absurd generall rules" (36).

Ch. 2 "Fancy" is the appearance of a thing. "Imagination" is the recollection of the appearance of a thing—the thing itself no longer an object of sense. "Memory" is the recollection of a thing that was an object of sense sometime (indeterminate) ago. "Experience" is the sum of one's memories.

"Ghostly" (19) = ecclesiastical.

The last paragraph hints at a kind of understanding unavailable to introspection, namely, an understanding that uncovers man's "conceptions and thoughts." This understanding involves the "sequell and contexture of the names of things into ... Speech" (19).

Ch. 3 God, he says, is *"Incomprehensible"* (23). Humans can know nothing of divine qualities. Men can conceive only that which has first been perceived by sense, and God is not an object of perception. But then neither are those small internal motions of the human body that Hobbes calls "Endeavour" (38). He will treat of religion at greater length in Chapters 12 and 31 and in Part III.

80 J. T. BOOKMAN

The incomprehensibility of God was the orthodox position for both Catholics and Protestants. Aquinas, for example, in *Summa Theologiae* (I. 12.12) states that God can be known only through "his relationship with creatures, that is, that he is the cause of all things." And, in the *Summa Contra Gentiles* (I. 14): "The divine substance exceeds by its immensity every form which our intellect attains." Calvin has no larger view of human knowledge in this regard: "The greatest geniuses are blinder than moles" (*Institutes of the Christian Religion.* II. 18–21). Hobbes castigates the "Schoolmen" here and throughout *Leviathan*— see especially Chapter 46. He is referring to a group of medieval Christian philosophers, all in holy orders and many in university faculty, hence "school-men" or "scholastics," who developed the system and method known as "scholasticism." Prominent among them were Anselm of Canterbury, Peter Abelard, Albert Magnus, Thomas Aquinas, Duns Scotus, and William of Ockham. Although the golden age of scholasticism had passed by Hobbes's time, many at Oxford and Cambridge and in the nation's pulpits remained under its influence. The scholastics contributed much to the recovery, translation, and promulgation of ancient texts. Chief among these were the works of Aristotle whose *Logic* alone, and that only a part, had been available until the thirteenth century. It was their effort, however, to reconcile faith and reason and to produce a synthesis of philosophy and theology that distinguishes the scholastics in the history of philosophy. Their method employed a dialectical approach: a close reading of the ancient philosophers and of the early church fathers, the identification of contradictions in their teachings, and the resolution of those contradictions in a new synthesis. In their attempt to secure a synthesis, the scholastics created a special vocabulary replete with words, Hobbes thought, of ambiguous meaning or uncertain reference. His difficulties with them extended well beyond the matter of definitions. He was a materialist. Everything for him was matter in motion. The Scholastics were all dualists: There is both substance and spirit, body and mind.

Ch. 4 Hobbes suggests that speech was a solitary, not social, invention (24).

- Do we know anything about the origins of speech?

He doubts not the significance of speech in the life of human beings. Without it, he says, there would be "neither Common-wealth, nor Society, nor Contract, nor Peace."

Universals are predicates that can be ascribed to many individual things, for example, "beauty," "good," "dog," and "triangle." On the question of universals, Hobbes is a nominalist: "[T]here being nothing in the world Universal but Names; for the things named, are every one of them Individuall and Singular" (26). He rejects the view, known as "realism," that universals name something independent of mind. Plato's theory of the Forms is a kind of realism. It much influenced Augustine, and many scholastics adopted the realist position.

By "accident" (26, 34, 35) is meant a quality, for example, color, that is not part of an object, as Hobbes understands things, but a consequence of perception.

In this chapter Hobbes begins to elaborate the method hinted at in Chapter 2, which will, he claims, enlarge understanding beyond that provided by introspection or prudence.

Ch. 5 This chapter will be addressed following Chapter 9.

Ch. 6 Hobbes asserts that "Sense, is motion in the organs and interiour parts of mans body." The "small beginnings of Motion … are commonly called ENDEAVOUR" (38). This mechanical view of human action received earlier expression in "The Introduction" where he likens the human body to an automaton (9) and in Chapter 3 where we were told that "[a]ll Fancies are motions within us" (20). Hobbes may believe that thought and emotion (his "passions") can be explained solely in terms of matter and motion. Indeed, he goes so far as to say that thought and emotion "are … anything else, but divers motions; (for motion, produceth nothing but motion)" (14). He is right to think that events like chemical reactions and electrical impulses are conditions of thought and emotion. Unless "Thomas Hobbes" named a once living human being, a body of flesh and blood, there would have been no *Leviathan*, no one to experience the fear that seized him at the beginning of the Long Parliament. Nevertheless, his claims are too large. It is worth noticing that in the ensuing four centuries no comprehensive physico-chemical theory has emerged to explain psychological states. It would seem, moreover, that any physico-chemical theory must ultimately founder on the fact that human beings have consciousness and intention.

82   J. T. BOOKMAN

Consider this example. The senses might perceive the rapid approach of a tornado or the presence of an armed robber. These perceptions trigger certain chemical reactions and electrical impulses associated with the emotion called "fear." That, of course, is not the whole story. Consciousness interprets these perceptions and imparts meaning to them. The same reactions and electrical impulses associated with fear occur, but the experiences are different. And, because they are different, the responses might also be different depending upon the intentions of the perceiver who is not a perceiver simply but also a conscious agent. Fortunately, the cogency of Hobbes's political philosophy does not hinge on the truth of his mechanistic materialism.

Hobbes proposes to found his political philosophy on an account of the passions. Thus, in Chapter 13 he argues that, in the absence of a coercive power to impose order, men and women would be "apt to invade, and destroy one another." This conclusion is an "Inference, made from the Passions" (89). He does not tell us here what he thinks the incidence to be of one or another passion or whether one is dominant over another.

The observation that "whatsoever is the object of any mans Appetite … make his sentence the Rule thereof" (39) is often understood as an expression of egoism, either ethical or psychological. Ethical egoism asserts that one ought always to act to promote one's self-interest. Psychological egoism denies the existence of motives like benevolence; all human conduct is motivated by self-interest. Hobbes certainly denies that the "good" can be discerned by reflection about the essence of things as Aristotle had contended (Nicomachean Ethics I. 7: 1097b22–1098a7). Words like "good" and "evil" are relative "to the person that useth them" (39).

"Deliberation" is the "alternate Succession of Appetites, Aversions, Hopes and Fears" (44). The role of reason in the thought process would seem to be confined to the estimation of consequences. Thus, "he who hath by Experience, or Reason, the greatest and surest prospect of Consequences, Deliberates best" (46). There is no suggestion that reason arbitrates among the passions and might even overrule some appetite or aversion in an act of will. Rather, "*Will* … is the last appetite in Deliberating" (45).

Ch. 7 Science is conditional—conditional in the sense that its conclusions take the form: "If this be, that is" (47). Only knowledge of fact can be absolute, and such knowledge is acquired by sense and is always particular.

Ch. 8 In Chapter 6, Hobbes maintains that differences in the objects of men's passions occur "because the constitution of a mans body, is in continuall mutation" (39). Here such differences "proceedeth partly from the different Constitution of the body, and partly from different Education" and "not onely from the difference of mens complexions; but also from their difference of customes, and education" (53).

Hobbes does not often allow himself to express a judgment about life beyond mere life, but in trying to explain how it was that the Jews believed that God spoke in the prophets, rather than to them, he suggests a "want of curiosity to search naturall causes; and their placing Felicity, in the acquisition of the grosse pleasures of the Senses" (57).

Ch. 9 Whatever coherence Hobbes's conception of the sciences may possess up to this point, this chapter pulls apart. The first distinction he makes in the diagram is between civil philosophy and natural philosophy, that is, between inquiry into the "Consequences from the Accidents of Bodies Naturall" and inquiry into the "Consequences from the Accidents of *Politique* Bodies."

- What informs this distinction?
- What distinguishes civil philosophy from inquiry into "Consequences from the Passions of Men" classified as a branch of physics?
- If civil philosophy involves the "apt imposing of Names ... a good and orderly Method ... till we come to a knowledge of all the Consequences of names appertaining to the subject in hand" (35), why is it not joined with "Mathematiques"? The commonwealth is not a natural body, but neither is a triangle or an equation.

Chs. 1–5, 7, and 9 In these chapters, Hobbes gives a brief account of his theory of scientific method and scientific truth. This account, he says, is "not very necessary to the business now in hand" (13), but if we are to acquire knowledge about the world, and politics in particular, the right method is necessary. Want of the right method results in "absurdity" (34, 35). There are two kinds of knowledge: knowledge of fact (prudence) and knowledge of consequences (60). The latter he calls "science" or "philosophy" (35, 60, 458); he uses the terms interchangeably. Prudence and science are both the products of reason, but science is superior, because some of its conclusions are "certain and infallible" (37). Prudence, on the other hand, is fallible "through the difficulty of observing all circumstances" (22, cf. 37, 458). All the conclusions of prudence are "uncertain" (37).

84   J. T. BOOKMAN

Hobbes divides the sciences into two types: *"Knowledge acquired by Reasoning from the Manner of the Generation of anything, to the Properties"* and knowledge acquired by reasoning *"from the Properties, to some possible Way of Generation of the same"* (458). In his Epistle Dedicatory to the *Six Letters to the Professors of the Mathematiques*, he makes the same distinction and notes a significant difference (E. W. VII, 184)· "When the causes are known there is place for demonstration [conclusions 'certain and infallible'], but not where the causes are to seek for. Geometry therefore is demonstrable, for the lines and figures from which we reason are drawn and described by ourselves. ... But because of natural bodies we know not the construction, but seek it from the effects, there lies no demonstration of what the causes be we seek for, but only of what they may be."

One such natural body is man. In Hobbes's diagram of the sciences in Chapter 9, "Consequences from the Qualities of *Men in Special*" is a branch of physics. This categorization reflects his conviction that human psychology can be reduced to motion (37, 38). His conception of science, then, comprehends what we would call axiomatic systems as well as the natural sciences. Geometry, mathematics, and logic are all axiomatic systems (28, 32). They alone provide knowledge that is demonstrable. This is so because "in Geometry [for example] ... men begin at settling the significations of their words; which settling of signification, they call *Definitions;* and place them in the beginning of their reckoning" (28, cf. 458, and E. W. VII: 184). The logical consequences of these "definitions" (we would say "axioms") may then be deduced and expressed as *"Theorems"* (34, cf. 28, 31–34). In those sciences, like physics, devoted to the study of natural bodies, the inferences made from the "Properties" or "effects" are about what the causes might be.

While the sciences may give us knowledge, the "ablest, most attentive, and most practised men, may deceive themselves, and inferre false Conclusions" (32). How is the truth of our conclusions to be determined? Hobbes replies that "truth consisteth in the right ordering of names in our affirmations." Inquiry must begin "at settling the signification of ... words" (28) and then "proceed from one consequence to another. For there can be no certainty of the last Conclusion without a certainty of all those Affirmations and Negations, on which it was grounded, and inferred" (33). The discovery of the truth, it would seem, requires, and only requires, careful attention to the specification of definitions and the application of logical rigor in drawing out the implications of those definitions. This account applies well enough to the axiomatic systems, but what of those sciences that make assertions about natural bodies?

LEVIATHAN   85

Hobbes is not altogether clear about the determination of truth in the natural sciences. In some places he seems to have in mind empirical confirmation. He characterizes the conclusions of the natural scientist as "[u]ncertain, when onely some particular events answer to his pretence, and upon many occasions so as he sayes they must" (37). Here, "pretence" might stand in for our "hypothesis"—Hobbes does not use the word—and his "events" and "occasions" for empirical confirmation. In an invidious comparison with prudence (35, 36, cf. 458), he says: "Science is the knowledge of Consequences, and dependance of one fact upon another: by which, ... we see how any thing comes about, upon what causes." Later, in *Leviathan*, he appeals to experience in confirmation of, or as not contrary to, his views about the passions (89) and about the relationship between absolutism and stable government (145, 221). These appeals, however, are addressed to those whose reason is confined to prudence. "The skill of making, and maintaining Common-wealths, consisteth in certain Rules ... or the method to find out" (145).

For Hobbes, civil philosophy is among the axiomatic systems like geometry. "Civil philosophy is demonstrable because we make the commonwealth ourselves" (*Six Letters to the Professors, E. W.* VII: 184). In such systems, knowledge of consequences is acquired by inferences made from definitions that state the causes. The definitions are determined by agreement: "Reckoning ... of the Consequences of generall names agreed upon" (32) and "Ratiocination from ... settled significations of their words" (34). The "definitions" upon which Hobbes founds his political philosophy are the "Natural Inclinations of Mankind" (489). The "definitions," however, are factual generalizations about the passions—the appetites and aversions of humankind.

- How likely is agreement about those generalizations?

Ch. 10 Power is not valuable in its own right but as a means to "some future apparent Good" (62). At one extreme, power is the means to compel others; at the other, receipt of a day's wages.

The *Value* of a man, is ... his Price" (63).

- Is Hobbes suggesting that there is a market in power?

86   J. T. BOOKMAN

Ch. 11 Hobbes contends that "the Felicity of this life, consisteth not in the repose of a mind satisfied" (70). Rather, felicity is "*Continuall* success in obtaining those things which a man from time to time desireth" (46). But, while there may be no utmost aim or greatest good, people "tend" to seek a "contented life," that is, "the repose of a mind satisfied." The realization of what desires might provide a "contented life" is unidentified. Given the diversity of passions and differences in knowledge or opinion about causes and effects, such a life would differ from person to person. "A contented life" remains a formal concept: "the repose of a mind satisfied." It is a life unobtainable because fear and desire are ever present (46).

That "general inclination" to acquire power (70) is an inclination to acquire the means to realize some future apparent good (62).

- What is the incidence of those passions among humankind that "inclineth to Contention, Enmity, and War" and those that "disposeth men to obey a common Power" (70)?

Ch. 12 "Peculiar to the nature of Man" is perception of the world as a world of causes and effects. Religion has its origins in the search for the causes of "good and evill fortune." Fruitless search for "the true causes of things" inspires fear, the creation of "some *Power*, or Agent *Invisible*" to which human beings attribute their fortune, the adoption of ceremonies by which to honor and propitiate that power, and prediction on contrived or faulty grounds. Although this chapter is largely a critique of pagan religion—gentilism—it contains other observations that deserve attention. Notice that both gentilism and monotheism develop from the same seed—the "Naturall seed of Religion" (79, 83). In the cultivation of that seed, gentiles and monotheists have had the same purpose: to make people "more apt to Obedience, Lawes, Peace, Charity, and civill Society" (79).

- Is this how Christ's purpose should be described?

"All formed Religion, is founded at first, upon the faith which a multitude hath in some one person ... to whom God himselfe vouchsafeth to declare his will supernaturally" (83, 84). The authenticity of claimants to divine revelation can only be attested by miracles. Some claimants are imposters and the religion they found or develop a sham.

- How are we to distinguish the true from the false?

In his discussion of the passions in Chapter 6, Hobbes described religion as a "*Feare* of power invisible, feigned by the mind or imagined from tales publiquely allowed." Fear of power invisible from tales not allowed is superstition. This does not, of course, answer the question just posed. It does indicate the authority that Hobbes proposes to invest in government to decide what practice may be followed as religion. That passage concludes in the observation that "when the power imagined, is truly such as we imagine, TRUE RELIGION" (42).

There is another way to God that does not begin in fear of power invisible. A natural curiosity "to know the causes of naturall bodies" (42) inspires some, a few (36), to undertake a profound pursuit of causes that "arrive to the acknowledgement of one Infinite, Omnipotent, and Eternall God." Reason concludes "that there must be … one First Mover … which is that which men mean by the name of God" (77).

- Is that so? Or do most people mean an anthropomorphic being whose attributes are the best human attributes magnified and who intervenes directly in human affairs, responds to petitionary prayer, and judges the worth of souls?

Hobbes's God as discovered by reason is abstract, remote, incomprehensible.

Ch. 13 Hobbes imagines human beings as individuals, shorn of any social attachments, who, in the absence of government, "have no pleasure, (but on the contrary a great deal of griefe) in keeping company" (88). Human interactions are characterized by "diffidence," that is, distrust, and violence. Consequently, people are unable to enjoy the benefits of civil society.

The state of nature is a fiction, a thought experiment, that describes social relations "where there is no power able to over-awe them all" (88). Hobbes's description of those relations is an "Inference, made from the Passions": a "Warre, where every man is Enemy to every man" (89). Anyone who doubts the reasonableness of his description is asked to consult his own experience and to take notice of the "savage people … in *America*" (89) and of the state of international relations (90).

- Do we accuse "mankind" when we lock our doors at night?

Chs. 6, 10, 11, and 13 In the "Review and Conclusion," Hobbes says that "I ground the Civil Right of Soveraigns and both the Duty and Liberty of Subjects, upon the known Natural Inclinations of Mankind" (489). These inclinations include objects of desire, emotions aroused in the pursuit of the objects of desire, and the means used to realize desires. Chapter 11 identifies a handful of inclinations that promote life in society and obedience to gov ernment and several inclinations that make for "Contention, Enmity, and War." With one exception, he does not tell us there of the incidence or intensity of those inclinations. The sole exception is "a generall inclination of all mankind, a perpetuall and restlesse desire of Power after power, that ceaseth onely in Death" (70). This inclination might, but does not necessarily, reduce the possibility of civil society. Power is one's "present means, to obtain some future apparent Good" and includes "eminence of the Faculties of Body, or Mind" and such things as "Riches, Reputation, Friends" (62). Power so defined is, and must be, pursued and exercised everyday in the state of nature and in civil society, if people are not to go hungry, to be exposed to the elements, and to be subjected to assault and fraud.

Human beings experience a wide range of emotions as they pursue their objects of desire: pleasure, hate, love, grief, hope, and fear among them. Fear, "continuall feare," particularly of violent death (89), provides in part the motivation to quit the state of nature and to live in civil association (90).

Hobbes describes as pervasive, or nearly so, certain objects of desire. Thus, it is "in the nature of man" "to invade," that is, to use force and fraud against one's fellows, "for Gain ... for Safety; and ... for Reputation" (88). "The pursuers of Wealth, Command, or sensuall Pleasure ... are the greatest part of Mankind" (99). "The Passions of Hate, Lust, Ambition, and Covetousnesse ... are infirmities ... annexed to the nature ... of man" (206). And, he says the "Business of the World ... consisteth almost in nothing else but a perpetuall contention for Honor, Riches, and Authority" (483). This last suggests that the desire for these things is quite intense as well as pervasive. Hobbes observes these inclinations in his fellow members of civil society, and they inform his view of human nature in the absence of government—the state of nature is an "Inference, made from the Passions" (89).

Ch. 14 Hobbes appropriates the term "right," which names a concept that had currency in his day and that had moral connotations (see the Leveller tracts, e.g., and his own comments at 149–150).

LEVIATHAN 89

- Does his right of nature impose obligations on anyone?
- What about the right-holder? Ought he or she to launch pre-emptive attacks? Defend himself or herself against such attacks?

He insists that every person has the same right and has that right as an individual simply, not as a citizen, or a child of God, or a peer of the realm. For earlier generations, rights were attached to status in the social order as in the Magna Carta. Hobbes's individualism does not come out of respect for human life or for people as moral agents, but out of a conception of human beings as actors who will. It is not reason that makes us right-holders but will. What we will is "the last Appetite in Deliberating" (45). The most pervasive and intense appetite is for life itself. Hobbes invests a right in "everyman ... to everything; even to one anothers body" (91). Such a right is "generally allowed" and "ought to be allowed him" because "necessary to a mans conservation" (88).

- Who recognizes such a right?
- Ought such a right to be recognized?

Renouncing or transferring right creates obligation (92). He who has laid aside right acquires an obligation to not hinder "another of the benefit of his own Right to the same" (92). Failure to honor an obligation is injustice (93, 100). Transferring of right is contract. Covenant is a particular kind of contract in which one or both parties agree to perform later. It is by means of a covenant that people are to extricate themselves from the state of nature. People become party to a contract and thereby acquire an obligation by the giving of consent—"Signes"—either express or by inference: "Whatsoever sufficiently argues the will of the Contractor" (94).

Furthermore, "Covenants entered into by fear, in the condition of meer Nature, are obligatory" (97). Thus, "if I covenant to pay a ransome ... the Covenant is valid" (97, 98, cf. 141–142, 154, 484–485). In these passages, Hobbes consistently maintains that the acquiring of obligation is a consequence of the giving of consent. Confronted by force, one might experience fear and be motivated to consent. It is not force, however, that obligates but consent. In responding to a contemporary critic, Hobbes says: "He [Bishop Bramhall] thinks, belike, that if a conqueror can kill me if he please, I am presently obliged without more ado to obey all his laws. May I not rather die, if I think fit? The conqueror makes no law over the conquered by virtue of his power; but by virtue of their assent, that promised obedience for the

90   J. T. BOOKMAN

saving [sparing] of their lives" (*The Questions Concerning Liberty, Necessity, and Chance in E. W. V*: 180). Contract creates obligation but "nothing is more easily broken than a mans word" (93), "the bonds of words are too weak to bridle mens ambition … and other Passions" (96), "the force of words, being … too weak to hold men to the performance of their Covenants" (99). Hobbes sometimes uses language suggesting that by the sword alone can people be brought to the performance of their covenants, that is, it is out of fear of punishment that most people obey, fear of "the Power of those men they shall therein offend" (99).

- Is any government strong enough to compel obedience from all? Most? Many?

Hobbes thinks that "the grounds of these Rights [of sovereignty as described in Chapter 18] have the rather need to be diligently, and truly taught; because they cannot be maintained by any Civill Law, or terrour of legall punishment" (232). And, in *Behemoth*, he asks, "If men know not their duty, what is there that can force them to obey the laws? An army, you will say. But what shall force the army?" (*E. W.* VI: 237).

Ch. 15 The "Foole" believes that he advances his own good by disobedience when he can do so with apparent impunity—when he can "neglect [avoid] not onely the dispraise, and revilings, but also the power of other men" (101). He takes advantage of the law-abidingness of his fellow subjects in using force and fraud. Hobbes contends that such behavior is against reason (102, 204).

The eleventh, seventeenth, and eighteenth laws of nature raise interesting questions for the ethical egoist. That theory argues that we ought always to act in our own self-interest.

- If advising and judging are a part of ethics, and Hobbes thinks they are, can the ethical egoist observe these laws of nature? In this regard, see Hobbes's comments about counsel (46 and 176 *passim*) and about judging (168 and 191 *passim*).

"*in foro interno*" = literally, in the internal court; or, in thought.

The obligation imposed by the laws of nature is different from that acquired as a consequence of covenant. The latter requires that one act in fulfillment of the terms of the covenant if the other party has already done his part or when there is a power to compel obedience from those who would otherwise not keep their promises (96–98). The laws of nature "bind to a desire they should take place" (110). He describes a law of nature as "a precept, or generall Rule, found out by Reason" (91), and the laws of nature as "dictates of Reason" (111). The laws of nature identify the conditions for the realization of peace, security, and commodious living (90, 91, 111). They are not laws, properly called, but principles— indeed, the "true and onely Moral Philosophy" (110, 111). "Law, properly is the word of him, that by right hath command over others" (111). Therefore, the laws of nature are laws properly called only if one regards them as commands of God. Hobbes does not say that obedience to the laws of nature is obligatory for that reason. They become obligatory as a consequence of the covenant creating the commonwealth, and "Covenant with God, is impossible" (97). Furthermore, one need not be a believer to discern the laws of nature. Unassisted reason is quite sufficient "even to the meanest capacity" (109, cf. 233) to reveal the basic principle.

Chs. 14 and 15 Hobbes recognizes that not all human beings want to exercise power over others. There are those who, were they not in the state of nature, "would be glad to be at ease within modest bounds" (88). And, in the preface to the second edition of *De Cive*, written in 1647 as he began work on *Leviathan*, he argues that "though the wicked were fewer than the righteous, yet because we cannot distinguish them, there is a necessity [in the state of nature] of suspecting, heeding, anticipating, subjugating, self-defending, ever incident to the most honest and fairest conditioned." Nevertheless, he emphasizes the anti-social inclinations of humankind and the war of everyman against everyman that issues from those inclinations. Thus, "*every* man [my emphasis] looketh that his companion should value him, at the same rate he sets upon himselfe" and, if he does not, "to make them destroy each other" (88). And, "if *any two* men [my emphasis] desire the same thing, which nevertheless they cannot both enjoy, they become enemies" (87). These desires for reputation, gain, and their preservation, safety, produce "a warre … of every man, against every man" (88). Given a prevailing uncertainty about how others will behave and equal vulnerability to murderous attack, people live in constant fear.

There is by definition no government to enforce prohibitions on anti-social behavior, and there are no prohibitions to enforce.

If people are to enjoy peace and the other benefits of civil society, they must institute government—a "power able to over-awe them all" (88).

92   J. T. BOOKMAN

- What authority must government have to control the use of force and fraud by self-seeking individuals acting alone, that is, by the people who populate Hobbes's state of nature?

Ch. 16 This chapter prepares the ground for the next in which Hobbes describes the nature of the covenant creating government. A person may by covenant authorize another to act on his behalf. Such a covenant creates an "artificial person" or representative. Those who "have no use of Reason" (113) lack the capacity to enter into such an agreement. All others are capable of authorship, that is, owning the words and acts of the representative or actor.

Hobbes is emphatic that "it is the *Unity* of the Representer, not the *Unity* of the Represented, that maketh the Person *One*. … And because the Multitude naturally is not *One*, but Many, they cannot be understood for one, but *many* Authors, of everything their Representative saith, or doth in their name" (114).

Ch. 17 The sovereign is created by covenant—an agreement among many individuals in the case of "Common-wealth by *Institution*" or an agreement between a conqueror and the conquered in "Common-wealth by *Acquisition*" (121). In both instances, fear provides the motivation to become party to the covenant (138). And, the consequences of the covenant are the same (139). The ruled lay down the right of nature to all things but retain the inalienable parts of that right (93). If this were the only change worked by the covenant, the sovereign it creates would not be very formidable, certainly no "great LEVIATHAN" or "Mortall God" (120). The sovereign would have acquired only unimpeded exercise of his or their right of nature. Such power would be insufficient to secure domestic peace, let alone to defend the commonwealth against a foreign enemy. The covenant, however, also authorizes the sovereign to act on behalf of the ruled, who "submit their Wills, every one to his Will, and their Judgements, to his Judgements" (120). The ruled have thereby an obligation to not just stand aside but to assist the sovereign in the administration of justice and in defense of the commonwealth.

Ch. 18 The theory of sovereignty laid out here elicited praise from Sir Robert Filmer: "No man that I know has so simply and judiciously handled [sovereign authority]. I consent with him about the rights of exercising government, but I cannot agree to his means of acquiring it" *(Observations*

*Concerning the Original of Government, Upon Mr. Hobs Leviathan, 1652).
In Patriarchia* (1680), Filmer espoused a divine right of kings. Hobbes rejects the idea that a monarch, or any other form of government, receives his, or its, authority from God. He also argues against the idea, put about by several proponents of parliamentary authority, that governments receive authority from the people and on condition. There is no people before the institution of government, no body that could take collective action, no civil society that could act in a constituent capacity. There is only a multitude whose members form no social attachments, with one exception—"small Families, the concord whereof dependeth on natural lust" (89). The covenant is an agreement *"every one, with every one"* (121) to which the sovereign is not party. The covenant does not bind the sovereign and, therefore, can impose no conditions on the sovereign.

- Hobbes asserts that the covenant creates "a reall Unitie of them all" (120). Is this so? In what sense? Has the multitude been transformed into a people who share a common life?

"Obnoxious" (128) = vulnerable.

Whatever the "inconveniences" of a government of absolute authority, it "is scarce sensible, in respect of the miseries, and horrible calamities, that accompany a Civill Warre; or that dissolute condition of masterless men" (128, cf. 144–145). Life under government is always better than civil war or anarchy.

- Is this true? Of Hobbesian men who are indistinguishable from one another in the state of nature? Of real people who are distinguished by race, ethnicity, language, religion, and gender among other things? Why?

Chs. 17 and 18 Hobbes nowhere suggests that civil society changes human beings in any significant way. Civil society does introduce a new consideration that must be taken into account in the thinking people do about how best to promote their interests. In the war that characterizes the state of nature, it is reasonable to engage in force and fraud to promote one's interests. In civil society, the use of force and fraud is not reasonable (101–103). As an enemy of public order, one might be apprehended and punished by government. Furthermore, it becomes in everyone's interest to support the government, at least when it is safe to do so, in its enforcement of the law against everyone else.

Hobbes recognizes that civil society makes it safe, or relatively safe, to associate with others. The isolated individuals of the state of nature are members of groups in civil society. All, or almost all, human beings have been members of groups that, more or less successfully, impart rules of right conduct, establish a set of roles, promote certain interests, and foster group loyalty. Familial, religious, professional, business, ethnic, and political groups are characteristic of societies everywhere. The significance of the social nature of humankind is slighted by Hobbes as can be seen in the obvious tension in his theory between the right of nature (91) and the obligation to defend the commonwealth (151–152). He does not recognize that the nation, another of those associations that humans create, can elicit a self-sacrifice that supersedes an individual's interest in self-preservation. Even when nationalism pales in war, as it often does for those at the tip of the spear, it is loyalty to one's buddies, the members, say, of one's platoon, that keeps soldiers in the field.

Smaller associations than the nation also inspire loyalty and promote interests larger than the individual. Indeed, it is with such associations in view that the Hobbesian state is in part erected. The "Foole" as robber or murderer or con man, that is, the unsocialized man, can be dealt with by a government whose authority is limited to the adoption and enforcement of laws against force and fraud. Another and far greater threat to domestic peace is posed by the socialized man—the man who is a member of associations. The gravest threats in seventeenth-century England came from the advocates of parliamentary authority who rebelled against the autocracy of Charles I and from the Puritans and Scottish Presbyterians who contended that only by obedience to a law higher than civil law could salvation be won. To the parliamentary rebels, Hobbes says, "it is manifest, that though the event follow … the attempt thereof is against reason" (103). He dismisses the claims of those acting out of religious principle as "frivolous," "because there is no naturall knowledge of mans estate after death … but onely a beliefe grounded upon other mans saying" (103, cf. 122). The remedy that Hobbes prescribes to deal with such groups is a government with unlimited authority. If government is to have the power to exercise such authority, it must win the support of many, particularly among the politically active. Hobbes recognizes that "the Actions of men proceed from their Opinions; and in the wel governing of Opinions, consisteth the well governing of mens Actions" (124). By writing *Leviathan*, he hopes to shape opinion. He urges the teaching of his views in the universities—the "Fountains of Civill and Morall Doctrine" (491, cf. 236–237). He hopes to persuade people that they have an obligation to obey and that their long-term interest is served by obedience. Disobedience is corrosive of the authority and power of the commonwealth, upon which all depend for peace and security. Civil society is in the long-term interest of all. He appeals, then, to reason, a reason, however, that remains prudential. It can caution against the immediate gratification of appetite at the expense of long-term interests. It does not, in Hobbes's view, determine ends for most people.

Hobbes's account of the covenant whereby commonwealth by institution is created raises questions. First, he denies that the persons living in the state of nature are anything more than a "disunited Multitude" before the establishment of government. Those persons cannot act in a collective way; they do not constitute a constituent assembly. He does provide, however, that "the Congregation of them that were assembled" (123) decides by majority vote whether to invest authority in a *"Man, or Assembly of Men"* (121).

- Why, if the majority of that congregation can decide that matter, cannot it decide other matters?
- Must it not also decide which man or assembly of men?

Second, Hobbes argues that, because the sovereign is not party to the covenant, "there can happen no breach of Covenant on the part of the Soveraigne" (122). The parties are individuals, *"Naturall Person[s]"* who *"Covenant, every one, with every one"* (121). The sovereign, of course, is an "Artificiall person" (111) which has no existence before the covenant and, therefore, could not act. The sovereign is an office or set of offices. It is all too easy to be misled into regarding the sovereign as a natural person by Hobbes's own frequent use of personal pronouns in referring to the sovereign.

- How does the relationship between Hobbes's sovereign and the covenant differ from the relationship between a corporation and its articles of incorporation?
- Does the fact that the corporation is not a party to the articles of incorporation imply that the natural persons who come to hold office in the corporation cannot breach the articles of incorporation?

96   J. T. BOOKMAN

Ch. 19 Hobbes dismisses the traditional distinctions among governments based upon number and the end pursued (see Aristotle. *The Politics*, III. 7: 1279a5–10). He discards as a criterion pursuit of the common good. Any government is preferable to civil war or anarchy. The difference among them is their "Convenience, or Aptitude to produce the Peace, and Security of the People" (131). He advances a handful of not very persuasive arguments in favor of monarchy. The sole difficulty in the case for monarchy he believes to be the problem of succession (136). It is worth noting that Hobbes makes no claim of any special competence in those who might exercise sovereign authority. The Stuarts, whom Hobbes found quite acceptable, were distinguished mostly by their licentiousness.

Ch. 20 A commonwealth by acquisition creates "dominion despoticall," that is, despotic rule. Like the commonwealth by institution, it rests on covenant—the consent of the vanquished (121). The ruled, earlier called "subjects" (121), are here called "servants" (141). The authority held by the sovereign is no different than that held by the sovereign by institution (139, 142), but the language that Hobbes uses to describe it is much more pointed: The "Vanquished" agree "that so long as his life, and the liberty of his body is allowed him, the Victor shall have the use thereof, at his pleasure" (141) and "the Master of the Servant, is Master of all he hath … as often as he shall think fit" (142).

Hobbes recognizes a "naturall inclination of the Sexes one to another, and to their children" (140). He does not allow this recognition to inform his view of the family. Familial relations for him raise questions, and only questions, of rule and obedience. His observation that "God hath ordained to man a helper" (139) does not presage claims of male superiority. He rejects the Aristotelian position that men are the superior sex (*The Politics*, I. 12: 1259b1–4). Force and contract regulate relations among family members. Indeed, a family is much like a commonwealth (142). Parental authority, he says, rests on the parent's power "to save, or destroy" the child (140).

Hobbes appears to invoke experience—"Practice" (145)—in support of his contention that absolute sovereignty offers the only hope for domestic peace (cf. 221). He adduces no evidence for his claim but directs us where to look: at commonwealths in which "the subjects never did dispute of the Soveraign Power" and at "long-lived" commonwealths (145). Even were we to learn, however, that the claimed association does not hold, experience is a poor teacher. "The skill of making, and maintaining Common-wealths, consisteth in certain Rules" (145, 221, 232).

Ch. 21 Following the definition given in Chapter 14 (91), Hobbes says liberty, or freedom, is "the absence of Opposition"—"external Impediments of Motion" (145). This "only is properly called *liberty*." He distinguishes this "natural *liberty*" from the liberty of subjects. Natural liberty is restricted by "walls, or chayns" (146); the liberty of subjects by "Artificiall Chains, called *Civil Lawes*" (147, 200). Civil liberty comprehends those rights that "cannot by Covenant be transferred" (151) and "those things, which in regulating their actions, the Soveraign hath praetermitted" (148). The latter "is in some places more, and in some lesse" (152). For many of his contemporaries, such differences were significant, and Hobbes's denial that they are significant provoked outrage. No difference between *Luca and Constantinople*? Hobbes believes people to be deceived who claim liberty as a "Birth right" (149) or who want to control the actions of their sovereigns (150).

- Can one have an obligation to defend the commonwealth (152) without violation of the right of nature?

"The Obligation of Subjects to the Soveraign, is understood to last as long, and no longer, than the power lasteth, by which he is able to protect them" (153). Just as a person acquires obligation upon consenting to the creation of a power to compel obedience from those who might otherwise disobey the law (96–98, 189) so that obligation ends when that power is insufficient to protect one against "Intestine Discord" (153) or a conquering enemy (154).

While the authority of the sovereign is unlimited, and the liberty of subjects is restrained by civil laws, this does not bar a subject from "controversie with his Soveraigne" whom he may sue and "demand the hearing of his cause" (152–153).

Ch. 22 "Letters" or "Letters Patent" (156 and *passim*) are documents issued by the king publicly disclosing the grant of an office, monopoly, or other special status to a person or an organization.

"Mulct" (157 and *passim*) = fine, a financial penalty.

"Bodies Politique" (155) refers to both governmental and non-governmental organizations. The sovereign is the only body politique that is regular, absolute, and independent (155). All others are "Subordinate to some Soveraign Power" (155).

98   J. T. BOOKMAN

In subordinate bodies dissent may be lawful, but "in a Soveraign Assembly, that liberty is taken away" (158).

- Why is this so? Might not the sovereign decide that peace and security are promoted by allowing dissent?
- Does dissent always challenge sovereign authority as Hobbes alleges?
- Is there any suggestion that these bodies foster identities that, if they do not supplant, compete with the asocial, self-interested qualities he ascribes to people in the state of nature?

Ch. 23 Hobbes makes the professoriate, indeed all teachers, and clerics public ministers who discharge their offices on the authority of the sovereign. He denies that these officials, and in particular Anglican bishops, Scottish Presbyters, and Puritan ministers, receive their authority from God. He elaborates on this view in Chapter 42.

Ch. 24 There is no property, "propriety," before the creation of government. The right that subjects may acquire in property under the law is "a right to exclude all other subjects from the use of them; and not to exclude their Soveraign" (172). The distribution, transfer, and conditions of possession of property are subject to governmental decision.

Ch. 25 Hobbes amplifies his earlier comments (46, 108, 109) about counsel.

Ch. 26 Law is command—the command of him whom one is obligated to obey. One acquires such an obligation by covenant and not because one can be compelled to obey (183). Fear of punishment might, of course, provide motivation to obey. "The Soveraign … is not subject to the Civill Lawes" (184). There is no higher law to which one might appeal. Neither custom (184), nor the laws of nature (185), nor common law (186), nor "the books of Morall Philosophy" (191) constitute such a law. As for a constitution, Hobbes regards that as not possible. Before the institution of government there is no people that could act in a constituent capacity, only a multitude.

Hobbes discusses the place of civil law and the laws of nature within categories made familiar by St. Thomas Aquinas in his *Summa Theologiae* (I–II: Qu. 90–97). "Naturall" law—Aquinas calls this law "eternal"— comes from God as First Cause: "Naturall Lawes being Eternall, and

LEVIATHAN 99

Universal, are all Divine" (197), according to Hobbes. For Aquinas, this law is identical with God's reason. It is the divine order that informs the whole universe. Everything is subject to its immutable necessity. It includes the laws of nature in the modern, scientific sense and also rules of right conduct like Hobbes's laws of nature. Humankind can discern such rules, Aquinas contends, by the use of unassisted reason and ought to be obeyed as commands of God. Unlike Aquinas, Hobbes regards the laws of nature as obligatory only under certain conditions. "Positive" laws "have been made laws by the Will of those that have had the Soveraign Power over others" (197). Such laws make obligatory at some point in time what was not obligatory before. Civil law is "Humane" positive law and may be penal or distributive (197). *"Divine Positive Lawes ...* are declared ... by those whom God hath authorized to declare them" (197), for example, Moses and the Ten Commandments. Except for those who have directly received supernatural revelation, no one else "can infallibly know by natu-rall reason" (198) that the claimed revelation is genuine. "Sanctity may be feigned; and the visible felicities of this world, are most often the work of God by Naturall and ordinary causes" (198). At best, one has only belief in the authenticity of a claim of revelation.

Ch. 27 "Fact" (201 and *passim*) = deed.

Sin is a religious concept. It is offense against God—a violation of his law (see, e.g., I Corinthians 6: 9–10 and Galatians 3: 5–6). On the tradi-tional Christian understanding, violation may occur in thought, word, or deed. Hobbes denies that it is sin "to be delighted in the Imagination onely" (201) by covetous thoughts. An intention to act on such thoughts is a sin of which God will take cognizance. Until intention is manifest in word or deed, there is no crime. Crime is a violation of civil law. In the absence of government, there is no crime but there might be sin. People might violate the laws of nature which, on Hobbes's understanding, com-prehend the Second Table. There is no sin in taking life, liberty, or prop-erty in the state of nature when one "cleared by the Uprightness of his own Intention" (202), that is, such acts are necessary for the preservation of one's own life.

Ch. 28 Hobbes holds that "the Right, or Authority of Punishing" that rests in the sovereign is "not grounded on any concession, or gift of the Subjects" (214). It is simply that right all possessed in the state of nature to inflict harm on another.

100   J. T. BOOKMAN

- Can this explanation be reconciled with what we were told earlier about the consequences of the covenant (see 98–100)?

By definition no one had authority in the state of nature to inflict harm. Authority is the just exercise of power and in the state of nature there is no just and unjust. Authority is acquired by the covenant. The covenant establishing government authorizes the sovereign to adopt laws prohibiting violation of the laws of nature and attaching penalties for their violation. Thus, Hobbes says, "a man may covenant thus, *Unless I do so, or so, kill me*" (98). He who violates civil law is unjust, and he authorizes his own punishment. In resisting punishment, he exercises the right of nature and acts justly in that "he cannot Covenant thus, *Unless I do so, or so, I will not resist you, when you come to kill me*" (98).

Ch. 29 This chapter is largely recapitulation of arguments made in Chapters 18, 21, and 26. Among the diseases that might infect a commonwealth, "a *Ghostly* [ecclesiastical] *Authority* against the *Civill*" (226) comes in for criticism. Hobbes refers to certain "Doctors" who have set up such an authority. Aquinas is among those doctors. He adopted the Gelasian doctrine of the two swords in which Pope Gelasius I at the close of the fifth century summed up the thinking of the church fathers on the proper relationship between church and state. That doctrine assumed a Christian society governed by two authorities. God entrusted to the state the care of secular interests and to the church the care of men's souls. Cooperation ought to prevail between them, and each should respect the jurisdiction of the other. On the Thomistic understanding, where the spheres overlap, as they do in man's mind and heart, the state should defer to the church because man's supernatural end of everlasting blessedness is higher than his natural end of temporal security and happiness.

Ch. 30 Hobbes reiterates the essentials of sovereign authority and emphasizes the importance of teaching all how such authority accords with reason. Government rests on opinion, not on force. Prevailing opinion in seventeenth-century England and elsewhere provided, he thought, a weak foundation for the commonwealth—a house built on sand (145; Matt. 7: 26–27). Gaining acceptance of the right political philosophy is impeded "not so much from the difficulty of the matter, as from the interest of them that are to learn" (233). At the conclusion of Chapter 31 (254), he expresses pessimism about the prospects for changing opinion.

The law of nature "obliges" the sovereign to provide for "*the safety of the people* ... but by Safety here, is not meant a bare preservation, but also all other Contentments of life" (231). This is not a right that subjects may claim, and the sovereign commits no injustice whatever policies it pursues (239, cf. 148). The sovereign is absolute. Nevertheless, sovereign authority must be exercised in a circumspect way. The sovereign's duties consist in not limiting or dividing sovereign authority (231–237; cf. 222–228, 127–128). In this regard, the sovereign should censor speech and press with particular attention to claims of ecclesiastical independence and to claims of popular participation in government (223–224, 226–228). The sovereign should provide equal administration of justice including equal taxation, which "consisteth ... in the Equality of that which is consumed" (238). He specifically mentions a consumption tax. Hobbes recommends no ambitious economic program to his absolute sovereign (125). He is to determine the laws of property (125), to protect against force and fraud (235), and "to secure them in such sort, as that by their owne industrie, and by the fruites of the Earth, they may nourish themselves and live contentedly" (120). The sovereign should also provide some minimum sustenance to those "unable to maintain themselves by their labour" (239) and employment opportunities for those "as have strong bodies" but are without jobs (239).

Ch. 31 Hobbes carries out his intention, announced in Chapter 12, "to speake more largely of the Kingdom of God" (83). There are two such kingdoms: natural and prophetic. The natural kingdom is the subject of this chapter, the prophetic in Chapter 35. God exercises a general superintendence of the world to which everything including all humankind is subject (245). God reigns by the right of nature. There is no covenant for none is necessary. Unlike the rough equality in power that prevails among humans in the state of nature, God has power irresistible (246–247). God's superintendence is manifest in the laws of physics and also in Hobbes's laws of nature. The laws of nature may be violated, but, if it is safe to observe them, one violates them at one's peril. Violation might have as a consequence the suffering of natural punishment. Such punishment is temporal, not spiritual (253–254). God's reign as just described is distinguished from the kingdom of God that comprehends those who "believe there is a God that governeth the world" (246). To them God "declareth his laws three ways" (246). Hobbes confines himself here to what people can learn "by their Naturall Reason onely, without other word of God" (248). They can

102   J. T. BOOKMAN

learn rules of right conduct, to wit, the laws of nature, and "those rules of Honour ... received from them" (249–250). He expresses skepticism about what can be known about God by natural reason, "that is, from the Principles of natural Science ... to do him the greatest Honour we are able" (252). He does insist that God exists.

- If God's nature is incomprehensible, how can natural reason know even that much? Must we not know something about God's nature before we could even identify the being whose existence is in question?
- If God's nature is incomprehensible, how can natural reason know what is appropriate or inappropriate to say about God?

Ch. 32 This chapter begins a long section in which Hobbes seeks in the light of Scripture to establish the authority of civil government in Christian nations and the duty of Christians to their sovereigns. In Parts I and II, he lays out his views of what unassisted reason teaches about authority and duty. Both, he argues, are the result of covenant. With respect to most men, fear alone will hold them to performance of their covenants. That fear might be of the "Power of Spirits Invisible" or the "Power of those men they shall therein offend" (99). Hobbes holds the former to be the greater power but the latter the greater fear. Perhaps. In any event, Britain was a nation of Christians ruled by a Christian monarch, and many British turned to the Bible and to their churches for answers to questions about authority and duty. If Hobbes were to gain wider acceptance of his views on these matters, he had to overcome two principal impediments: the belief that the church as minister to man's higher end, the salvation of his soul, is independent of, if not superior to, the state and the belief that a Christian jeopardizes his salvation by obedience to civil laws thought to violate God's law. Both these beliefs relied on Scripture, described in the "Epistle Dedicatory" as the "Outworks of the Enemy, from whence they impugne the Civill Power" (3). Hobbes allows that Scripture, subject to "wise and learned interpretation, and careful ratiocination [provides] all rules and precepts necessary to the knowledge of our duty both to God and man" (259). The Bible is God's word "by mediation of the Prophets, or of the Apostles, or of the Church" (256–257). Furthermore, God has not spoken since. No purported prophet since the time of Christ has satisfied the two criteria of authenticity: the doing of miracles and not teaching any but the established religion (257).

LEVIATHAN 103

Much of the argument in Part III is given over to biblical exegesis. In this, Hobbes insists that neither our sense, nor experience, nor reason should be abandoned, for these are the God-given resources by which we are to live our lives and to realize "Justice, Peace, and true Religion" (255–256). Nevertheless, "we are bidden to captivate [that is, to permit domination of] our understanding to the Words." This is necessary because "there be many things in Gods Word above Reason," although "nothing contrary to it" (256). Hobbes is quick to criticize the Schoolmen for propounding doctrines contrary to reason—for "converse in questions of matters incomprehensible" (59), but here he is ready to suspend reasoned judgment, "though the mind be incapable of any Notion at all from the words spoken" (256, 292).

Ch. 33 The text of the Bible that Hobbes interprets is that authorized by the Church of England. This text, the King James version, is the subject of Adam Nicolson's *God's Secretaries* (2003). Hobbes does not doubt that it is the "True Register" of those things said and done by the prophets and apostles. Bart Ehrman takes up the matter in *Misquoting Jesus* (2005). "None can know they are Gods Word, (though all true Christians believe it) but those to whom God himself hath revealed it supernaturally" (267). Biblical principles, with the qualifications noted (268), are made law by the sovereign. Hobbes is most concerned to deny to the Church of Rome any authority to interpret Scripture—a subject to which he returns in Chapter 42.

Ch. 34 Hobbes seeks to make sense of some biblical terms that, interpreted "in the language of the Schools" (269), are contrary to reason. In his explication of "Spirit," his materialism is much in evidence. He denies that there are substances incorporeal. All is body including God himself. A literal reading of Genesis 1:2 lends support to his position (271).

Ch. 35 The kingdom of God, the "Prophetique" kingdom (246), is a commonwealth—a civil, temporal government (282, 284). By covenant between God and Abraham, the Jews became God's "*peculiar* Subjects, whom he commanded by a Voice" (280, 246). After the rejection of God's civil government and the election of Saul as king, the prophetic kingdom was suspended and will remain suspended until the Second Coming "when Christ shall come in Majesty to judge the world, and actually to govern his owne people" (284). For Hobbes, "the Kingdome ... of God, is a reall,

104   J. T. BOOKMAN

not a metaphoricall Kingdome" (283). This "literal interpretation of the *Kingdome of God*" (284) leads him to dismiss St. Augustine's idea of a City of God, a kingdom whose subjects are united by their love of God (The City of God. XI. 1; XIV. 1–7, 28; XIX. 17, 21–24; and XXII. 22). Membership in that kingdom is universal, open to all irrespective of status, race, ethnicity, or gender, and includes the good angels and the elect in heaven and those who are still on their pilgrimage on earth The church and the City of God are not conterminous. The church is a visible, human organization. It has some members who do not love God but only themselves. Nevertheless, since the Fall one can become a member of the City of God only by the conferment of grace, and the usual means of the conferment of grace are the sacraments of the church. While the state exists to provide "earthly peace for the sake of enjoying earthly goods" (*City of God*. XV. 4), the church has care of a higher end—the salvation of souls. Augustine is indefinite about church-state relations. He does say that the Christian state will recognize and respect the boundary between the temporal and spiritual spheres. Centuries later, after many border disputes, Aquinas concludes in *On Kingship* (Ch. 14): "So that spiritual and earthly things may be kept distinct, the ministry of this kingdom [of God] is entrusted not to earthly kings but to priests, and especially to … the Roman Pontiff, to whom all kings over Christian peoples should be subject as to Christ himself." Hobbes could count on his fellow Protestants to reject papal supremacy, as he does, but he is no less hostile to the idea of the two kingdoms, temporal and spiritual, with jurisdiction over the latter in the hands of the church. He regards this as a recipe for disaster. Sovereignty would then be divided, and, quoting Mark 3:24, "*a Kingdome divided in it selfe cannot stand*" (127). Hobbes, of course, insists on civil supremacy.

- Given the differences over religious doctrine, governance, and worship that prevailed at the time and the intensity with which these views were held, can peace be realized along Hobbesian lines?

Ch. 36 Hobbes revisits matters broached in Chapter 32. In particular, he addresses him who claims that "God hath spoken to him in the Holy Scripture" or that "he [God] hath spoken to him in a Dream" (256–257). Scripture is the word of God as mediated by the prophets, the Apostles, or the church. He asserts that "all Prophecy supposeth Vision, or Dream" (297). Presumably this applies to all those who mediate God's word, with

LEVIATHAN 105

the exception of "our Saviour who was both God that spake, and the Prophet to whom he spake" (295). We are advised that visions and dreams are suspect (257). Scripture itself cautions against false prophets, of which there have been many more than true prophets (298). Worldly motives, like ambition, inspire some to pretend to be prophets (297). Furthermore, there is disagreement among the prophets of both Old and New Testaments (298). The question is: What are we to understand to be God's word? Even if we assume Scripture to be the Word, it speaks in many voices. Whose interpretation is to be authoritative? For Hobbes, the choice is between one's Christian sovereign or the "first Chaos of Violence, and Civill warre" (299–300). He is not proposing that anyone relinquish his or her own judgment about God or the meaning of the Scripture to the sovereign, but to "not by act or word to declare I beleeve him not" (256, cf. 306, 323, 471).

Ch. 37 The performance of miracles is one of the two marks of true prophecy (257–259, 298). Miracles came to an end with the coming of Christ. Therefore, there can be no more true prophecy (259). Even with regard to this earnest of earlier prophets, Hobbes advises skepticism (304–306).

Ch. 38 Hobbes revises the estimate made in Chapter 14 (99) about the fears that conduce to obedience, at least in Christian nations. Upon our religious understanding hinges the very possibility of commonwealth (306–307, 311). He seeks to mitigate the asperities of "Eternal torment" and to diminish the ecstasy of beatitude. Eternal torment is a "Second Death of every one that shall be condemned at the day of Judgement, after which he shall die no more" (315). This is another instance of that literal interpretation adopted by Hobbes and favored by other Protestant commentators. Here "dead" means dead and an end to everlasting torment. He suggests an alternative reading of the relevant biblical texts in Chapter 44, wherein the wicked live as they have always lived after the Fall (432–433). Eternal life is a life "resembling that which we lost in Adam in the point of marriage" (308).

Hobbes advances his reading of the Bible as provisional until such time as the government shall make the interpretation that should be obeyed. "For the points of doctrine ... under God have the Soveraign Power" (311).

106   J. T. BOOKMAN

- Does Hobbes subordinate the end of salvation to that of temporal peace?

Chs. 39–41 In these chapters, Hobbes addresses what he regards as a fundamental error in scriptural interpretation: "The greatest ... abuse of Scripture ... is the wresting of it, to prove that the Kingdome of God ... is the present church" (419). Against that understanding, he defines "church" as *"[a] company of men professing Christian Religion, united in the person of one Soveraign"* (321). Earlier (246, 280), he described God's kingdom as natural when He rules by the laws of nature and prophetic when He rules by positive laws over a special people. His examination of the Old Testament in Chapter 40 leads him to conclude that God had ruled over a prophetic kingdom: the church ruled "by authority immediate from God" (327). The election of Saul brought an end to that kingdom, not to be seen again until the Second Coming (280–284, 333). Hobbes contends in Chapter 41 that the coming of Christ represents no reinstitution of the prophetic kingdom. In support he cites John 18:36: *"My Kingdome is not of this world"* (333). He argues that Christ "was not King of those that he Redeemed, before he suffered death" (333) and that, during his time on earth, he made no challenge to civil authorities (335)—"Render therefore unto Caesar the things which are Caesar's" (Matt. 22:21). There is, then, no prophetic kingdom over which the church might rule. In God's natural kingdom, the church has no authority to rule. God rules in that realm by the laws of nature. Just as Saul and his successors ruled by the consent of the people, so have civil authorities always ruled. Hobbes summons the testimony of the Apostles who admonished the faithful to obey the powers that be (Rom. 13:1–6; Titus 3:1; I Peter 2:13–15).

Ch. 42 This is by far the longest chapter in *Leviathan*. On his account in the previous three chapters, the church is not the institutional manifestation of God's kingdom in either the natural or the prophetic sphere. Its role "is to make men Beleeve, and have Faith in Christ" (342) by preaching and by administering the sacraments (346–353). In this the church follows the example of Christ, whose office is "called, not a Reigning, but a Regeneration" (341–342, 335). The performance of this office is not dependent on state support: "Faith hath no relation to, nor dependence at all upon Compulsion, or Commandement" (342). Indeed, until rulers became Christians, the church had to win converts in the face of governmental opposition. Christian

LEVIATHAN 107

rulers may, if they choose, command obedience to the rules of the church (342), but "any other Rules, which the Soveraign Ruler hath not prescribed, they are but Counsell, and Advice" (360).

The state is to govern by making laws, obedience to which is compulsory. The church is to win converts by persuasion. In distinguishing these tasks, Hobbes intends no separation of church and state. On the contrary, he enlists the church and Christianity in the cause of civil peace. Government rests on opinion, as he reminds us again and again. The church helps to shape opinion. The stability of government must not "depend ... on the skill, and loyalty of Doctors, who are no lesse subject, not only to Ambition, but also to Ignorance, than any other sort of men" (373, 403). Therefore, the "Civill Soveraign is the Supreme Pastor." All other pastors are subordinate, even though ordained by another. The church, then, is made a department of government. No special task is reserved exclusively to the church. The sovereign may even administer the sacraments (374–375).

In the final third of the chapter (378–402), Hobbes attacks Cardinal Robert Bellarmine, who in *De Summo Pontifice* (1581) set out the Jesuit position on papal supremacy. It coincided in most respects with that of St. Thomas (see comments on Ch. 35).

Ch. 43 Two things only are necessary for salvation: "*Faith in Christ, and Obedience to Laws*" (403).

- Is there anything that the sovereign might command "as cannot be obeyed, without being damned to Eternall Death"?

Remember that a command to profess something in which one does not believe is not among those things that jeopardizes salvation (343).

- Would failure to obey the sovereign in anything, subject of course to the usual qualifications (93, 98, 99) constitute injustice (100)?

Hobbes concedes that beliefs in addition to the belief that "Jesus is the Christ" are necessary for salvation. Those beliefs, he says, are implied by the "Foundation," even "though he [the believer] have not skill enough to discern the consequence" (412–413). "There can ... be no contradiction between the Laws of God, and the Laws of a Christian Common-wealth"

108 J. T. BOOKMAN

(414). Hobbes does not attempt to construct the Nicene Creed, the orthodox statement of Christian belief, upon that foundation—a project, one suspects, beyond even his formidable powers.

Ch. 44 This is the first of the four chapters that comprise Part IV, the "Kingdome of Darkness." Hobbes describes that kingdom as a "*Confederacy of Deceivers ... to dis-prepare them for the Kingdome of God to come*" (417–418). It is synonymous with the kingdom of Satan. Non-Christians make up part of that kingdom. Another part is made up of Christians: "We cannot say, that ... the Church enjoyeth ... all the light" (418). It is the darkness in which many Christians live with which Hobbes is concerned and for which he holds the Roman Catholic Church largely responsible. The confederacy of deceivers has taken advantage of our "naturall Ignorance" (418). Natural ignorance has two aspects: "Ignorance of causes" and "Ignorance of the signification of words" (73). This condition has several consequences. It "constraineth a man to rely on the advise, authority of others" (73); it "disposeth a man to make Custome and Example the rule of this actions" (73); it "disposeth a man to Credulity" (74); and it inspires "Feare of Things invisible" (75). This last is the "natural seed" of religion.

- Can we expect, then, with advances in the natural sciences and the spread of literacy, a decline in religious belief and sentiment?

Hobbes adduces what he regards as the principal causes of religious error—in this chapter, the misinterpretation of Scripture. He attacks on scriptural grounds and in arguments now familiar Catholic doctrines concerning the kingdom of God as the present church, papal supremacy, the sacraments—transubstantiation, for example, eternal torment, purgatory, and the immortality of the soul.

Ch. 45 "Daemonology" is the belief that immaterial spirits, good and bad, can possess persons. He regards demonology and idol worship as relics of gentilism, the religion of the pagans. Roman Catholicism, as the first expression of Christianity, inherited these and many other relics that have no scriptural support (453).

He tries in this chapter to allay the fears of Puritans that, in worshiping before, or in the presence of, images, they violate the Second Commandment. Puritans regarded the images—paintings and sculpture, for

LEVIATHAN 109

example—of the Anglican Church as idols, and they destroyed many during the civil war. Hobbes contends that such worship is not idolatry unless the worshiper regards the image as "inanimated" or inhabited by God (450). Nor is it idolatry to observe the idolatrous practice of worship commanded by the sovereign (449, 452) as long as one intends no "internall, and reall honour" (452) to the person or image. This would seem to make what is in the mind and heart of the worshiper the crucial determinant of idolatry. It is not the only determinant. If "the Place, or Image be dedicated ... not by the authority of them that are our Soveraign Pastors, is Idolatry" (450).

Ch. 46 Vain philosophy, according to Hobbes, has its origins in Aristotle. It has been perpetuated by the universities which accord him so much authority that their teaching is "not properly Philosophy ... but Aristotelity" (462). Aristotle has also had a baneful effect on Christian theology. In particular, Hobbes criticizes the "doctrine of '*Separated Essences*'" as productive of much foolishness that "would fright them [men and women] from Obeying the Laws of their Countrey" (465) and that is confounded by modern science (466–468, 473–474). He explains the currency of the doctrine of separated essences as a consequence of the copula "is" as in "Socrates is a man." In that statement, "man" has been misunderstood as naming an essence, something distinct from "Socrates." As a criticism of Aristotle, it is misplaced. For him, essence has no existence apart from the concrete, individual object. Aristotle is also faulted, wrongly, for teaching that all government, except for popular government, is tyrannical and, presumably, not deserving of obedience. Aristotle regarded the best government, at least under ideal circumstances, as rule by the best—those who have practical wisdom. Ideal circumstances, however, rarely prevail, and, therefore, other claims to authority must be considered. Book III of *The Politics* finds merit in the claim of the many to a share in government. Like the claims of all others—the wealthy, the well-born, and those who fight, for example—the claim of the many is flawed. This leads Aristotle to conclude that, if those of practical wisdom cannot rule, rule by law is best because "law is reason unaffected by desire" (1287a32–33). Hobbes accuses Aristotle of naiveté because he recognizes that law, understood, as Aristotle understood it, not just as command but as the settled principles that inform the very life of a society, is a measure against which to hold rulers accountable and a ground for thinking "it lawfull to raise warre against them" (471).

110   J. T. BOOKMAN

Ch. 47 The Roman Catholic Church is a beneficiary of the ideas that inform the kingdom of darkness. It is not the only beneficiary (474–476). The Presbytery against which Hobbes rails was the ministry of the Church of Scotland. The Reformation in England was initiated by the crown in the person of Henry VIII. The Church of England, the Anglican Church, preserved much of the doctrine and liturgy of the Roman Church and its episcopal governance with the king at its head. In Scotland, ministers and laity, strongly influenced by Calvinist ideas, organized a new church in place of the old. In the absence of any real Parliament of their own, Scots made the Presbyterian Church the agent of Scottish nationalism and, more particularly, religious independence. It was the attempt of Charles I to impose the Book of Common Prayer on the Presbyterian Church that provoked Scottish revolt and marked the beginning of the civil war.

Hobbes claims for believers the "Independency of the Primitive Christians" (479). The preceding analysis makes clear in what this "independency" consists: freedom from ecclesiastical punishment for departure from orthodox doctrine. Authority formerly exercised by the church Hobbes invests in the state. The sovereign, however, in demanding observance of a particular liturgy, even profession of certain doctrines, does so for the sake of domestic peace and not because it knows the only path to salvation. One may doubt that those who fell afoul of the "Clarendon Code" drew much solace from this qualification. The Clarendon Code, adopted soon after the Restoration, was a set of laws that imposed stiff penalties on those dissenting from Anglicanism.

Review Hobbes, satisfied that he has said nothing "contrary either to the Word of God, or to good Manners; or tending to the disturbance of the Publique Tranquillity" (491), recommends that his book be published and its ideas taught in the universities. He did not disturb the public tranquility, but he did disturb the private tranquility of many royalists who regarded his comments (484) about obligation to a conqueror as a currying of favor with the Cromwellian regime and as abandoning the king's cause. He does neither or, at any rate, trims no principles to do so. Earlier in *Leviathan*, as he notes, but also in earlier works, Hobbes stresses the connection between obligation and protection. As for his abandoning of the king's cause, he can consistently maintain both that one has an obligation to obey Cromwell and the Rump Parliament and that the monarchy of Charles I was the legitimate government and Cromwell was a usurper

LEVIATHAN 111

and unjust in effecting its downfall. Just as the "Rights of the Kings of England did [not] depend on the goodnesse of the cause of *William* the Conqueror" (486), so the authority of the Cromwellian regime does not depend upon the goodness of its cause. "There is scarce a Commonwealth in the world, whose beginnings can in conscience be justified" (486). Hobbes also defends those who took the "Engagement," among them his long-time patrons, the Cavendishes, against the charge that they were assisting the enemy. He points out that they "assist the Enemy but with part of their estates," that is, taxes, but those who refused the Engagement, "assist him with the whole" (485); the latter had their estates confiscated.

Apart from these contemporary matters, the "Review" adds a twentieth law of nature to those set out in Chapters 14 and 15. Hobbes contends that there is no contradiction between this law and the right of nature (see Chapter 14: 91). He mentions Sidney Godolphin as a man for whom there was "no ... Inconsistence of Humane Nature, with Civill Duties" (484). Godolphin, however, must number among those whom Hobbes mentions as having "a Feare of the consequence of breaking their word; or a Glory, or Pride in appearing not to need to breake it" (99). The rest of us are caught up in "a perpetual contention for Honor, Riches, and Authority." This passage expresses again Hobbes's take on the problem: Somehow the competing desires of individuals must be reconciled. The laws of nature, enforced by an absolute sovereign, provide the foundation for that reconciliation. In what follows, he takes up a different perspective: The locus of conflict is the individual within whom there are competing inclinations (see Chapter 11). The conditions are, of course, related, but for the conflicted individual some kind of psychotherapy will be necessary. Hobbes believes that by "Education, and Discipline" the antagonistic forces, social and individual, can be reconciled (483).

A Bibliographical Essay

Leviathan came before the English-speaking public in the spring of 1651. Tuck (82) recounts the complicated history of its publication in a "Note on the Text." Macdonald and Hargreaves (4) describe in detail the differences among the three early editions brought out by Andrew Crooke. They also identify all editions of Hobbes's works and all collected editions published before 1726. For each edition they provide a table of contents, a brief description of the circumstances of its publication, and depiction of the title page. They list among Hobbes's works *The Last Sayings, or Dying Legacy of Mr. Thomas Hobbs of Malmesbury and Memorable Sayings of Mr. Hobbes*, now thought to be the work of Charles Blount (1654–1693). Sacksteder (6) devotes several sections of his bibliography to editions, reprints, and translations published 1879–1979. His attribution to Hobbes of "Considerations Touching the Facility or Difficulty of the Motions of a Horse on Streight Lines & Circular" is spurious according to Malcolm (30). The attribution to Hobbes of *A Short Tract on First Principles* is questionable. Tuck and Malcolm (29) believe it to be from the hand of Robert Payne (1595–1651), chaplain to the Duke of Newcastle and associate of the Welbeck Academy. Zagorin (204) contends that the traditional attribution is correct.

The *Cambridge Companions* edited by Sorell (7) and Springborg (8) have useful bibliography. They include foreign publications and are among the more recent efforts at a reference guide. Another recent guide is Malcolm (5). He includes only work cited in his collection of essays. As many as half the entries are in foreign languages, and he covers all aspects of Hobbes's thought. Despite its length, some 52 pages, the utility of the bibliography for students of Hobbes's political philosophy, indeed of his thought generally, is compromised by the inclusion of what are, at best, tangential contributions and the omission of important pieces by much-cited scholars. Much the same can be said of the 30-page bibliography appended to volume 1 of his edition of *Leviathan* (76). It is confined to works cited in the text or in the notes. Sacksteder (6) and Hinnant (3) brought out bibliographies in the early 1980s. Sacksteder is comprehensive of studies done in languages using the Roman alphabet over the period 1879–1979. He lists 155 entries for books on Hobbes and 1015 articles. Hinnant is more selective than Sacksteder and covers a much longer period. The year-by-year list of books and articles includes foreign language publications and editions of Hobbes's works. He annotates secondary works and cites reviews of major monographs. Eccleshall and Kenny (2) also annotate their 186 entries for Hobbes.

There are three modern biographies: Martinich (32), Reik (39), and Rogow (41). Martinich pays more attention to the whole of Hobbes's philosophy than does Rogow who is principally concerned with his political philosophy. Martinich says that *Leviathan* "deserves to be called 'A Bible for Modern Man' because no other work of his or any of his contemporaries presents such a forceful, eloquent, and comprehensive statement of the doctrine that expresses the spirit of modern thought." He neglects, however, to make the case for that characterization. Rogow, in addition to his Ph.D. in political science, was trained as a psychoanalyst. He contends that "Hobbes's great contribution to political philosophy cannot be fully explained or understood without reference to the vicissitudes of his life." He acknowledges that too little is known about Hobbes's life to permit a psychoanalytic interpretation, but he is "tempted to conclude that Hobbes's whole political theory, in terms of its psychological motivation or inspiration, can be seen as a repudiation of Malmesbury and much that it represented." Such speculation does not mar an informative, although sometimes misinformed, well-written biography. Reik addresses the question: "How did the early humanist scholar become, in a seemingly abrupt manner, the author of *Leviathan* and the philosopher whose method is modelled on rigorous scientific thinking?" The question seems not particularly apposite for investigation, since, one might observe, Hobbes never ceased to be a humanist interested in literary pursuits; seventeenth-century humanists regarded natural philosophy as closely tied to morality, and Hobbes's political philosophy is not very scientific. Nevertheless, her "feasible reconstruction of the development of his thought" issues in the valuable observation that "Hobbes's science is based on the correct use of words, and it is … his awareness of speech as the means by which social order is both created and destroyed … that leads us back to … classical humanism."

Hobbes himself wrote two short autobiographies in Latin: one in verse entitled "*Vita Carmina Expressa*," the other in prose. Both are available in translation in Gaskin (22, 23). In the same volume, Gaskin also has an abstract in modernized English of John Aubrey's brief life. The abstract is serviceable and certainly easier to read than Aubrey's original notes. The original is readily available in Dick (11), who selected 134 of the more notable lives from the 426 in Aubrey's *Brief Lives* (12).

Particular aspects of Hobbes's life are addressed by Malcolm (28) and Milton (33). Malcolm seeks to explain the exclusion of Hobbes from the Royal Society. That body is the subject of Purver's volume (38). Two members who exchanged polemics with Hobbes, Robert Boyle and John Wallis, are central figures, respectively, of books by Shapin and Schaffer (42) and Jesseph (24). They identify the rational differences that separated the antagonists and describe the irrational terms in which much of the controversy was carried on. Milton is concerned with the charges of heresy levied against Hobbes in 1666 and the role Henry Bennet, Lord Arlington, played in their dismissal. Malcolm (26) has compiled Hobbes's extant correspondence in two volumes for the Clarendon works. Unfortunately, much of Hobbes's correspondence is lost, perhaps destroyed by Hobbes himself, and there is nothing in what remains regarding the development of his political ideas. Of the 211 letters, 70 are from Hobbes. Sumners and Pebworth (45) and Trevor-Roper (47) discuss the Welbeck Academy and the Great Tew Circle, with which Hobbes associated before the civil war. Lucius Cary, Viscount Falkland, who provided the meeting place for the Great Tew Circle, his estate at Great Tew, is the subject of a biography by Marriott (31). William Cavendish, Earl of Newcastle and host of the Welbeck Academy, appears in Bickley's account (13) of the Cavendish family. Newcastle was a sometimes patron of Hobbes, but it was the Devonshire branch of the family that employed him for nearly the whole of his adult life and whose story is told by Pearson (37).

Several of those whose lives intersected with that of Hobbes and whose actions affected him are the subjects of biographies. Consult Ashley (10) on Charles II, Coward (19) on Cromwell, and Ollard (35) and Trevor-Roper (46) on Edward Hyde, Earl of Clarendon, Lord Chancellor to Charles II, and fierce critic of *Leviathan*. The views of Hugo Grotius, Marin Mersenne, and Pierre Gassendi, all of whom influenced or encouraged Hobbes, are analyzed in Chappell's volume (15). Sorell (44) has written a short introduction to the life and thought of Descartes. Clarke (17) fills out the portrait in his extended intellectual biography. Tuck (48) describes the relationship between Hobbes and Descartes.

Leviathan offended many. Mintz (34) in an appendix lists over 100 critical works that appeared in the latter half of the seventeenth century alone. Much of the contemporary criticism was directed at his religious ideas. And much of it was polemical and, seemingly, unbound by an actual reading of Hobbes. Rogers (40) reproduces substantial excerpts from the works of several of the more sober and cogent critics: Sir Robert Filmer, Bishop John Bramhall, Lord Clarendon, and Reverend George Lawson. In their book-length analyses, Bowles (14), Mintz (34), and Parkin (36) accord those critics attention, but they also take notice of the views of others: Ralph Cudworth and Henry More, the Cambridge Platonists, and John Whitehall, the London barrister, for example. Parkin is the most comprehensive in this regard. Springborg (114) includes four essays on the reception given Hobbes by his contemporaries, and Goldie (21) also addresses the matter.

Wootton (50) surveys the ideological context in which Hobbes wrote by reproducing short excerpts from seventeenth-century works. His introduction is a helpful guide to that literature. Skinner (43), too, seeks to establish that context as essential to an understanding of Hobbes's theory of political obligation. This essay, reprinted in abbreviated form in Cranston and Peters (97), exemplifies his contextualist approach to reading a text. Appleby (9), Clark (16), Kenyon (25), Wilson (49), and Wrightson (51) describe the social, political, and economic conditions of the times.

The Clarendon Press began publication of a collected works in 1983 under the general editorship of Howard Warrender. He has been succeeded by Noel Malcolm and others. Individual works have appeared sporadically under separate titles. Ten volumes have been published out of a projected 27. Upon completion of this project, scholars will have a collected works that reflects modern scholarship and omits spurious attributions. The Clarendon edition will displace Molesworth (56), which for so long has been the source for material to be found only in libraries or private collections holding early editions and manuscripts. The Clarendon edition, moreover, will include works omitted by Molesworth: *The Elements of Law, Critique of Thomas White's De Mundo*, and the correspondence.

There are several collections of one and another of Hobbes's works. Cromartie and Skinner (52) bring together *A Dialogue between a Philosopher and a Student of the Common Law of England and Questions Relative to Hereditary Right*. Nelson provides Hobbes's translations of the *Iliad* and the *Odyssey*. Both Cromartie and Skinner and Nelson are part of the Clarendon works. Tönnies (59) first joined under the title *The Elements of Law, Natural and Politic* two works first published under separate title in 1650: *Human Nature: or, the Fundamental Elements of Policy* and *De Corpore Politico, or, The Elements of Law, Moral and Politic*. The Cambridge University Press in 1928 and Frank Cass in 1969 reprinted the Tönnies edition. Gaskin (53) makes corrections to Tönnies particularly in the epistle dedicatory. He also includes, as earlier noted, Hobbes's autobiographical sketches and Aubrey's brief life. Gert (54) pulls together *De Homine* and *De Cive*. Those two works and *De Corpore* make up Hobbes's "Elements of Philosophy," from which Peters (58) makes selections. Reynolds and Saxonhouse (73) edit three discourses from the *Horae Subsecivae*, a work whose authorship has long been disputed. They identify Hobbes as author on the basis of statistical analysis of the text.

The Clarendon works includes editions of most of Hobbes's major political treatises: *De Cive, Leviathan, and Behemoth. The Elements of Law* has yet to appear. Tuck (143) faults Warrender's *De Cive* (67) for reproducing an English translation wrongly attributed to Hobbes. Gert (54)

116   J. T. BOOKMAN

adopts the same translation. Malcolm (27) makes a case for Charles Cotton as translator of what has been the standard text. Tuck and Silverthorne (68) make their own translation. *Behemoth*, like other editions in the Clarendon works, includes a useful introduction—in this instance by Seaward (65). The Tönnies edition (63) was reprinted by Frank Cass in 1969, with a new introduction by M. M. Goldsmith and by the University of Chicago Press in 1990, with an introduction by Holmes (64). Hobbes's criticism of Edward Coke's contention that the common law limits monarchical authority can be found in Cropsey (71) and in the Clarendon edition (52). There are many editions of *Leviathan*. Some reproduce only a part of the whole, for example, Flathman (85), which is mentioned here because, as a Norton critical edition, it has excerpts from the works of Hobbes's contemporary critics and essays by modern scholars. Know that *Leviathan* has an epistle dedicatory, an introduction, 47 chapters comprising four parts, and "A Review and Conclusion." Shapiro (81) also combines the text, the whole of it, with several essays of commentary and an introduction of his own.

Malcolm (76) edits the Clarendon edition of *Leviathan* in three volumes. The English and Latin versions appear on facing pages in Volumes 2 and 3. Textual variants are given below the text and explanatory notes define the meaning of terms and identify references and allusions. Volume 1 describes the biographical and historical contexts in which Hobbes wrote, gives an account of the several forms of the text, and reviews earlier modern editions. Curley (84) has select variants from the Latin version. Oakeshott's edition (79) is distinguished by his famous introduction. Minogue (80) also has insightful things to say in his introduction. Tuck (82) provides a 27-page glossary of proper names with biographical notes and a concordance with the Macpherson (78), Oakeshott, and Molesworth editions. Differences in the text of *Leviathan* among those editions mentioned above are slight, and those differences have not affected interpretation. Differences among the several editions in scholarly apparatus are large. Malcolm is certainly the most elaborate in this respect. Virtually all the editions have introductory essays from which one can learn much.

A modern edition of Hobbes's essay on free will, along with Bishop Bramhall's retort, is Chappell (87). Schlatter (93) and Grene (89) have brought out Hobbes's translation of Thucydides. The translations of Homer that occupied Hobbes in the last years of his life make up a volume in the Clarendon works edited by Nelson (57).

King (104) and Dunn and Harris (99) have compiled extensive collections of scholarly articles on Hobbes. Both are multi-volume collections of over 75 articles and more than 1500 pages. King concentrates on Hobbes's ethics, politics, and religion. Dunn and Harris cast their net more widely to include essays on Hobbes's epistemological and scientific views. Both the King and Dunn and Harris volumes came out in the 1990s. For more recent articles, consult Foisneau and Sorell (101), Foisneau and Wright (102), Lloyd (105), and Springborg (114). It would be a mistake to neglect earlier collections like Brown (95) and Cranston and Peters (97) because in them can be found expression, in some cases, classic expression, of most of the main lines of interpretation. Neglected by those earlier collections are feminist interpretations and interpretations of Hobbes on international relations. For the former, see Hirschmann and Wright (103). For the latter, see Caws (96) and Airaksinen and Bertman (94). The contributors to Caws maintain only a tenuous connection with Hobbes. The other volume is a collection of papers presented at a conference in 1987 that respond to the question of whether world government can be justified on Hobbesian principles. Most conclude that it cannot. Three scholars who have contributed much to Hobbes studies have each assembled his essays under one cover: Malcolm (106), Oakeshott (107), and Skinner (111). Skinner's essays appear in revised form. Articles in the appended bibliography that appear in one or another collection bear such reference.

A recent review of the secondary literature appears as Chapter 3 of Tuck (143), although the most recent work of which he takes notice is that of Skinner. He regards Skinner's contextualist approach as having great promise. Raphael (137) devotes two chapters to exposition and criticism of the literature as of 1977. With one exception, he confines his attention to books in English. Strauss, Taylor, Warrender, Macpherson, and Watkins, among others, receive scrutiny. In an appendix to his edition of *Leviathan*, Minogue (80) describes in broad terms the criticism of Hobbes by his contemporaries and those who followed down to the present. Curley (158) wrote a two-part piece consisting of a bibliographical essay of some 50 pages and a bibliography with over 500 entries in English and Continental languages to which the essay makes reference. He concentrates on work from the years 1975–1989 concerned with the psychological presuppositions that underlay Hobbes's moral and political theories. Hampton (125) and Kavka (129) dominate the discussion. Goldsmith (163) also accords Hampton a prominent place in his survey of the literature. Baumgold (116) gets much attention. In his wide-ranging review, Zagorin (204) divides Hobbes scholars into textualists and contextualists. Not much is made of this. Zagorin's sympathies are with the textualists. He has interesting things to say about the work of Johnston (128), Hampton, Kavka, and Baumgold.

Raphael (137) and Tuck (143) have written very good, short introductions to Hobbes's life and thought. Raphael is most concerned with showing the connections between Hobbes's metaphysical and psychological views and his ethical and political theories. Tuck seeks to locate the whole of Hobbes's philosophy in the intellectual context of the time with particular stress on the challenge from skepticism and on Hobbes's appropriation of a "right of nature" from Grotius upon which to found a new moral order.

At the beginning of his review of the literature, Goldsmith (163) noted the great outpouring of work on Hobbes occasioned by the centenaries of his birth in 1988 and of his death in 1979. He hoped that the danger of overproduction might be averted. Alas, there has been no abatement in the volume of publication, both of the works of Hobbes and of work on Hobbes. As a consequence, we have better primary texts and a fuller, although still spare, biography. What has not emerged is anything like a consensus on Hobbes's teaching. Baumgold (147) identifies the difficulties that have prevented the emergence of such a consensus as three: (1) the production of multiple versions of Hobbes's books, (2) uncertainty about the relationship of the three major texts in political philosophy, and (3) Hobbes's style of writing, wherein he sometimes inserts material from earlier work without reconciliation with the new. She appends annotated outlines of the chapter organization in *The Elements of Law, De Cive, and Leviathan.* Gaskin (53) in his introduction to *The Elements of Law* lays out a similar scheme. Such an outline permits ready comparison of Hobbes's reflections on a subject across the three texts.

The so-called Taylor-Warrender thesis has attracted few adherents. Warrender (144) develops an idea first set out by Taylor (192); namely, Hobbes's laws of nature are commands of God and, as commands of God, are obligatory. Men and women, they contend, could extricate themselves from the state of nature only if they are morally bound to do so. This view comes under attack from Barry (150), S. M. Brown (153), Oakeshott (107), and Plamenatz (180), who show that there is little textual support for it. Warrender (200) replies to Plamenatz's criticism. Skinner (186) and Mintz (34) object to the Taylor-Warrender thesis on contextual grounds: Placing Hobbes within the natural law tradition or, as Hood (127) does, placing his political theory on Christian foundations makes inexplicable

LEVIATHAN 119

the contemporary response to *Leviathan* as inimical to all religion and morality. Skinner also objects to Hood's interpretation for making distinctions among kinds of obligation that have no basis in the text. Trainor (195) defends Warrender against Skinner's criticism. Skinner (187) replies. Martinich (133) is one of the few who find merit in the Taylor-Warrender thesis. He argues that Hobbes "had a strong commitment to the Calvinist Christianity of Jacobean England. ... Theological concepts, especially those of English Calvinism, are an inextricable part of his philosophy."

Macpherson (132), too, has largely dropped out of the conversation. His Marxist interpretation came under attack on both textual and contextual grounds. Macpherson (172) responds to some of the criticism. He argues that Hobbes's views on human nature are informed by the behavior of men and women in the possessive market society then developing in England. In such a society, all acquire a desire for gain and glory; everyone competes with one another for their acquisition; land and labor are commodities; and some are advantaged in the competition by the possession of superior powers. Macpherson's critics, Carmichael (154), Letwin (171), and Thomas (194), contend that the qualities that he regards as distinctive of market society have been far more common historically in different societies than he thinks. Furthermore, while England in the seventeenth century had some of the attributes of a market society, it was, suggests Letwin, "a mixture of status, custom, and innovation, of freedom and restraint, of efficiency and carelessness, and was not any simple thing fit to be summed up by a ragged and emaciated model." For Macpherson, Hobbes develops a morality for bourgeois man—the morality of the market. Oakeshott (107), on the other hand, characterizes Hobbes's morality as that of the "tame man," but he also finds suggestion of another morality in the character of Sidney Godolphin, that exemplar of aristocratic values.

It is too bad that Macpherson is now largely ignored, not so much for his Marxism but for his focus on the character of civil society in Hobbes's thought. Considerable attention has been given to the character of the state of nature and the problem of the first performer; namely, if the absence of trust is as pervasive and profound as Hobbes thinks, how can people institute the sovereign by a covenant that requires trust for its execution? Macpherson suggests that this attention is misplaced. He points out that for Hobbes the state of nature is a fiction and that he dismisses a mutual covenant as the means whereby any civil society was actually created. He faults Hobbes for failing to recognize that the possessive market society is a class society. In such a society, the bourgeoisie discern their shared interests

120   J. T. BOOKMAN

and recognize that the state is necessary for their promotion. This imparts to civil society a cohesiveness that it would otherwise not have.

From the first, *Leviathan* was criticized for its absolutist doctrine of sovereignty—see Mintz (34) and Parkin (36), among others. As Skinner (138) points out, Hobbes's definition of "Liberty, or Freedom" comprehends only the "absence of Opposition" and "opposition" is "external Impediments of motion." Such an understanding makes Hobbes "the most formidable enemy of the republican theory of liberty." That theory regards as unfree choices burdened particularly by the existence of arbitrary government, government that does not respect and protect rights. It is of course the pursuit of things like republican freedom and religious salvation that Hobbes regards as destructive of social peace. Kateb (169) maintains that, for Hobbes, jeopardizing social peace is irrational because it weakens a nation's capacity to conduct international relations. "The supreme irony is that Hobbes encourages nations to be what he wants individuals not to be: activist, uncontented, and ambitious. ... Only docile individuals provide the matter out of which an audacious nation can be fabricated."

Some have seen in Hobbes a despot—even a totalitarian. Strauss (142), Macpherson (132), and Oakeshott (107) all dismiss that idea. Indeed, Strauss says that "if we may call liberalism that political doctrine which regards as the fundamental political fact the rights, as distinguished from the duties, of man and which identifies the function of the state with the protection ... of those rights ... the founder of liberalism was Hobbes." Oakeshott expresses his dissent differently: "Law as the command of the Sovereign holds within itself a freedom absent from law as Reason or custom: it is Reason, not Authority, that is destructive of individuality. ... Hobbes is not an absolutist precisely because he is an authoritarian ... [and this] separates him from the rationalist dictators of his or any age." Tuck (196) and Ryan (185) find a defense of toleration and individuality in the prudential restrictions of the sovereign's authority. Ryan (183) picks up on Oakeshott's suggestion: No sovereign can require us to believe propositions that may not be true. Belief is not under the control of the will and cannot be commanded. This, of course, is true, but, as Ball (149) and Wolin (202) point out, since the sovereign is authorized to define the terms of the moral and political lexicon and to establish the definitive interpretation of Scripture, the sovereign can influence belief. For Ball, Hobbes is "the precursor of a conceptually sanitized and scientized society largely immune from internal criticism and deaf to dissent." While Ball and Wolin have the better part of the argument with respect to the authority of the sovereign, they, along with many other commentators, neglect to address the question of power. Hobbes distinguishes between power and authority. In *Leviathan* (Ch. X), "the Power *of a Man*, (to take it Universally,) is his present means, to obtain some future apparent Good." Power may be natural or instrumental. "*Natural Power*, is the eminence of the Faculties of Body, or Mind," such as extraordinary strength, prudence, and eloquence. "*Instrumentall* are those Powers, which acquired by these, or by fortune, are means ... to acquire more," such as wealth, reputation, friends, and good luck. Authority is the just exercise of power. We are told (Ch. XV) that "Injustice" is "*the not Performance of Covenant. And whatsoever is not Unjust, is Just.*" In the case of commonwealth by institution, the sovereign is not party to the covenant and, therefore, cannot violate it. In the case of commonwealth by acquisition, the sovereign keeps his side of the bargain by not killing the conquered forthwith. The sovereign makes no promises about his future conduct. In both cases Hobbes (Ch. XVIII) describes the establishment of government as an authorization of "all the Actions and Judgements, of that Man, or Assembly of men, in the same manner, as if they were his own, to the end, to live peaceably amongst themselves, and be protected against other men."

As a consequence, the sovereign's authority is absolute in the sense that subjects have no moral ground upon which to object to governmental action; no charge of injustice can be brought against the sovereign. Tuck (143) concedes that Hobbes invests no right of resistance in the sovereign's subjects, but he claims that "at some point a sovereign might try to introduce policies which could not be justified ... and at that point ... to say that he had exceeded his rights [authority]." Thus Tuck finds moral restrictions on the sovereign's authority that Barry (150) denies. Whatever the scope of governmental authority, nothing follows about the power of government. More particularly, it does not follow that the sovereign is powerful, that government can realize domestic peace and provide defense against foreign enemies. Even after the establishment of the commonwealth, people remain isolated individuals in pursuit of "wealth, command and sensual pleasure" and, above all, their own self-preservation. It is from such a populace that the sovereign must raise an army, hire a police force, and recruit an administration. The power that the sovereign possesses to act is an effect of the covenant. The parties to it agree not to impede the sovereign in his exercise of the right of nature. Tarlton (193) identifies ways in which the sovereign can augment his power. Even as she or they accomplish this, the subjects remain a passive lot. Gauthier (123) argues that everyone recognizes that it is in his or her interest to support the sovereign against everyone else and, therefore, "the sovereign will always

122   J. T. BOOKMAN

have numbers on his side, at least as long as he seeks to punish only a few offenders on any one occasion." He doubts that the sovereign can "compel acceptance of his authority in war." Baumgold (148) traces the development of Hobbes's position from *The Elements of Law* to *Leviathan* on a subject's obligation to defend the commonwealth against attack. She concludes that Hobbes came to separate military service from the civic obligation of all subjects. Even the achievement of domestic peace may prove difficult because no one can alienate his right to defend himself and to secure the means to sustain life. Moreover, everyone is her own judge as to the severity of the threat posed by the sovereign's actions. It is upon this point that some of his contemporaries seized. Clarendon in his *A Brief View and Survey of the Dangerous and Pernicious Errors to Church and State ... in Leviathan* observed: "What greater insecurity can any Prince be in or under, then to depend upon such subjects? And alas! What security to himself or them can the Sword in his hand be, if no other hand be lift on his behalf, or the Swords in all other hands be directed against him?" Given that right of self-defense, Hampton (125) concludes that "the kind of ruler Hobbesian people are able to create is not good [that is, powerful] enough to secure [even domestic] peace." Even if we side with Gauthier on this matter, it is worth noticing that Hobbes imposes many prudential restrictions on the sovereign's authority, and this may reflect a recognition that the sovereign, at any rate in his preferred form, will not be powerful and, therefore, unable to undertake ambitious projects.

Hobbes's contemporaries also attacked *Leviathan* for its perceived atheism. Curley (157) dismisses the charge as a misunderstanding. Martinich (32, 133), too, finds a good deal of Calvinist doctrine in Hobbes's works. Tuck (143), on the other hand, regards Hobbes's theology as "Christian atheism." Theist or atheist, Gaskin (53) writes that "Hobbes is not concerned primarily with glorifying God, advancing his kingdom on earth, or making vivid and urgent man's concern with what needs to be done to secure salvation." What does concern him primarily, according to Pocock (181), is the establishment of secular authority over the church. In this important essay, Pocock bemoans the neglect by modern scholars of Parts III and IV of *Leviathan* which make up fully half its pages. Springborg (189) has been one of the few who have responded to Pocock's challenge. As editor, she (114) includes eight essays on Hobbes's theology and ecclesiology in the *Cambridge Companion*. Johnston (128) and Martinich (133) are also well worth consulting for their careful exposition of Hobbes's religious views.

A much controverted question has been the relationship between Hobbes's political and moral philosophy and his metaphysics and epistemology. Hobbes himself suggests in *De Cive* (see the preface) that his political philosophy "grounded on its own principles sufficiently known by experience ... would not stand in need of [*De Corpore and De Homine*]." And, at the close of the "Introduction" to *Leviathan*, Hobbes asks the reader to consider, not the force of the argument from science in confirmation of his reading of "Man-kind," but "if he also find not the same in himself." It is also the case that in both *De Cive and Leviathan* he adduces as evidence for his psychology the common experience of his fellows who travel armed on the highway and lock their houses at night. Nevertheless, Hobbes obviously thinks that his political and moral philosophy is implied by or is in some sense founded on the rest of his philosophy. Strauss (142) and Sorell (140) deny a connection between the two. Gauthier (123), Macpherson (132), Peters (135), and Watkins (145) affirm a connection. Oakeshott (107) suggests that "the coherence of his philosophy, the system of it, lies not in an architectonic structure but in a single 'passionate thought' that pervades its parts ... the thread, the hidden thought, is the continuous application of a doctrine about the nature of philosophy ... philosophy is reasoning ... the world as it appears in the mirror of reason; civil philosophy is the image of the civil order reflected in that mirror."

There are at least two gaps in the Hobbesian system that must be bridged in order to connect its several parts. First, no one, including Hobbes, has shown how to get from his account of human physiology, which is materialistic and mechanistic, to his psychology. Thus, Hobbes tells us in *Leviathan*, Ch. VI, that sensation "is Motion in the organs and interiour parts of mans body, caused by the action of the things we See, Heare, & c." And this motion causes "walking, speaking, striking"—all *"Voluntary motion* ... as is first fancied in our minds." His account of human physiology, however, does not imply the psychological qualities such as desire of power, ease, and praise and fear of death and dishonor, which he attributes to men and women. Secondly, moral terminology enters into his political works that is absent from the rest of his philosophy. Propositions about causes and effects do not imply, for example, that human beings are morally obligated to observe agreements into which they have entered, as Hobbes stipulates in *Leviathan*.

Hobbes's account of human psychology is closely connected with his moral and political theories. He founds his argument for the institution of the state and absolute sovereignty on the desire of all human beings for

124   J. T. BOOKMAN

self-preservation, for example. Taylor (192) and Warrender (144) deny any such connection. Hobbes's ethics, including the obligation to keep the covenant creating the sovereign, has "no logically necessary connection" with his psychology in Taylor's view. In response, Nagel (176) points out that, in light of Hobbes's insistence that people act, at least largely, out of self-regarding desires, this robs morality of any motivational force. I say "largely" because Gert (54) and Watkins (145) argue persuasively that Hobbes is not a psychological egoist. That doctrine denies, as Gert puts it, "the existence of certain kinds of motives, viz., genuine benevolence, or the belief that an action is morally right." Sorell (140), Hampton (125), Johnston (128), Gauthier (123), and Kavka (129) agree that Hobbes is not a psychological egoist. They do acknowledge that he has a pessimistic view of human nature and that self-regarding motives figure to the exclusion of other motives in the generation of the state.

There is no such agreement on the character of Hobbes's ethics. Peters (135), Goldsmith (124), and Watkins (145) regard Hobbes as an ethical egoist, that is, as espousing the principle that one always ought to act to promote one's self-interest. No explicit expression of such a principle is to be found in Hobbes's works, but it is consistent with his psychology, at least for the most part. His insistence that the "good" is relative to a particular person at a particular time and place can also be understood to assert such a principle. Alongside this subjectivist interpretation, Hampton (125) suggests that "Hobbes can even regard himself as a 'moral objectivist' of sorts, because he has shown that moral propositions can be understood to be objectively true and necessary ... as assertions of a causal connection between certain actions and a desired common goal." Gauthier (123) has a similar view. For Hobbes himself, "The Science of them [his laws of nature], is the true and onley Moral Philosophy" (*Leviathan*, Ch. 15). This makes moral philosophy a matter of prudence. Strauss (142) argues that Hobbes rejects "natural right," the doctrine that nature supports justice and that nature's teaching about the ends of humankind can be discerned by reflection. The rejection of natural right leads to relativism and nihilism. In place of natural right, Hobbes founds morality, according to Tuck (143), on a right of nature, a right of self-preservation.

Gauthier (123), Hampton (125), and Kavka (129) devote much attention to the coherence of Hobbes's explanation of the establishment of the sovereign. They find his explanation not to be coherent. Given his psychology, rational people acting to promote their own good would be unable to institute or maintain the sovereign. All three commentators engage in a reconstruction of Hobbes's theory in an attempt to secure coherence. These reconstructions are carried out in the "spirit" of Hobbes's philosophy and are informed by modern social science. Dunn (159) regards these efforts as wrong-footed. "He [Hobbes] could scarcely be further from espousing a rational choice model for explaining most of human performance." Dunn shares with all the foregoing scholars the conviction that Hobbes's emphasis on mortality and vulnerability "renders his body of thought permanently pertinent across space and time."

A SELECT BIBLIOGRAPHY OF WORKS IN ENGLISH

1. "Bulletin Hobbes" in *Archives de Philosophie*, annually.
2. Eccleshall, Robert and Michael Kenny, comp. *Western Political Thought: A Bibliographical Guide to Post-War Research*. New York: Manchester University Press, 1995.
3. Hinnant, Charles H. *Thomas Hobbes: A Reference Guide*. Boston: G. K. Hall, 1980.
4. Macdonald, Hugh and Mary Hargreaves. *Thomas Hobbes; a Bibliography*. London: The Bibliographical Society, 1952.
5. Malcolm, Noel. "Bibliography" in his *Aspects of Hobbes*. Oxford: Clarendon Press, 2002, 553–605.
6. Sacksteder, William. Hobbes Studies (1879–1979): *A Bibliography*. Bowling Green, OH: Philosophy Documentation Center, 1982.
7. Sorell, Tom. "Bibliography" in *Cambridge Companion to Hobbes*. Cambridge: Cambridge University Press, 1996, 381–98.
8. Springborg, Patricia. "Select Bibliography" in *Cambridge Companion to Hobbes's Leviathan*. Cambridge: Cambridge University Press, 2007, 501–21.

HIS LIFE AND TIMES

9. Appleby, Joyce O. *Economic Thought and Ideology in Seventeenth Century England*. Princeton: Princeton University Press, 1978.
10. Ashley, Maurice. *Charles II*. London: Panther Books, 1973.
11. Aubrey, John. *Aubrey's Brief Lives*. Oliver Lawson Dick, ed. London: Secker and Warburg, 1960.
12. ——— *Brief Lives, Chiefly of Contemporaries, Set Down by John Aubrey, between the Years 1669 and 1696*. Andrew Clark, ed. 2 vs. Oxford: Clarendon Press, 1898.

126 J. T. BOOKMAN

13. Bickley, Francis, *The Cavendish Family*. London: Constable, 1911.
14. Bowles, John. *Hobbes and His Critics; a Study in Seventeenth Century Constitutionalism*. New York: Barnes and Noble, 1969 [1951].
15. Chappell, Vere, ed. *Grotius to Gassendi*. New York: Garland, 1992.
16. Clark, J. C. D. *Revolution and Rebellion. State and Society in England in the Seventeenth and Eighteenth Centuries*. Cambridge: Cambridge University Press, 1986.
17. Clarke, Desmond. *Descartes: A Biography*. Cambridge: Cambridge University Press, 2006.
18. Coffey, John. *Persecution and Toleration in Protestant England 1558–1689*. New York: Longman, 2000.
19. Coward, Barry. *Oliver Cromwell*. London: Longman, 1992.
20. Daly, James. *Sir Robert Filmer and English Political Thought*. Toronto: University of Toronto Press, 1979.
21. Goldie, Mark. "The Reception of Hobbes" in *Cambridge History of Political Thought, 1450–1700*. J. H. Burns and Mark Goldie, eds. Cambridge: Cambridge University Press, 1991, 589–615.
22. Hobbes, Thomas. "Prose Life" in J. C. A. Gaskin, ed. *The Elements of Law Natural and Politic*. Oxford: Oxford University Press, 1994, 245–53.
23. ――― "Verse Life" [Vita Carmina Expressa] in J. C. A. Gaskin, ed. *The Elements of Law Natural and Politic*. Oxford: Oxford University Press, 1994, 254–64.
24. Jesseph, Douglas M. *Squaring the Circle: The War between Hobbes and Wallis*. Chicago: University of Chicago Press, 1999.
25. Kenyon, J. P. *Stuart England*. London: Penguin Books, 1978.
26. Malcolm, Noel, ed. *The Correspondence of Thomas Hobbes*. 2 vs. New York: Oxford University Press, 1994.
27. Malcolm, Noel. "Charles Cotton, Translator of Hobbes's *De Cive*" in his *Aspects of Hobbes*. Oxford: Oxford University Press, 2002, 234–58.
28. ―――. "Hobbes and the Royal Society" in his Aspects of Hobbes. Oxford: Oxford University Press, 2002, 317–35.
29. ―――. "Robert Payne, the Hobbes Manuscripts, and the 'Short Tract'" in his *Aspects of Hobbes*. Oxford: Oxford University Press, 2002, 80–145.
30. ―――. "A Summary Biography of Hobbes" in his *Aspects of Hobbes*. Oxford: Clarendon Press, 2002, 1–26.

31. Marriott, J. A. R. *Life and Times of Lucius Cary, Viscount Falkland.* 2d ed. New York: Putnam's, 1907.
32. Martinich, A. P. *Thomas Hobbes.* New York: St. Martin's Press, 1997.
33. Milton, P. "Hobbes, Heresy, and Lord Arlington." *History of Political Thought,* 14 (1993), 501–46.
34. Mintz, Samuel I. *The Hunting of Leviathan: Seventeenth-Century Reactions to the Materialism and Moral Philosophy of Thomas Hobbes.* Cambridge: Cambridge University Press, 1962.
35. Ollard, R. *Clarendon and His Friends.* New York: Atheneum, 1987.
36. Parkin, Jon. *Taming the Leviathan: The Reception of the Political and Religious Ideas of Thomas Hobbes in England 1640–1700.* Cambridge: Cambridge University Press, 2007.
37. Pearson, John. *Stags and Serpents: The Story of the House of Cavendish and the Dukes of Devonshire.* London: Macmillan, 1983.
38. Purver, Margery. *The Royal Society: Concept and Creation.* Cambridge, MA: MIT Press, 1967.
39. Reik, Miriam. *The Golden Lands of Thomas Hobbes.* Detroit: Wayne State University Press, 1977.
40. Rogers, G. A. J., ed. *Leviathan: Contemporary Responses to the Political Theory of Thomas Hobbes.* Bristol, Engl.: Thoemmes, 1995.
41. Rogow, Arnold. *Thomas Hobbes: Radical in the Service of Reaction.* New York: Norton, 1986.
42. Shapin, Steven and Simon Schaffer. *Leviathan and the Air-Pump: Hobbes, Boyle, and the Experimental Life.* Princeton: Princeton University Press, 1985.
43. Skinner, Quentin. "The Ideological Context of Hobbes's Political Thought." *Historical Journal,* 9 (1966), 286–317.
44. Sorell, Tom. Descartes: *A Very Short Introduction.* New York: Oxford University Press, 2000.
45. Summers, Claude and Ted-Larry Pebworth, eds. *Literary Circles and Cultural Communities in Renaissance England.* Columbia, MO: University of Missouri Press, 2000.
46. Trevor-Roper, Hugh. *Edward Hyde, Earl of Clarendon.* Oxford: Clarendon Press, 1975.
47. ———. "The Great Tew Circle" in his *Catholics, Anglicans, and Puritans.* Chicago: University of Chicago Press, 1988, Ch. 4.

128   J. T. BOOKMAN

48. Tuck, Richard. "Hobbes and Descartes" in G. A. J. Rogers and Alan Ryan, eds. *Perspectives on Thomas Hobbes*. Oxford: Clarendon Press, 1988, 11–41.
49. Wilson, Charles H. *England's Apprenticeship*, 1603–1763. Rev. ed. London: Longman, 1985.
50. Wootton, David, ed. *Divine Right and Democracy. An Anthology of Political Writing in Stuart England*. Harmondsworth, Middlesex: Penguin, 1986.
51. Wrightson, Keith. *English Society, 1580–1680*. London: Hutchinson, 1982.

COLLECTED WORKS

52. Cromartie, Alan, ed. *A Dialogue between a Philosopher and a Student of the Common Law of England; and Quentin Skinner, ed. Questions Relative to Hereditary Right*. Oxford: Clarendon Press, 2005.
53. Gaskin, J. C. A., ed. *The Elements of Law, Natural and Politic: Part I, Human Nature, Part II, De Corpore Politico*. Oxford: Oxford University Press, 1994.
54. Gert, Bernard, ed. *Man and Citizen, De Homine and De Cive*. Garden City, NJ: Anchor, 1972. Rpt. Indianapolis: Hackett, 1991.
55. Malcolm, Noel et al., eds. Clarendon Edition of the Works of Thomas Hobbes. V. 1–(27 vs. projected). Oxford: Clarendon Press, 1983–.
56. Molesworth, Sir William, ed. *The English Works of Thomas Hobbes*. 11 vs. London: J. Bohn, 1839–1845. Rpt. London: Routledge Thoemmes, 1992.
57. Nelson, Eric, ed. *Translations of Homer: The Iliad and the Odyssey*. 2 vs. Oxford: Clarendon Press, 2008.
58. Peters, Richard S., ed. *Body, Man, and Citizen: Selections*. New York: Collier, 1962.
59. Tönnies, Ferdinand, ed., *The Elements of Law, Natural and Politic*. London: Simpkin Marshall, 1889. Rpt. London: Frank Cass, 1969.

INDIVIDUAL WORKS

60. *An Answer to a Book Published by Dr. Bramhall, late Bishop of Derry; called the Catching of the Leviathan. Together with an Historical Narration Concerning Heresy, and the Punishment Thereof.* London: W. Crooke, 1682.

LEVIATHAN 129

61. *The Art of Rhetoric, With a Discourse of the Laws of England.* London: W. Crooke, 1681.
62. *Behemoth: the History of the Causes of the Civil-Wars of England and the Counsels and Artifices by Which They were Carried on from the year 1640 to the year 1660.* London: W. Crooke, 1682.
63. *Behemoth, or the Long Parliament.* Ferdinand Tönnies, ed. London: Frank Cass, 1969 [1889].
64. ———— Stephen Holmes, ed. Chicago: University of Chicago Press, 1990.
65. ———— Paul Seaward, ed. Oxford: Clarendon Press, 2010.
66. *Decameron physiologicum; or, Ten Dialogues of Natural Philosophy.* London: 1678.
67. *De Cive: The English Version.* Howard Warrender, ed. Oxford: Clarendon Press, 1983.
68. *On the Citizen [De Cive].* Richard Tuck and Michael Silverthorne, eds. and trans. Cambridge: Cambridge University Press, 1998.
69. *De Corpore Politico; or. The Elements of Law, Moral and Politik.* London: 1650.
70. *[De Corpore] The Metaphysical System of Hobbes in Twelve Chapters from Elements of Philosophy Concerning Body.* Mary Whiton Calkins, ed. LaSalle, IL: Open Court, 1963.
71. *Dialogue Between a Philosopher and a Student of the Common Law of England.* Joseph Cropsey, ed. Chicago: University of Chicago Press, 1971.
72. *An Historical Narration Concerning Heresy, and the Punishment Thereof.* Stanford, CA: Academic Reprints, 1954.
73. *[Horae Subsecivae] Three Discourses: A Critical Modern Edition of Newly Identified Work of the Young Hobbes.* Noel B. Reynolds and Arlene Saxonhouse, eds. Chicago: University of Chicago Press, 1995.
74. *Human Nature: or, The Fundamental Elements of Policie.* London: 1650.
75. *Leviathan, or the Matter, Form and Power of a Common-Wealth, Ecclesiasticall and Civill.* London: Andrew Crooke, 1651. Rpt. Oxford: Clarendon Press, 1909.
76. ————. Noel Malcolm, ed. 3 vs. Oxford: Clarendon Press, 2012.
77. ————. J. C. A. Gaskin, ed. Oxford: Oxford University Press, 1996.
78. ———— C. B. Macpherson, ed. Harmondsworth, Middlesex: Penguin, 1985.
79. ———— Michael Oakeshott, ed. Oxford: Basil Blackwell, 1946.

130   J. T. BOOKMAN

80. ———. Kenneth Minogue, ed. London: J. M. Dent (Everyman), 1994.
81. ———. Ian Shapiro, ed. New Haven, CT: Yale University Press, 2010.
82. ——— Richard Tuck, ed. Cambridge: Cambridge University Press, 1991.
83. *Leviathan: A Critical Edition*. G. A. J. Rogers and Karl Schuhmann, eds. 2 vs. Bristol, Engl.: Thoemmes Continuum, 2003.
84. *Leviathan: With Selected Variants from the Latin Edition of 1668*. Edwin Curley, ed. Indianapolis: Hackett, 1994.
85. *Leviathan: The Authoritative Text*. Richard E. Flathman, ed. New York: Norton, 1997.
86. *Of Liberty and Necessity: A Treatise Wherein All Controversie Concerning Predestination, Election, Free-Will, Grace, Merits, Reprobation, etc. Is Fully Decided and Cleared, In Answer to a Treatise Written by the Bishop of London-Derry, on the Same Subject*. London: W. B. for F. Eaglesfield, 1654.
87. *Hobbes and Bramhall on Liberty and Necessity*. Vere Chappell, ed. Cambridge: Cambridge University Press, 1999.
88. *Mr Hobbes Considered in his Loyalty, Religion, Reputation, and Manners. By Way of a Letter to Dr. Wallis*. London: 1662.
89. *The Peloponnesian War: The Complete Hobbes Translation*. David Grene, ed. Chicago: University Press, 1989.
90. *Reasons of State, Propaganda, and the Thirty Years War: An Unknown Translation*. Noel Malcolm, ed. Oxford: Clarendon Press, 2007.
91. *Six Lessons to the Professors of the Mathematiques: One of Geometry and the Other of Astronomy*. London: J. M. for Andrew Crooke, 1656.
92. *Thomas White's De Mundo Examined*. H. W. Jones, trans. London: Bradford University Press, 1976.
93. *Hobbes's Thucydides*. Richard Schlatter, ed. New Bruinswick, NJ: Rutgers University Press, 1975.

COMMENTARY: COLLECTIONS

94. Airaksinen, Timo and Martin A. Bertman, eds. *Hobbes: War Among Nations*. Aldershot, Hants: Avebury, 1989.
95. Brown, Keith C., ed. *Hobbes Studies*. Oxford: Basil Blackwell, 1965.

96. Caws, Peter, ed. *The Causes of Quarrel: Essays on Peace, War, and Thomas Hobbes.* Boston: Beacon Press, 1989.
97. Cranston, Maurice and Richard S. Peters, eds. *Hobbes and Rousseau: A Collection of Critical Essays.* Garden City, NY: Anchor, 1972.
98. Dietz, Mary G., ed. *Thomas Hobbes and Political Theory.* Lawrence, KS: University of Kansas Press, 1990.
99. Dunn, John M. and Ian Harris, eds. *Hobbes.* 3 vs. Lyme, NH: Edward Elgar, 1997
100. Finkelstein, Claire, ed. *Hobbes on Law.* Aldershot, Hants: Ashgate, 1999.
101. Foisneau, Luc and Tom Sorell, eds. *Leviathan After 350 Years.* Oxford: Clarendon Press, 2004.
102. ——— and George Wright, eds. *New Critical Perspectives on Hobbes's Leviathan Upon the 350th Anniversary of Its Publication.* Milan: Franco Agnelli, 2005.
103. Hirschmann, Nancy J. and Joanne H. Wright, eds. *Feminist Interpretations of Thomas Hobbes.* University Park, PA: Penn State University Press, 2012.
104. King, Preston, ed. *Thomas Hobbes: Critical Assessments.* 4 vs. London: Routledge, 1993.
105. Lloyd, S. A., ed. *The Bloomsbury Companion to Hobbes.* London: Bloomsbury Academic, 2013.
106. Malcolm, Noel. *Aspects of Hobbes.* Oxford: Clarendon Press, 2002.
107. Oakeshott, Michael. *Hobbes on Civil Association.* Oxford: Basil Blackwell, 1975 [1946].
108. Rogers, G. A. J. and Alan Ryan, eds. *Perspectives on Thomas Hobbes.* Oxford: Clarendon Press, 1988.
109. Ross, Ralph, H. Schneider, and T. Waldman, eds. *Thomas Hobbes in His Time.* Minneapolis: University of Minnesota Press, 1974.
110. Shaver, Robert, ed. *Thomas Hobbes.* Aldershot, Hants: Ashgate, 1999.
111. Skinner, Quentin. *Visions of Politics III: Hobbes and Civil Society.* Cambridge: Cambridge University Press, 2002.
112. Slomp, Gabriella, ed. *Thomas Hobbes.* Aldershot, Hants: Ashgate, 2008.
113. Sorell, Tom, ed. *The Cambridge Companion to Thomas Hobbes.* Cambridge: Cambridge University Press, 1996.

132 J. T. BOOKMAN

114. Springborg, Patricia, ed. *The Cambridge Companion to Hobbes's Leviathan*. Cambridge: Cambridge University Press, 2007.
115. Walton, C. and P. J. Johnson, eds. *Hobbes's Science of Natural Justice*. Dordrecht: M. Nijhoff, 1987.

COMMENTARY: BOOKS

116. Baumgold, Deborah. *Hobbes's Political Theory.* Cambridge: Cambridge University Press, 1988.
117. Botwinick, Aryeh. *Hobbes and Modernity: Five Exercises in Political Philosophical Exegesis.* Lanham, MD: University Press of America, 1983.
118. Brandt, Frithiof. *Thomas Hobbes's Mechanical Conception of Nature.* Vaughn Maxwell and Annie I. Faus cpll, trans. Copenhagen: Levin and Munksgaard, 1928.
119. Coleman, Frank M. *Hobbes and America: Exploring the Constitutional Foundations.* Toronto: University of Toronto Press, 1977.
120. Collins, Jeffrey R. *The Allegiance of Thomas Hobbes.* Oxford: Clarendon Press, 2005.
121. Cooke, Paul D. *Hobbes and Christianity: Reassessing the Bible in Leviathan.* Lanham, MD: Rowman & Littlefield, 1996.
122. Flathman, Richard E. *Thomas Hobbes's Skepticism, Individuality, and Chastened Politics.* Newbury Park, CA: Sage, 1993.
123. Gauthier, David. *The Logic of Leviathan: The Moral and Political Theory of Thomas Hobbes.* London: Oxford University Press, 1969.
124. Goldsmith, M. M. *Hobbes's Science of Politics.* New York: Columbia University Press, 1966.
125. Hampton, Jean. *Hobbes and the Social Contract Tradition.* Cambridge: Cambridge University Press, 1986.
126. Hirschmann, Nancy J. *Gender, Class, and Freedom in Modern Political Theory.* Princeton: Princeton: Princeton University Press, 2007, Ch.2.
127. Hood, F. C. *The Divine Politics of Thomas Hobbes: An Interpretation of Leviathan.* Oxford: Clarendon Press, 1957.
128. Johnston, David. *The Rhetoric of the Leviathan.* Princeton: Princeton University Press, 1986.
129. Kavka, Gregory S. *Hobbesian Moral and Political Theory.* Princeton: Princeton University Press, 1986.
130. Kraynak, Robert P. *History and Modernity in the Thought of Thomas Hobbes.* Ithaca, NY: Cornell University Press, 1990.

131. McNeilly, F. S. *The Anatomy of Leviathan*. London: Macmillan, 1958.
132. Macpherson, C. B. *The Political Theory of Possessive Individualism: Hobbes to Locke*. Oxford: Clarendon Press, 1962.
133. Martinich, A. D. *The Two Gods of Leviathan: Thomas Hobbes on Religion and Politics*. Cambridge: Cambridge University Press, 1992.
134. Malnes, Raino. *The Hobbesian Theory of International Conflict*. New York: Oxford University Press, 1993.
135. Peters, Richard S. *Hobbes*. Harmondsworth, Middlesex: Penguin, 1956.
136. Plamenatz, John P. *Man and Society*. 2 vs. New York: McGraw-Hill, 1963, v. 1, ch. 4.
137. Raphael, D. D. *Hobbes: Morals and Politics*. London: George Allen & Unwin, 1977.
138. Skinner, Quentin. *Hobbes and Republican Liberty*. Cambridge: Cambridge University Press, 2008.
139. Sommerville, Johann. *Thomas Hobbes: Political Ideas and Historical Context*. New York: St. Martin's Press, 1992.
140. Sorell, Tom. *Hobbes*. London: Routledge and Kegan Paul, 1986.
141. Spragens, Thomas A., Jr. *The Politics of Motion: The World of Thomas Hobbes*. London: Croom Helm, 1973.
142. Strauss, Leo. *The Political Philosophy of Hobbes, Its Basis and Its Genesis*. Elsa M. Sinclair, trans. Oxford: Clarendon Press, 1936.
143. Tuck, Richard. *Hobbes: A Very Short Introduction*. New York: Oxford University Press, 2002.
144. Warrender, Howard. *The Political Philosophy of Hobbes: His Theory of Obligation*. Oxford: Clarendon Press, 1957.
145. Watkins, John W. *Hobbes's System of Ideas; a Study in the Political Significance of Philosophical Theories*. Rev. ed. London: Hutchinson, 1989.

COMMENTARY: ARTICLES

146. Ashcraft, Richard. "Ideology and Class in Hobbes' Political Theory." *Political Theory*, 6 (Feb., 1978), 27–62 and in Dunn and Harris, v.2, 234.
147. Baumgold, Deborah. "The Difficulties of Hobbes Interpretation." *Political Theory*, 36 (2008), 827–55.

148. ———. "Subjects and Soldiers: Hobbes on Military Service." *History of Political Thought*, 4 (Spr., 1983), 43–64 and in Dunn and Harris, v. 2, 465 and King, v. 3, 59.

149. Ball, Terence. "Hobbes's Linguistic Turn." *Polity*, 17 (1985), 739–60 and in Dunn and Harris, v. 2, 513, and Slomp, 429.

150. Barry, Brian. "Warrender and His Critics." *Philosophy*, 42 (Apr., 1968), 117–37 and in Cranston and Peters, 37, Dunn and Harris, v. 1, 479, King, v. 2, 177, and Chappell, 1.

151. Brown, Keith C. "Hobbes's Grounds for Belief in a Deity." *Philosophy*, 37 (Oct., 1962), 336–44 and in King, v. 4, 40.

152. Brown, J. M. "A Note on Professor Oakeshott's Introduction to the *Leviathan*." *Political Studies*, 1 (1953), 53–64, and in King, v. 2, 75.

153. Brown, Stuart M., Jr. "Hobbes: The Taylor Thesis." *Philosophical Review*, 68 (July, 1959), 303–25 and in Brown, *Hobbes Studies*, 57, and King, v. 2, 99.

154. Carmichael, D. J. C. "C. B. Macpherson's Hobbes, A Critique." *Canadian Journal of Political Science*, 16 (1983), 61–80 and in King, v. 1, 359.

155. ———. "Hobbes on Natural Rights in Society: The *Leviathan* Account." *Canadian Journal of Political Science*, 23 (1990), 3–21.

156. Cropsey, Joseph. "Hobbes and the Transition to Modernity" in Joseph Cropsey, ed. *Ancients and Moderns*. Chicago: University of Chicago Press, 1964, 213–37.

157. Curley, Edwin. "Calvin and Hobbes, or Hobbes as an Orthodox Christian." *Journal of the History of Philosophy*, 34 (1996), 257–71 and in Slomp, 399.

158. ———. "Reflections on Hobbes: Recent Work on His Moral and Political Philosophy." *Journal of Philosophical Research*, 15 (1990), 169–250.

159. Dunn, John. "The Politics of Imponderable and Potentially Lethal Judgment for Mortals: Hobbes's Legacy to the Understanding of Modern Politics" in Ian Shapiro, ed. *Leviathan*. 433–52.

160. Forsyth, Murray. "Thomas Hobbes and the Constituent Power of the People." *Political Studies*, 29 (1981), 191–203 and in King, v. 3, 575.

161. ———. "Thomas Hobbes and the External Relations of States." *British Journal of International Studies*, 5 (Oct., 1979), 196–209 and in Dunn and Harris, v. 2, 291, and Slomp, 485.

LEVIATHAN   135

162. Gert, Bernard. "Introduction" in his *Man and Citizen*. Garden City, NY: Anchor, 1972, 3–32.
163. Goldsmith, M. M. "The Hobbes Industry." *Political Studies*, 39 (1991), 135–47.
164. ———. "Hobbes's Mortal God: Is There a Fallacy in Hobbes's Theory of Sovereignty?" *History of Political Thought*, 1 (1980), 33–50 and in King, v. 3, 768.
165. ——— "Hobbes on Liberty." *Hobbes Studies*, 2 (1989), 23–39.
166. Hoekstra, Kinch. "The *de facto* Turn in Hobbes's Political Philosophy" in Luc Foisneau and Tom Sorell, eds. *Leviathan After 350 Years*. Oxford: Clarendon Press, 2004, 33–74.
167. ———. "Hobbes and the Foole." *Political Theory*, 25 (1997), 620–54 and in Slomp, 291.
168. International Hobbes Association. *Hobbes Studies*, v. 1–, 1988–.
169. Kateb, George. "Hobbes and the Irrationality of Politics." *Political Theory*, 17 (1989), 355–91 and in Dunn and Harris, v. 3, 126.
170. Krook, Dorothea. "Mr. Brown's Note Annotated." *Political Studies*, 1 (1953), 216–27.
171. Letwin, William. "The Economic Foundations of Hobbes' Politics" in Maurice Cranston and Richard Peters, eds. *Hobbes and Rousseau: A Collection of Critical Essays*, Garden City, NY: Anchor, 1972, 143–64.
172. Macpherson, C. B. "*Leviathan* Restored: Reply to Carmichael." *Canadian Journal of Political Science*, 16 (1983), 795–809 and in King, v. 1, 380.
173. Malcolm, Noel. "Hobbes's Theory of International Relations" in his *Aspects of Hobbes*, 432–56 and in Slomp, 499.
174. Milner, B. "Hobbes on Religion." *Political Theory*, 16 (1988), 400–425.
175. Missner, M. "Skepticism and Hobbes's Political Philosophy." *Journal of the History of Ideas*, 44 (Jul-Sep., 1983), 404–27.
176. Nagel, Thomas. "Hobbes's Concept of Obligation." *Philosophical Review*, 68 (Jan., 1959), 68–83 and in Dunn and Harris, v. 1, 336, and King, v. 2, 116.
177. Olafson, Frederick A. "Thomas Hobbes and the Modern Theory of Natural Law." *Journal of the History of Philosophy*, 4 (Jan., 1966), 15–30 and in King, v. 3, 361.

178. ———. "A Reply to Mr. Taylor." *Philosophical Review*, 68 (July, 1959), 373–79.
179. Pitkin, Hanna F. "Hobbes's Concept of Representation." *American Political Science Review*, 59 (1964), 328–40 and 902–18 and in King, v. 3, 443 and 465.
180. Plamenatz, John P. "Mr. Warrender's Hobbes." *Political Studies*, 5 (1957), 295–308 and in Brown, 73.
181. Pocock, J. G. A. "Time, History and Eschatology in the Thought of Thomas Hobbes" in his *Politics, Language and Time: Essays on Political Thought*. New York: Atheneum, 1971, 148–201 and in Dunn and Harris, v. 2, 1, and Slomp, 327.
182. Polin, Raymond. "The Rights of Man in Hobbes and Locke" in D. D. Raphael, ed., *Political Theory and the Rights of Man*. Bloomington, IN: Indiana University Press, 1967, 16–26.
183. Ryan, Alan. "Hobbes and Individualism" in Rogers and Ryan, 81–106, Dunn and Harris, v. 3, 24, and Chappell, 207.
184. ———. "Hobbes, Toleration, and the Inner Life" in David Miller and Larry Siedentop, eds. *The Nature of Political Theory*. Oxford: Clarendon Press, 1983.
185. ———. "A More Tolerant Hobbes" in Susan Mendus, ed. *Justifying Toleration: Conceptual and Historical Perspectives*. Cambridge: Cambridge University Press, 1988, 37–59 and in Dunn and Harris, v. 3, 1
186. Skinner, Quentin. "Hobbes's *Leviathan*." *Historical Journal*, 7 (1964), 321–33, and in Dunn and Harris, v. 1, 368, and King, v. 1, 77.
187. ———. "Warrender and Skinner on Hobbes: A Reply." *Political Studies*, 38 (1988), 692–95, and in King, v. 1, 467.
188. Sorell, Tom. "Hobbes without Doubt." *History of Philosophy Quarterly*, 10 (1993), 121–35.
189. Springborg, Patricia. "*Leviathan* and the Problem of Ecclesiastical Authority." *Political Theory*, 3 (1975), 289–303 and in Dunn and Harris, v. 2, 145, and King, v. 4, 136.
190. ———. "*Leviathan*, the Christian Commonwealth Incorporated." *Political Studies*, 24 (June, 1976), 171–83 and in Dunn and Harris, v. 2, 199.
191. Strauss, Leo. "On the Basis of Hobbes's Political Philosophy" in his *What is Political Philosophy and Other Studies*. Glencoe, IL: Free Press, 1959, 170–96.

192. Taylor, A. E. "The Ethical Doctrine of Hobbes." *Philosophy*, 13 (Oct., 1938), 406–24 and in Brown, 35, Dunn and Harris, v. 1, 117, and King, v. 2, 22.
193. Tarlton, C. D. "The Creation and Maintenance of Government: A Neglected Dimension of Hobbes's *Leviathan*." *Political Studies*, 26 (Sept., 1978), 307–27 and in Slomp, 270.
194. Thomas, Keith. "The Social Origins of Hobbes's Thought" in Brown, 185–236 and in Dunn and Harris, v. 1, 381.
195. Trainor, B. T. "Warrender and Skinner on Hobbes." *Political Studies*, 38 (1988), 680–91, and in King, v. 1, 453.
196. Tuck, Richard. "Hobbes and Locke on Toleration" in Dietz, 153–71 and Dunn and Harris, v. 3, 401.
197. ———. "Introduction" in his *Leviathan*, ix–xlv.
198. ———. "Optics and Sceptics: The Philosophical Foundations of Hobbes's Political Thought" in Edmund Leites, ed. *Conscience and Casuistry in Early Modern Europe*. Cambridge: Cambridge University Press, 1988, 235–63 and in Dunn and Harris, v. 3, 49, and Chappell, 299.
199. ———. "Warrender's *De Cive*." *Political Studies*, 33 (1985), 308–15, and in King, v. 1, 421.
200. ———. Warrender, Howard. "The Place of God in Hobbes's Philosophy: A Reply to Mr. Plamenatz." *Political Studies*, 8 (1960), 48–57 and in Brown, 89.
201. Weiner, Jonathan M. "Quentin Skinner's Hobbes." *Political Theory*, 2 (Aug., 1974), 251–58, and in King, v. 1, 184.
202. Wolin, Sheldon S. "Hobbes and the Culture of Despotism" in Dietz, 9–36 and in Dunn and Harris, v. 3, 420.
203. Zagorin, Perez. "Hobbes on Our Mind." *Journal of the History of Ideas*, 51 (1990), 317–35.
204. ———. "Hobbes's Early Philosophical Development." *Journal of the History of Ideas*, 54 (1993), 505–18.

CHAPTER 4

The *Second Treatise*

LOCKE (1632–1704): A BRIEF SKETCH OF HIS LIFE

In late 1666, at the age of 34, Locke declined an offer of an ecclesiastical post in Ireland.[1] The offer came from the Dean of Christ Church in Dublin, the brother of a woman to whom he had been attracted and who had followed her brother to Dublin. Locke's affections for the woman were insufficiently keen to overcome his reservations about the job. Those reservations, he explained in a letter, were his reluctance to make a lifelong commitment to a profession, his uncertainty as to his fitness for the clergy, and his desire to pursue his scientific studies. He added that "the same considerations have made me a long time reject very advantageous offers of several very considerable friends in England."[2] One of those offers, another ecclesiastical living, had been made three years earlier. It too would have required him to take holy orders. At that time, Locke was under increasing pressure to enter the clergy and to take a vow of celibacy as conditions for keeping his fellowship at Oxford. Anglican clerics could marry, but the universities also required celibacy of their fellows. Relief

---

[1] I have drawn upon Roger Woolhouse, *Locke: A Biography* (Cambridge: Cambridge University Press, 2007) and Maurice Cranston, *John Locke: A Biography* (London: Longmans, Green, 1957) in the writing of this sketch.

[2] E. S. de Beer, ed., *The Correspondence of John Locke*, 8 vs. (Oxford: Clarendon Press, 1976–1989), v. 1, 303–304:#219.

© The Author(s) 2019
J. T. Bookman, *A Reader's Companion*
to The Prince, Leviathan, *and the* Second Treatise,
https://doi.org/10.1007/978-3-030-02880-0_4

139

140   J. T. BOOKMAN

from this pressure came in the form of a dispensation from the King, obtained, at least in part, by the intercession of his new friend Anthony Ashley Cooper (later Earl of Shaftesbury and Lord Chancellor), who had influence at the royal court. As a result, Locke was able to continue to enjoy the living afforded by his fellowship and the time it provided for his research. None of this reflects any lack of religious conviction.

Locke's commitment to reason was large. He announces in the *Essay Concerning Human Understanding* that "reason must be our last Judge and Guide in every thing."[3] He perceived no conflict between reason and religion. Indeed, he often expresses the view that reason, not revelation, offered the surer path to God and to the rules that he would have us obey. For Locke, writing in the early 1660s, "God shows Himself to us as present everywhere ... as much in the fixed course of nature now as by the frequent evidence of miracles in time past." It is to such a wise and powerful creator that man owes his own existence. All other things in the universe cannot have created man "who is far more perfect than they are." Nor could men and women have created themselves. "Nothing is its own cause," save God himself. He thinks too that "the existence of God cannot be denied if we acknowledge the necessity for some rational account of our life, or that there is a thing that deserves to be called virtue or vice." That account can be inferred in part from the wisdom of God who must not have created the world, and humankind in particular, without purpose, and that purpose is "no other end than His own glory." Therefore, one purpose of humankind is to "render praise, honour, and glory" to God.[4]

A rational account of our life can also be known by reflection about human nature: consciousness, rationality, and sociability, all impel men "to procure and preserve a life in society with other men." If the end of peaceful social relations is to be realized, then men and women must observe certain moral precepts. Without them, "men can have no social intercourse or union among themselves." These precepts are expressions of God's will. We can learn these precepts either as a law of nature by the light of reason or as the revelations of Scripture by faith. The law of nature can be known by "anyone ... who is willing to apply diligent study and to direct his mind to the knowledge of it."[5] Locke held to these beliefs throughout his life.

---

[3] IV.xix.14.
[4] W. von Leyden, ed., *John Locke: Essays on the Law of Nature* (Oxford: Clarendon Press, 1954), 109, 153, 109, 157, 157.
[5] *Ibid.*, 157, 119, 187.

The *Essay Concerning Human Understanding* (1690) expresses his conviction that he shows in Book IV, Chapter 10 that "the existence of a God, reason clearly makes known to us." And God "hath spread before all the world, such legible characters of his works and providence, and given all mankind so sufficient a light of reason, that they to whom this written word [the Scriptures] never came, could not (whenever they set themselves to search) either doubt of the being of a God, or of the obedience due to him."[6]

Locke's relationship with the Church of England was uneasy. In a commentary in 1681 on a published sermon by the Dean of St. Paul's, he describes himself as belonging to the Church of England.[7] And, as a public official in later years, he had to attest to his status as an Anglican communicant. His writings suggest, however, that his commitment to the Anglican Church had been given much earlier—for prudential reasons if no other. Thus, following the restoration of the monarchy in 1660 and the re-establishment of the Church of England, Locke wrote that the state acts within its authority in imposing the practice of the Anglican Church with regard to ritual and church organization.[8] These are "matters indifferent" in religious worship as opposed to doctrine—matters required by God's law. In his view, differences over "matters indifferent" (e.g., the episcopal organization of the church, the wearing of a surplice in preaching, placing the altar behind rails, and kneeling at communion) had contributed to bringing about the events of the civil war and the Cromwellian regime "which have so wearied and wasted this poor nation."[9] The "peace and settlement [order]" of the people, he believed, would benefit from conformity to Anglicanism. He persisted in this belief in the "Second Tract on Government" written two years later. He there expresses the hope that "nobody will be so obstinate and stiff- necked as to attempt further civil changes or to disparage the magistrate's power in respect of indifferent things."[10] Clearly, the civil war and Cromwell's Commonwealth much affected Locke's thinking. In the "First Tract on Government," he

---

[6] Roger Woolhouse, ed., (Harmondsworth: Penguin, 1997), IV.xi.1, III.ix.23.

[7] John Locke, "A Defence of Non-conformity" in Lord Peter King, *The Life and Letters of John Locke* (New York: Garland, 1984 [1884]), 346–358.

[8] Philip Abrams, ed., *John Locke: Two Tracts on Government* (Cambridge: Cambridge University Press), 117–181.

[9] *Ibid.*, 118.

[10] *Ibid.*, 211–212.

142   J. T. BOOKMAN

recalls the impression those events had on him in 1642 at the age of ten: "I no sooner perceived myself in the world but I found myself in a storm, which has lasted almost hitherto."[11] In the same place, he welcomes the restoration of the Stuart monarchy: "All the freedom I can wish my country or myself is to enjoy the protection of those laws which the prudence and providence of our ancestors established and the happy return of his Majesty has restored."[12] While the Restoration may have brought the peace that Locke so hoped for—at least for a while,[13] it was the storm that had created an opportunity to significantly advance his prospects.

Locke was born and raised in a Puritan household in a village near Bristol. How strong the beliefs and severe the practices of his parents were is unknown. His father, also John Locke, fought on the parliamentary, and Puritan, side in the war against King Charles I. The senior Locke was attorney to Alexander Popham, a prominent local official. It was as captain in a regiment raised by Popham that Locke's father served the parliamentary cause. After the revolution and beheading of the king, Popham became Member of Parliament from Bath, which gave him the chance to reward his attorney and friend by naming the 14-year-old Locke to a place at Westminster School, one of the best in the country. There the young Locke was exposed to the decidedly royalist and Anglican views of the school's headmaster who retained his place despite the Puritan triumph. In the course of his six years at Westminster, Locke distinguished himself by winning election as a King's Scholar and the award's provision of free room and board and then a scholarship to Christ Church. In Oxford Locke found himself among fellow students and a faculty purged by Cromwell of its Anglican administrators but otherwise divided in their loyalties to church and crown. Christ Church conferred upon him a B.A. in 1656 and an M.A. in 1658. After receiving his M.A., he won a fellowship and appointment as tutor in classics and in 1663 as censor in moral philosophy. The latter post required him to give a series of lectures. Out of these lectures came his "Essays on the Law of Nature." Like so many of his writings, the "Essays" circulated among friends but were unpublished during his lifetime. Of those he did publish, several of the important works—*Letter Concerning Toleration, Two Treatises of Government*, and

[11] *Ibid.*, 119.
[12] *Ibid.*, 121.
[13] De Beer, *Correspondence*, v. 1, 124–126:#82 and 136–137:#91.

the *Reasonableness of Christianity*—were published anonymously. Although many had well-founded suspicions about the identity of the author, only after his death did Locke acknowledge authorship in his will.

However Locke may have come to join the Anglican Church, he did not regard as important in securing salvation the matters that so agitated his fellow-communicants and the religious dissenters, chief among them the Puritans. God requires of those who worship him, according to Locke, only the "sacrifice of a broken and contrite heart, which may be willingly and acceptably given to God in any place or posture."[14] This view, first expressed in the "First Tract on Government" (1660), he held for the rest of his life. He did reflect anew about the authority of the state with regard to "matters indifferent," that is, liturgy and dogma.

In 1667, Locke composed an essay on toleration that set out much of the argument of his later and better-known *Letter Concerning Toleration*. The essay contends that the "manner of worshiping my God" has a just claim "to an unlimited toleration." He had changed his mind about the threat posed to civic peace by differences in ritual and church organization: "[K]neeling or sitting in the sacrament can in itself tend no more to the disturbance of the government or injury of my neighbor than sitting or standing at my own table." Furthermore, since we cannot will our beliefs, the state cannot force us to do so. Therefore, he concludes, the state ought to confine itself to "the quiet and comfortable living of men in society one with another" but not with "their concernments in another life."[15] This constraint on state authority put Locke at odds with the Church of England, which held that the state should insure orthodoxy. But he had seen that the Act of Uniformity (1662) had not produced the hoped-for unity among Protestants. The subsequent passage by Parliament of other legislation to punish the non-conforming had only increased disquiet. And Locke had also seen during a three-month stay in Cleves as a member of a diplomatic mission to the Elector of Brandenburg that it is possible for Christians as different as Lutherans, Catholics, and Calvinists to live peacefully together. Nevertheless, he was not prepared in the essay or the later *Letter* to extend toleration to Catholics whom he regarded as owing their first allegiance to a foreign prince, namely, the pope, and

---

[14] Abrams, *Two Tracts*, 146.

[15] "An Essay on Toleration" in Mark Goldie, ed., *Locke: Political Essays* (Cambridge: Cambridge University Press, 1997), 138, 144, 137.

therefore as constituting a threat to the security of the state. Locke denied toleration to atheists as well because he regarded belief in God as "the foundation of all morality ... without which a man is ... one of the most dangerous sorts of wild beasts, and so incapable of all society."[16] Locke's freedom of religion is freedom to choose a religion.

Locke's published work, particularly the *Essay Concerning Human Understanding* (1689), which bore his name, the *Letter Concerning Toleration* (1689), and the *Reasonableness of Christianity* (1695), drew the fire of some Anglican clergymen. He did have his supporters among his fellow-communicants and in the church clergy including most prominently Samuel Bold, the rector of Steeple in Dorset, who defended Locke against criticism of the *Reasonableness of Christianity*. There was never any effort in the Anglican hierarchy to excommunicate him for his departures from orthodoxy.

What comes through in Locke's essays and his exchanges with his Anglican critics is anti-clericalism. He did not want the Anglican clergy to impose a misguided orthodoxy, misguided because the orthodox held essential a particular ritual and a particular church organization that, in Locke's view, are not essential to salvation. Indeed, the imposition of any orthodoxy is misguided for that reason. The Church of England offered one way to heaven, and Locke adopted it as his own, but he did not think it the only way. His aversion to taking holy orders suggests that he did not want to be subject to superiors who would insist on orthodoxy and that he did not want to be an advocate of the orthodox. However such considerations may have figured, if at all, in his thinking as a young man at Oxford in the 1660s, Locke's principal interests lay elsewhere.

As an undergraduate Locke began to pursue in earnest an interest in natural philosophy—what we today would call the "natural sciences." This interest continued throughout his life, although the time he could devote to it declined as he became involved in political affairs. Nevertheless, until very nearly the day he died, he could be found taking readings of temperature, barometric pressure, and humidity; he suspected a connection between the weather and epidemics. In his travels within England and on the continent—three-and-a-half years in France and five years in

---

[16] *Ibid.*, 137. See also *A Letter Concerning Toleration* in Raymond Klibansky and J. W. Gough, eds., *Epistola de Tolerantia: A Letter on Toleration* (Oxford: Clarendon Press, 1968), 135.

THE *SECOND TREATISE*   145

Holland—Locke sought out his fellow-scientists to exchange ideas about the diagnosis and treatment of disease and to compare notes about operations and recipes for medicines. While his interests ranged across the natural sciences, medicine commanded first attention. Between 1658, the year he was awarded the M.A., and 1667, the year he joined Ashley Cooper, almost two-thirds of his reading was devoted to the natural sciences and most of that to medicine. Theology and religion came in a distant second; law and politics barely figured.[17] In 1661 and 1662 he attended lectures in medicine and in 1663 enrolled in a course on pharmacology.

Inside the university Aristotle and Galen dominated the curriculum in medicine. Outside the university study had become more empirical. First among those keen to apply the findings of research to medical problems was Robert Boyle, who had established a laboratory in Oxford. Locke met Boyle in early 1660. That meeting began a long association between him and the father of modern chemistry. Boyle's experiments involving blood and respiration contributed to a paper that Locke wrote in 1664 in Latin about the function of respiration in sustaining life. Over the winter of 1665–1666, Locke and his friend and medical student, David Thomas, set up a small lab to do chemical experiments. Thomas, upon receiving his license to practice medicine, enlisted Locke's assistance when he began to treat patients. Had not a chance meeting occurred, Locke might himself have taken up a career in medicine.

Through his friend, Thomas, he met Lord Anthony Ashley Cooper in July 1666. They hit it off immediately. So rapidly did the friendship develop that within a year Locke joined Ashley's household in London where he served as part-time physician, secretary, and advisor. From that time forward, he spent his life in the company of the English ruling class: the educated, the wealthy, the powerful. He tutored the children of his patrons and accompanied the child of a friend of Lord Ashley to the continent. He enjoyed the patronage of a succession of nobles. Locke never married. He fathered no children. He never lived in a house of his own. He was an absentee landlord of the property his father bequeathed to him.

At the time of their meeting, Ashley was in his mid-40s, married with a 14-year-old son. He was a seasoned veteran of England's political wars and currently serving King Charles II as Chancellor of the Exchequer. In

---

[17] J. R. Milton, "Locke at Oxford" in G. A. J. Rogers, ed., *Locke's Philosophy: Content and Context* (Oxford: Oxford University Press, 1994), 29–47.

146   J. T. BOOKMAN

1672, Charles awarded him a peerage as Earl of Shaftesbury and later in the year made him Lord Chancellor, chief minister to the king. Shaftesbury, however, was a defender of parliamentary authority and advocate of a Protestant monarchy. Those views led to his dismissal three years later. He then set about organizing the opposition to a king grown more and more autocratic in his rule and more Catholic in his sympathies. That opposition marked the beginning of the Whig Party. The king suspected him of involvement in a plot to overthrow the government and sought unsuccessfully to secure an indictment on charges of treason. Undeterred by the failure of the grand jury to indict, Charles renewed his effort. Shaftesbury, frightened no doubt by the months he had spent in the Tower awaiting the decision of the grand jury and by the resolve of the king, fled the country in late 1682 and died within a few months in Holland.

Locke's association with Shaftesbury marked a turn in his attention away from medicine. The turn, however, was far from complete. It was at Exeter House, Shaftesbury's London home, that he met Dr. Thomas Sydenham, the leading physician of his day. His conversations with Sydenham led him to accompany the doctor on his visits to patients. So impressed was Locke with Sydenham's thinking about medicine and his approach to patient care that he wrote "Anatomie" (1668) in which he rejected his earlier views and advocated an experiential approach. "De Arte Medica," begun the following year but never completed, gave increased emphasis to such an approach. The essay is in Locke's handwriting, but he may have been serving as secretary in the composition of a work by Sydenham.[18] It is some measure of Locke's standing in the scientific community that he was elected in 1668 a Fellow of the recently established Royal Society for the Improving of Natural Knowledge. And Shaftesbury was sufficiently confident of Locke's skills to ask him to participate in an operation for the relief of Shaftesbury's acute abdominal pain. The operation involved the removal of a tumor on the liver and the insertion of a drainage tube. The operation was successful. Nevertheless, Shaftesbury then encouraged Locke to devote himself to the study of "whatsoever is related to the business of a Minister of State."[19]

[18] Kenneth Dewhurst, *John Locke (1632–1704), Physician and Philosopher: A Medical Biography* (London: Wellcome Historical Medical Library, 1963), 38.

[19] Benjamin Rand, ed., *The Life, Unpublished Letters and Philosophical Regimen of Anthony, Earl of Shaftesbury* (New York: Macmillan, 1900), 328–334.

THE *SECOND TREATISE*   147

While Shaftesbury sought his counsel on matters of concern to him as Chancellor of the Exchequer, he also involved Locke in a more personal enterprise. Shaftesbury was one of eight proprietors to whom the king had conveyed the colony of Carolina in 1663. Locke became secretary to the Lords Proprietor in 1669, a position he retained until 1675. During that period he had a hand in the drafting of the *Fundamental Constitutions of Carolina*, which sought to keep a good deal of authority in the hands of the proprietors themselves rather than in the hands of those about to sail to America. How large a hand is uncertain.[20] The proprietors, particularly Shaftesbury, were forceful, articulate men with views of their own. Nevertheless, Locke seemed to evince pride in authorship when he circulated copies among his friends, revised the document, and kept it among his papers. However much influence he may have had, he would have found congenial that provision conferring freedom of worship: "It shall be lawful for slaves, as all others, to enter ... what church ... any of them shall think best, and ... be as fully members as any freemen. But yet, no slave shall hereby be exempted from that civil dominion his master has over him."[21] The *Fundamental Constitutions* did countenance slavery. In this period too, Locke, more aware of the profit to be had, invested £100 in an initial stock offering (the total required was £1600) for the development of the Bahamas. He also invested £400 in the Royal African Company, which was much involved in the slave trade. It does not affect the moral reckoning, but appreciate how large a sum that is: A few years later Locke engaged a man-servant for £5 a year and a few years earlier he had sublet his Christ Church rooms for £10 a year.

In 1672, Shaftesbury, as Chancellor of the Exchequer, appointed Locke to his first government post—one of slight responsibility, but it paid well and allowed him to dispense some patronage of his own. Later that year Shaftesbury acquired his peerage and became Lord Chancellor. Locke's official responsibilities increased as well. He served as secretary and treasurer to the Council of Trade and Plantations, a group charged with the management of economic affairs and trade with Britain's colonies. Locke

---

[20] K. H. D. Haley, The First Earl of Shaftesbury (Oxford: Clarendon Press, 1968), 242–248; J. R. Milton, "John Locke and the Fundamental Constitutions of Carolina," *Locke Newsletter*, 21 (1990), 111–133; and David Armitage, "John Locke, Carolina and the Two Treatises of Government," *Political Theory*, 32 (2004), 602–626.

[21] Goldie, *Locke*, 179–180.

148   J. T. BOOKMAN

was unable to breath the air of high politics for long. By 1675, Shaftesbury had fallen out of favor. The king dismissed him and disbanded the Council of Trade and Plantations. In November of that year, Locke left England with friends for the south of France. He had already begun to suffer from the respiratory problems (asthma and bronchitis) that would afflict him for the rest of his life—problems made worse by breathing all that coal dust emitted by the fireplaces of the Big Smoke. He hoped that getting away from the smoke and damp of a London winter would restore him to health. He ended up staying in France for three-and-a-half years where he filled his journal with observations about local government, the economy, technology, the state of religion, the terrain through which he passed, plant life, and, of course, medical thought and practice.[22]

Upon his return from France in May 1679, Locke found himself in an England increasingly anxious about the future of parliamentary government and the Protestant religion. King Charles II, encouraged by his Catholic brother James, had for some time sought to rule without Parliament, and he had shown Catholic sympathies by his toleration of Catholics and an alliance with France's Louis XIV in a war against Holland. These policies aroused fears exacerbated by the discovery of a purported "Popish Plot." The plot aimed at the assassination of Charles and the installation of James on the throne. The revelation that Louis had been secretly subsidizing Charles only made matters worse. In response, Parliament took up bills that would have excluded James, the heir apparent, from the throne. Over the course of several years, however, the king, determined to keep James in the line of succession, prevented further action by postponing the meeting of Parliament or dissolving it. The opposition, frustrated by the king's maneuvers, began to discuss revolution. Locke may well have not been party to these discussions, but he must have known of them; he certainly knew many of the principals. The rising tension induced Charles in July 1681 to order the arrest of Shaftesbury and a search of his house—including, one assumes, Locke's rooms.

These were the circumstances in which Locke wrote the *Two Treatises of Government*. The immediate occasion for the *First Treatise* was the publication in 1680 of *Patriarcha; or the Natural Power of Kings* by Sir Robert

---

[22] John Lough, ed., *Locke's Travels in France, 1675–1679* (Cambridge: Cambridge University Press, 1953), has extracts from Locke's journal. Dewhurst, *John Locke*, provides the medical entries which Lough omits entirely.

THE *SECOND TREATISE*   149

Filmer. Filmer argues that monarchs have their authority by divine right as successors to the authority invested by God in Adam over his children. According to Filmer, this authority is absolute and admits of no limitation by the monarch's subjects or their representatives. The *First Treatise* entitled *The False Principles and Foundation of Sir Robert Filmer, and his Followers Are Detected and Overthrown* is Locke's reply. Contrary to Filmer's contention that the natural state of humankind is subjection to another, Locke in the *Second Treatise* asserts that people enjoy a natural state of freedom and that government acquires its authority from the consent of the governed. Furthermore, while Locke in his earlier "Essay Concerning Toleration" (1667) allows only civil disobedience to the religious dissenter whose right to worship in his own way had been infringed by government, he is now prepared to support revolution against a government that had abused the trust reposed in it, as Locke clearly believed Charles II had done. This was strong stuff. The *Two Treatises* were not published until 1689, that is, after the "Glorious Revolution," and even then anonymously.

In what state the *Two Treatises* may have been at the time (July 1681) of the search of Shaftesbury's house is unknown. We know only that Locke probably wrote them in the period 1679–1683. Had the king's agents found the *Two Treatises*, he would have been in deep trouble. They found nothing apparently that cast doubt on his loyalty. By 1683, the times had grown more dangerous. The discovery in April of a plot (the Rye House Plot) to kill the king brought Locke under suspicion. He was not named as a co-conspirator but was known as an associate of some who were named. Locke set about destroying some papers and hiding others. A good thing too for he was under surveillance. Oxford, royalist as ever, drew up a list of pernicious doctrines and withdrew from the Bodleian Library books that espoused those ideas—ideas that could have been found in the *Second Treatise*: The king is subject to law, the authority of government is derived originally from the people, and the abuse of power justifies revolution. Ideas like those were found in Algernon Sidney's *Discourses Concerning Government*, and they cost him his life. Locke left England for Holland in September where he would spend the next five years.

Exile provided him with the time and safety to complete a project that he had begun years before (1671) and to which, in the intervening years, he had been able to give only passing attention: *An Essay Concerning Human Understanding* (1690). He maintained a correspondence with

150   J. T. BOOKMAN

friends still in England including Edward Clarke and his wife Mary whom he had met at Shaftesbury's. This younger couple asked Locke for suggestions for the upbringing of their eldest child, aged about three. These "directions in education," set out in a series of letters over several years, Locke later compiled in a book published anonymously under the title *Some Thoughts Concerning Education* (1693). It was from his English correspondents that Locke learned of his expulsion from Christ Church and the loss of his fellowship on the order of King Charles. It was from his correspondents too that he learned of the death of Charles in 1685 and the succession of James to the throne. The threat to Protestantism in England and the revocation by Louis XIV of the Edict of Nantes which had given some protection to French Protestants inspired Locke to reflect again on religious toleration. The *Epistola de Tolerantia* was the product of those reflections. Written in 1685 but first published in Latin in 1689, it then appeared in English later that year as the *Letter Concerning Toleration*—both anonymously.

The coronation of James II stirred some among the English emigrants to mount several failed insurrections in England. James in response asked the Dutch government to expel a long list of dissidents. Locke's name, at the direction of a local agent, appeared on the list of those to be seized. Cautious as ever, Locke moved around Holland under several aliases, Johnson and van der Linden among them, and became very guarded in his movements, at one point venturing out only at night. The Protestant community in England was distressed at the crowning of James. Nevertheless, for the sake of civic peace, Protestants were prepared initially to accept his rule in light of the fact that he had no heir and the Protestant Mary of Orange was next in line. James, however, quickly frittered away the support that he had by advancing policies to place Roman Catholics in the officer corps of the army, on the bench of the judiciary, on the Privy Council, and in Anglican parish houses. The last straw came in June 1688 when the Queen gave birth to a son. Encouraged by these events and at the invitation of leaders in the Anglican Church and in both the Whig and Tory parties, William of Orange set sail for England with a fleet of 400 ships. Their landing in November and the subsequent march of the insurgent troops to London were largely unopposed. James fled to France. In February 1689, Locke left Holland in the company of Princess Mary— soon to be crowned Queen of England. Her husband Locke describes as "our Great Restorer" in the preface to the *Two Treatises* and observes in a

THE *SECOND TREATISE* 151

letter to a friend that England would be best served "by restoreing our ancient government, the best possible that ever was if taken and put together all of a peice in its original Constitution. If this has not been invaded [by Charles II] men have don very ill to complain."[23]

Upon his return to England, Locke hoped to live a quiet life of leisure among his books and his friends. That first year, 1689, saw three works upon which he had long labored at the printers: the *Essay Concerning Human Understanding*, the *Two Treatises*, and the *Letter Concerning Toleration*. From this accomplishment he derived much satisfaction, but publication provoked critical comment and involved him in unwelcome controversy. For two years Locke exchanged volleys with the Anglican cleric Jonas Proast over the *Letter*. On Locke's side the fire appeared as the *Second Letter Concerning Toleration* (1690) and the *Third Letter for Toleration* (1692). After a ceasefire of 12 years, a renewal of the controversy brought a *Fourth Letter for Toleration* (1704). Throughout the controversy, Locke added little to the argument of the *First Letter*, but added much of a polemical nature. Proast in his anonymous pamphlet *The Argument of the "Letter Concerning Toleration" Briefly Considered and Answered* (1690) denies the Lockean principle that state authority ought to be confined to secular matters; spiritual concerns also fall under the state's jurisdiction. The question for him was how the state might exercise its authority to bring people to the true religion. He agrees with Locke that any direct application of force would be wrong and probably ineffective. Force, however, might be applied, in the form of some unspecified penalty, to encourage dissenters to consider the arguments for the true religion. Most people, he thought, come to their religious beliefs without any reasoned consideration of the alternatives.[24] Locke replies in the *Second Letter* that, since there is no agreement about what is the true religion, the state will exercise its power on behalf of its preferences. And, he asks: If a dissenter conforms or, for that matter, when a communicant of the Church of England conforms, is he or she to be examined to determine the reasons for allegiance? Locke thinks not. In practice, the state is not concerned about the convictions, reasoned or otherwise, of its subjects but about their conformity.

---

[23] De Beer, *Correspondence*, v. 3, 545–547:#1102.
[24] Jonas Proast, *The Argument of the Letter Concerning Toleration* (New York: Garland, 1984 [1690]).

152   J. T. BOOKMAN

Although the *Two Treatises* largely escaped attack at the time, Locke was kept busy responding to criticism of the *Essay Concerning Human Understanding*. His principal critic was the Bishop of Worcester, Edward Stillingfleet. The *Essay* neither affirms nor denies the doctrine of the Trinity. The absence of an affirmation was enough to inspire the Bishop to accuse Locke of Socianism (what we today would call in this regard "Unitarianism"), a heresy to the Church of England. In a *Letter to the Bishop of Worcester* (1697), Locke replies that Stillingfleet attacks him for holding views that he does not hold. He does not respond head-on to the charge of anti- Trinitarianism. He does say that the *Essay* was written "without any thought" of the Trinitarian controversy and that he is able to believe in mysteries, like the immortality of the soul, that are beyond reason. Locke's *Letter* did not satisfy the Bishop who renews his charges in an *Answer to Mr. Locke's Letter* (1697); Locke followed with a *Reply to the Bishop of Worcester's Answer* the same year. Both parties were warmed by the exchange, but there was no meeting of the minds.[25]

In a series of books, John Edwards, another Anglican clergyman, accused the anonymous author of the *Reasonableness of Christianity* (1695) of Socianism, if not atheism. In that work, Locke contends that the miracles worked by Jesus, as recounted in the Gospels, establish Christ's divine authority and, therefore, that the Gospels are an expression of divine revelation. Christianity recommends itself to those of faith by its promise of forgiveness of sins and everlasting life. It recommends itself to reason by confirming the principles of natural religion—that which can be known by unaided reason. Furthermore, the message of Christianity is intelligible to the ordinary person. And what makes Christianity intelligible is the simplicity of its message: Jesus is the Messiah, the son of God. That belief constitutes the essential tenet of the Christian faith. According to Edwards, in reducing the fundamental tenets to one, Locke neglects equally important beliefs like original sin, Christ's redemption of sin, and the Trinity.[26] Locke responded twice to Edwards: in *A Vindication of the Reasonableness of Christianity, etc. from*

[25] *The Works of John Locke. A New Edition, Corrected*, 10 vs. (Aalen: Scientia Verlag, 1963 [1823]), Volume 4 has the whole exchange.

[26] John Edwards, *Some Thoughts Concerning the Several Causes ... of Atheism ... With Some Brief Reflections on Socinianism: and on ... The Reasonableness of Christianity*, etc. (New York: Garland, 1984 [1695]).

Mr. Edwards' Reflections (1695) and *A Second Vindication of the Reasonableness of Christianity* (1697). In these essays Locke distinguishes between beliefs required to make one a Christian and beliefs required of Christians. Belief in Jesus as the Messiah, the son of God, makes one a Christian. Belief in other truths to be found in the Gospels are required of Christians. Just what those other truths are, however, can only be decided by the individual. Anyone who accepts Christ as the Messiah and seriously undertakes to live a Christian life as he or she understands the scriptural requirements "is a true and faithful subject of Christ's kingdom; and cannot be thought to fail in any thing necessary to salvation." Those who regard the Scriptures as containing a "set bundle of fundamentals" have caused "[s]chisms, separations … blood and butchery, all the train of mischiefs which have so long harassed and defamed Christianity, … and which must still continue as long as any … shall take upon him to be the dispenser and dictator to others of fundamentals."[27]

The controversial nature of his books was not the only thing keeping Locke from a quiet life. Public affairs engaged him as well. The newly crowned King William offered him a diplomatic post. He declined, pleading ill-health, while acknowledging a responsibility to serve the country and an interest in doing so. Appointment as Commissioner of Appeals for Excise followed a few months later in May 1690. Not quite a sinecure, it required little of him but paid £200 per year. His friends at court and in Parliament also sought his views on contemporary issues. In the main these issues concerned economics. Locke produced papers in response to such inquiries in which he supported the maximization of labor power, promotion of the export trade, and the opening up of the market.[28] He also weighed in on the renewal in 1695 of the Licensing Act, which regulated the printing of books. His arguments contributed to repeal of the Act, which provided for the censorship of "heretical" or "seditious" books. Locke's principal objection was to the monopoly accorded a few publishers and the consequent high price of books.[29]

---

[27] *A Second Vindication of the Reasonableness of Christianity* in Locke, *Works*, v. 7, 233 and 358.

[28] Patrick Hyde Kelly, *Locke on Money*, 2 vs. (Oxford: Clarendon Press, 1991); "Venditio" in David Wootton, ed., *Political Writings of John Locke* (Harmondsworth: Penguin, 1993), 442–446; and in the latter "Labour," 440–442.

[29] "Liberty of the Press" in Goldie, *Locke*, 330–339.

154   J. T. BOOKMAN

Despite his failing health, Locke accepted a royal appointment to a newly formed Council of Trade charged with the promotion of trade and manufacturing, colonial trade and administration, and the problem of the unemployed poor. He had familiarity with these matters acquired as secretary to Shaftesbury's Council of the early 1670s. The burdens of this post far exceeded those imposed upon him as an Excise Appeals commissioner. In a short period, June–October 1697, the Council met 26 times; Locke missed only one session. He was unable, however, to sustain such an effort. Despite the pleas and admonitions of his fellows, his health, the cold and damp of winter, and the London smog permitted him to attend only sporadically thereafter. He resigned in June 1700.

During his tenure on the Council of Trade, Locke wrote a report for the consideration of the members on the problem of the unemployed poor. Now he does assert in the *First Treatise* that "God ... has given no one of his Children such a property in his peculiar Portion of the Things of this World, but that he has given his needy Brother a Right to the Surplusage of his Goods; so that it cannot justly be denied him, when his pressing Wants call for it."[30] The report is a concrete policy proposal for the discharge of that duty the better-off have to a needy brother and, more generally, the duty imposed upon all by the law of nature "to preserve the rest of Mankind."[31] The report aims not only at the provision of necessities, but Locke also wants to reduce the number of those "who live like drones upon the labour of others" and to "make England ... richer" by employing as many of the poor as possible.

He contends that pauperism is not a consequence of "scarcity of provisions nor from want of employment for the poor." Rather, "it can be nothing else but the relaxation of discipline and corruption of manners." He estimates that "upon a very modest computation ... above one half of those who receive relief from the parishes are able to get their livelihood." These last are the immediate problem, and he urges vigorous execution of existing law for "suppression of this ... sort of begging drones." As this might prove insufficient, he proposes that able-bodied men between the ages of 14 and 50 caught begging outside their own parishes without a pass be impressed into the navy for three years. A beggar who has counterfeited a pass should lose an ear the first time convicted and for a second

---

[30] Peter Laslett, ed., Locke: *Two Treatises of Government*, Student Edition (Cambridge: Cambridge University Press, 1988), §42.

[31] *Second Treatise*, §6 in *ibid.*; see also Von Leyden, Essays, 195.

THE *SECOND TREATISE* 155

such offense "transported to the plantations." Men "maimed or above fifty" caught begging "shall be sent to the next [nearest] house of correction, there to be kept at hard labour [probably breaking rocks for the roads] for three years." Women and children were to be subject to lesser punishment. Children under 14 caught begging should be sent to a working school "soundly whipped" and "kept at work till evening." By such measures, Locke believes, the able-bodied who will not work "may be greatly reduced to a very small number, or quite extirpated."

In addressing the enduring problem of pauperism, Locke distinguishes among three classes of people. Those who "can do nothing at all towards their own support" should be supported at public expense. He recommends that they "be lodged three or four or more in one room, and yet more in one house, where one fire may serve, and one attendant may provide for many of them, with less charge than when they live at their own choice." These people would qualify for a pass permitting them to solicit "broken bread and meat, or other charity, from well- disposed people." A second class is made up of "those who … cannot maintain themselves wholly." This includes those "decayed from their full strength" and "most of the wives of day labourers with two or more children." Locke proposes the establishment of working schools to which children, ages 3–14, from families on relief should be sent. There they are to be taught some job in the manufacturing of wool and thereby become "inured to work." They are to receive a daily ration of bread and "in cold weather, if it be thought needful, a little warm water-gruel." Such schools also allow enforcement of church attendance, "whereby they may be brought into some sense of religion." Freed from child-rearing responsibilities, many mothers will be "at more liberty to work." The remaining class of the unemployed poor, the able-bodied, much reduced in number by the threat of service in the Royal Navy or incarceration in a house of correction, should be provided a job, at less than market wages if necessary, by the better-off in the parish. Over this system, Locke sets the "guardians of the poor," whom he authorizes to set up working schools, to decide who shall receive relief, to decide who shall receive a pass to beg and what shall be the hours for begging, to send the recalcitrant to houses of correction or to impress them into the navy, and to arrange employment for those out of work.[32] Parliament dismissed the scheme as too ambitious and too punitive.

---

[32] "An Essay on the Poor Law" in Goldie, *Locke*, 183–198.

156   J. T. BOOKMAN

In his declining years, marked by a persistent cough and painful respiration, an ear abscess, legs so sore that he was often confined to bed, and "so great a pain in my arm when I write that I am often fain to give off," Locke wrote a study of St. Paul's Epistles. This work, published posthumously, he regarded as a "study of the way of salvation, in those holy writings wherein God has revealed it from heaven."[33] Close to death and reflecting on his life with a friend, he allowed that "he looked upon this life to be nothing but vanity" and advised her "to look on this world only as a state of preparation for a better."[34] These sentiments were not very different from those he had expressed years before in the *Letter Concerning Toleration*: One "must exercise ... utmost care, application, and diligence, in seeking out and performing [those things prescribed by God]; for nothing belonging to this mortal condition is in any way comparable with eternity."[35] He died in 1704 at the age of 72 while, at his request, a friend read aloud the Psalms.

SECOND TREATISE: A COMMENTARY

Locke The Second Treatise of Government: An Essay Concerning the True Original, Extent, and End of Civil Government in Peter Laslett, ed. *Two Treatises of Government*. Student ed. Cambridge: Cambridge University Press, 1988.

Two Treatises of Government is a single work. History, however, has treated its two parts very differently. The *Second Treatise* with its claims of natural rights, the consent of the governed, and representative government has become a standard text for students of politics the world over. *The First Treatise* on the other hand is largely devoted to exegesis in aid of an attack on the doctrine of the divine right of kings. The appeal of that doctrine, the divine right of kings, and that kind of argument, biblical interpretation, at least in the West barely survived the century after Locke's death. Consequently, the *First Treatise* is ignored by all except scholars of

---

[33] *An Essay for the Understanding of St. Paul's Epistles by Consulting St. Paul himself* in Arthur W. Wainwright, ed., *John Locke: A Paraphrase and Notes on the Epistles of St. Paul* (Oxford: Clarendon Press, 1987), 115.

[34] H. F. R. Bourne, *The Life of John Locke*, 2 vs. (Aalen: Scientia Verlag, 1969 [1876]), v. 2, 559–560.

[35] Klibansky and Gough, *Epistola*, 123–125.

THE *SECOND TREATISE* 157

Locke's political philosophy. And, indeed, the *Second Treatise* provides the focus of attention here. We will not neglect the *First Treatise* entirely. It will be necessary to refer to the *First Treatise* and Locke's other works to explicate the meaning of one and another passage in the *Second Treatise*. The numbers below in bold on the left margin refer to paragraphs of the *Second Treatise*.

Preface The preface precedes the *First Treatise*. It was added well after the composition of the body of the work. Locke announces his intention to make good in the consent of the people the title to the throne "of our Great Restorer," the recently crowned William III. That reference to William, who acceded to the throne in February 1689, some allusions to events of James II's reign, and the publication of the *Two Treatises* in late 1689 long misled many to regard the *Two Treatises* as written to justify the Glorious Revolution. The research of Peter Laslett has established that Locke wrote it in the circumstances of the Exclusion Crisis of 1679–1681 and its immediate aftermath. Thus, Locke wrote to justify a revolution in prospect against Charles II (which of course never came off) rather than to justify a revolution after the fact. To be sure, Englishmen could invoke the ideas of the *Second Treatise* to justify the Glorious Revolution. *The Second Treatise*, then, was a radical document in its call, albeit a guarded one, for revolution in response to abuse of power by government. It was radical, too, for its time in its deployment of arguments general in character that could apply anywhere. Unlike so much of the polemical literature inspired by the Glorious Revolution, the *Second Treatise* has nothing to say about the English constitution. There is no invocation of Magna Carta and other events that distinguish English history from that of other nations.

§1 Locke denies that rulers may claim "Authority" from the biblical Adam's "*Private Dominion and Paternal Jurisdiction*." He also dismisses the idea that government is the "product only of Force and Violence." In what follows he intends to "find out another rise of Government, another Original of Political Power, and another way of designing and knowing the Persons that have it."

§2–3 Locke makes a distinction between political power and the power of a "*Father* over his children, a *Master* over his Servant, a *Husband* over his wife, and a *Lord* over his Slave." In subsequent paragraphs (cf. §22–24, 63–74, and 84–86), he will set out the bases of these distinctions. When

158   J. T. BOOKMAN

"Political Power" exists, men are in civil society and government has the authority to make laws and to employ force in their execution. Men have an obligation to obey a government that has political power. How some men acquire political power and all acquire an obligation to obey the law as made by government are matters taken up in subsequent paragraphs but particularly §§95–122.

§4 Locke uses the state of nature to determine, as he says at §1, how states come to be, how they can be justified, and what form the state should take. He defines the state of nature as a "state of perfect Freedom" in which people may dispose of themselves and their possessions as they see fit "within the bounds of the Law of Nature, without asking leave, or depending upon the Will of any other Man" (cf. §87:1–8). He emphasizes here and in §5–6 that all have an equal claim to freedom. God as "Lord and Master of them all" has not conferred political power upon anyone; this is the thesis of the *First Treatise*. Here the state of nature should be understood as a moral condition in which all are placed by God.

§5 The term "men" refers to all of humankind not just to males (see the essay "Virtue B in Mark Goldie", ed. *Locke: Political Essays*, 287–288). Locke is not concerned here to argue for gender equality. He is concerned to establish that by nature no one has authority over another (cf. §22, 95) except that exercised by parents over children (§55).

§6 The limits of the freedom enjoyed by all in the state of nature are given by the law of nature. That law teaches everyone *"to preserve himself"* and *"to preserve the rest of Mankind"* at least "when his own Preservation comes not in competition." Everyone has a right to dispose of himself and his possessions as he sees fit and a duty to respect that right in everyone else. That right and its correlative duty are obligatory because the law of nature is an expression of God's will, and we are all his creatures "sent into the World by his order and about his business" (cf. "Essays on the Law of Nature" in Goldie, Locke, 119–120; and *Essay Concerning Human Understanding*, II. xxviii. 8).

Hobbes, too, spoke of laws of nature that men could discover by the use of reason, and he spoke of a right of nature. Hobbes's laws of nature, however, answer a question in his theory different than that answered by Locke's law of nature. Hobbes asks, "How must men behave toward one another in order to realize peace?" His answer is: (1) seek peace, (2) be

THE *SECOND TREATISE*   159

willing to give up your right of nature in so far as others are willing to do so, and (3) keep your agreements. Locke asks, "How ought men to behave toward one another?" He answers: Respect the rights of others and support others in the exercise of their rights at least when it is safe to do so. Locke's law of nature is morally obligatory both in the state of nature and in civil society. Hobbes's laws of nature, on the other hand, are morally obligatory only for those who have become party to a contract transferring or renouncing part of their right of nature. The rights that men enjoy under the law of nature are, as Locke understands them, different in an important respect from the right of nature exercised by men in Hobbes's theory. Hobbes's right of nature entails no correlative duty to respect the same right in others. Locke's conception of rights is in this respect our own: one's rights are limited by the rights of others.

In another respect their conceptions of rights have an apparent similarity. Hobbesian men possess equally the right of nature, and Lockean men under the law of nature have equal rights. Nevertheless, there is a real difference. Locke's understanding of equality of rights requires not only that the rights of others be taken into account but that no infringement be made on the rights of others. Hobbes's right of nature provides that all are equally free of any obligation when threatened by loss of life, wounds, or imprisonment. Hobbes would say that one should take into account another's right, but the force of that "should" is not moral but prudential. One "should" do so because of another kind of equality of which he speaks, namely, an equality in strength and intelligence. By virtue of that kind of equality, it would be dangerous not to take into account another's right.

Their conceptions of the law of nature point to another difference between them. Hobbes, as we have seen, conceives of reason merely as a calculating faculty for most men. Once the passions have established ends, then reason in the light of experience can determine the means to realize those ends. Now, for Locke too, reason performs this function. Surely, Lockean men must also discover and observe those principles that Hobbes calls the first three laws of nature (set out above) if they are to live in peace with one another. In the *First Treatise* (§86), he speaks of reason as serving this prudential function in self-preservation. But for Locke reason also provides knowledge of ethical principles.

- What is it that makes a right natural?
- Can natural rights have some foundation other than revelation?
- May natural rights sometimes be overridden? For what reason?
- Just what are our natural rights?

160 J. T. BOOKMAN

Reason, we are told, teaches the law of nature to "all Mankind who will but consult it." This suggests that not all can or do consult reason. Locke allows that neither minors nor the mentally defective are capable of freedom because they lack the capacity to discover the law of nature (§60–65). Such persons are not morally responsible. All other persons are morally responsible because they can consult reason. But, he observes, not all do consult reason. "For how few there are who in matters of daily practice or matters easy to know surrender themselves to the jurisdiction of reason or follow its lead, when, either led astray by the violence of passions or being indifferent through carelessness or degenerate through habit, they readily follow the inducements of pleasure or the urges of their base instincts" ("Essays on the Law of Nature" in Goldie, *Locke*, 85, cf. 127).

In this and other passages in which he explains non-observance of the law of nature (e.g., §124), Locke makes no mention of irreligion as a bar to the exercise of reason. And yet in *A Letter Concerning Toleration* (Raymond Klibansky and J. W. Gough, eds., *Epistola de Tolerantia*, 135), he denies toleration to atheists: "Promises, covenants, and oaths, which are the bonds of human society, can have no hold upon an atheist, for the taking away of God, even only in thought, dissolves all" (cf. *The Fundamental Constitutions of Carolina* in Goldie, Locke, 177). Locke thinks that if men consult reason, then they "could not ... either doubt of the being of a God, or of the obedience due to him" (*Essay Concerning Human Understanding*, III. ix. 23). On this understanding, atheism is a consequence, even the most pernicious consequence, of a failure to consult reason.

§7 Locke shares Hobbes's view that a law without a power to enforce it is in vain and no law at all ("Essays on the Law of Nature" in Goldie, *Locke*, 113, and "Of Ethic in General" in Goldie, *Locke*, 304). He invests everyone with a right to enforce the law of nature. This is more than a right of self-defense. If it were simply that, then a man could only enforce the law when someone attempted to deny his rights. Those who have suffered no infringement of their rights may enforce the law of nature. Indeed, this is one of the principal ways, if it is not too dangerous, in which one may preserve the rest of mankind (cf. §171). Another way is to respect the rights of others.

The law of nature "willeth the Peace and *Preservation of all Mankind*" (see also §16, 134–135, 149, 159, 171, 183). This is as close as Locke gets to a summary expression of the law of nature. All its injunctions of particular rights and duties are aimed at that end.

THE *SECOND TREATISE*   161

§8 The punishment meted out to the transgressor of the law of nature must be proportionate to the crime.

§9 The state has no authority, no political power, over an alien. Nevertheless, a state may punish an alien for criminal activity, that is, transgressions against the law of nature, by exercising the executive power that all possess in the state of nature. Thus, a policeman (and all other citizens of the host state) is simultaneously in civil society with respect to his fellow citizens (and they with one another) and in the state of nature with respect to aliens.

§10 Atheists are not to be tolerated. They have varied from the "right Rule of Reason" in denying the existence of God and, if Locke's strictures are adopted, have violated civil law should they be so bold as to express their views. By doing so, the atheist becomes a "noxious Creature" to be dealt with accordingly (cf. §8).

- Does the atheist as an atheist do injury to another?

§12 The law of nature is "as intelligible and plain to a rational creature, and a studier of that law" as the statute books "nay possibly plainer." Locke had long insisted that moral precepts are expressions of God's will and that men and women can learn his commands as either a law of nature by the use of reason or the revelations of Scripture (cf. First Tract on Government in Goldie, *Locke*, 10–11; and "Essays on the Law of Nature" in Goldie, Locke, 119–120). What remained uncertain for him was whether reason or revelation afforded the surer way for most people to apprehend those precepts (cf. *Essay Concerning Human Understanding*, III. ix. 23 and IV. iii. 18; and *Reasonableness of Christianity*, §241–243).

§13 Investing an executive power in everyone to enforce the law of nature puts in jeopardy the peace and preservation of mankind: "Self-love will make men partial to themselves and their Friends. And on the other side, That Ill Nature, Passion and Revenge will carry them too far in punishing others." These human failings Locke characterizes as the "inconveniences" of the state of nature for which government is the remedy. These passages offer a glimpse into what Locke thinks about how men would behave in the absence of government. He returns to the matter in §123–124 and 131 (cf. *First Tract on Government* in Goldie, *Locke*, 39; and *A Letter*

162   J. T. BOOKMAN

Concerning Toleration in Klibansky and Gough, Epistola, 125). Thus men when they judge in their own cases are partial and violent. And, Locke emphasizes, "*'Absolute Monarchs'* are but Men."

- Would it be rational for men to grant unlimited power to anyone? Why?
- In light of §6 and its conception of humankind, may men invest unlimited power in any person?

§14 The relative character of the state of nature is evident in this example. Independent governments with respect to one another and, we learned in §9, individual members of different civil societies with respect to one another are in the state of nature. It is true that, in the absence of agreements establishing civil society, the parties are, on his definition in §4, in the state of nature.

- Are these examples quite to the point?

Locke seeks here to reply to a question regarding historical instances of men living in a "*[s]tate of perfect Freedom* ... without asking leave or depending upon the will of any other Man." His examples show that the institution of civil society has not proceeded so far as to bring all people under the authority of the *same* common judge. But everyone, or so it would seem, is a member of some civil society or other and, therefore, subject to the law of that government in whose jurisdiction he finds himself. Certainly that is the case today and would seem to have been so in Locke's day, although he may have thought the American Indian lived without government.

- Is it possible for large numbers of human beings to live without government (cf. §127)? It is worth recalling Aristotle's observation (*The Politics*, 1253a1–7) that human beings are "political animals." Any being who lives outside the *polis* is either a beast or a god. The *polis* is a condition for the development of those qualities that distinguish human beings from beasts. Without the *polis* human beings would remain mere beasts. Gods are not dependent on the *polis*.
- In the absence of government, what would relations among people be like?

THE *SECOND TREATISE* 163

§*16–18* The fundamental law of nature is the preservation of humankind. This would seem to require the restraint imposed by §7 in the exercise of the executive power in the state of nature, namely, punishment proportionate to the offense. Locke removes that restraint here. A state of war exists when one has declared by word or action a "sedate settled design, upon another Mans Life." Such a person may be killed. And yet a thief "who has not in the least hurt him [his victim] nor declared any design upon his Life" may also be killed.

§*19* Locke's language in this paragraph has encouraged much misunderstanding. He says: "Men living together according to reason, without a common Superior on Earth, with Authority to judge between them, is *properly the State of Nature.*" Now, if men are "living together according to reason," that is, observing the law of nature, then relations among them would be a "State of Peace." If men do not live according to reason, relations among them would be a "State of Enmity, Malice, Violence, and Mutual Destruction." It would seem that there are two mutually exclusive conditions: the former is the state of nature, and the latter is the state of war. The final sentence demands close attention. The state of war might occur "both where there is, and is not, a common Judge." Locke does not, then, respond here to the question put at the end of §14 above. He does describe the extremes that might obtain both in the state of nature and under government.

§*20* A state of war occurs whenever force is used without right. It might occur between those who have not agreed to establish civil society. It also might occur in civil society under either of two sets of circumstances. I might be unable to appeal to our common judge because you seek to rob me in the absence of a policeman. This, Locke says, "permits me my own defence, and the Right of War" (§19). The state of war also occurs when the government works "a manifest perverting of Justice … however coulored with the Name, Pretences or Forms of Law." In such a case, those who suffer under the law can only appeal to heaven, that is, rebel.

§*21* We learn a bit more about relations among men in the absence of government. "Every the least difference is apt to end" in war. This observation joined with that of §13 (men are prone to partiality and violence when they judge in their own cases) suggests just how hazardous life in a state of nature might be.

164   J. T. BOOKMAN

§23–24 Locke justifies the enslavement of captives taken in a just war (cf. §85). "By some Act that deserves Death," they have "forfeited their Lives, and with it their Liberties, and lost their Estates." The power that is acquired over slaves is "Absolute, Arbitrary, Despotical," and slaves are outside civil society. The power of the slave-master is not political. Political power is created only by consent.

What is an act that deserves death? It is the use of force without right (§16–18). The thief who robs me at gun point certainly uses force without right, and, as we have seen, I may kill him if we have no common judge with authority, or, if we are in civil society, there is no policeman to whom I can appeal (§18–19). May criminals who are subjects of the law made by government be enslaved? They may not. "When the actual force is over, the *State of War ceases* between those that are in society, and are equally on both sides Subjected to the fair determination of the Law" (§20). It is only when the parties have no common judge with authority that "*the State of War once begun, continues*" (§20). Locke describes slavery as "nothing else, but *The State of War continued, between a lawful Conqueror, and a Captive.*"

- What acts deserving of death were committed by the Africans enslaved by the English slave-traders?

Locke held black slavery to be justifiable. The *Fundamental Constitutions of Carolina* (Goldie, *Locke*, 181) to which he contributed provide that every freeman "shall have absolute power and authority over his negro slaves." He could scarcely, however, in his own views justify the whole of it. Even a lawful conqueror acquires no power over those who took no part in the war (§170), over the children or wives of those who did take part (§182–183 and 189), or over the possessions of those who did take part beyond what is necessary to secure reparation for damages (§183–184).

§27 Locke uses the term "property" in two senses: The broader sense refers to "Life, Liberty and Estate" (cf. §87 and 123); the narrower sense, as used in §27, refers to material possessions alone. He adopts the biblical and medieval view that God gave the world to men in common (§26) and he undertakes to justify how individuals may come to possess things for their exclusive use. Locke contends that whatever a man has mixed his labor with becomes his property. He argues against the contention

THE *SECOND TREATISE*   165

advanced by some of his contemporaries that universal consent is required to appropriate something held in common. "If such a consent as that was necessary, Man had starved, notwithstanding the Plenty God had given him" (§28).

There are limits to what may be appropriated in this way. He who invests labor in a thing makes it his property "at least where there is enough, and as good left in common for others" (cf. §33, 36, and 37). A second limitation is that nothing appropriated may be permitted to spoil or go to waste (cf. §31, 37, and 38). Private property acquired in this way and within those limitations, Locke argues, would occasion little conflict among men (cf. §31 and 39). There certainly might be differences among men in the amount of property appropriated, but the differences could not be great given the limitations. Furthermore, those who do acquire more do not thereby acquire any power over those with less.

- Would there be any reason for an able-bodied person to work for someone else?

§28 Not only the turfs with which I have mixed my labor become my property, but the "Turfs my Servant has cut" also become my property.

- How well does this accord with the justification for private property set out at the beginning of §27?

§29 Let us assume that Locke's "Fountain" is a spring, that is, a source of water upon which no improvements have been made.

- May someone appropriate the fountain by, say, improving access to it or increasing its flow?
- What if this is the only source of water within a day's walk?

§32 Locke extends his labor theory of appropriation to land. He recognizes that property in land is different from property in apples or fish; land "takes in and carries with it all the rest."

§34 Locke asserts that "God gave it [the world] to the use of the Industrious and Rational." In obedience to God's command, they "subdue the Earth, i.e., improve it for the benefit of Life."

166   J. T. BOOKMAN

- Do all who are industrious and rational have equal opportunity to appropriate land?
- Can we assume that all who might object to Locke's principles of appropriation are the "Quarrelsome and Contentious" who have no good reason to object?

§36 Appropriation of land on the measure stipulated "may be allowed still, without prejudice to any Body." An increase in population, however, might deny you the opportunity to till a parcel of land in England, all the land in England having been appropriated by others. You could, Locke suggests, move to some unoccupied land elsewhere in the world. We are asked, it would seem, to take a worldview in determining if there is enough land and as good left for others. Leaving aside the objection that there are today no unoccupied territories, how satisfactory is Locke's position? Say, you cannot afford to move, you must support an elderly parent who cannot travel, you do not want to leave friends, you know the language here but not there, you simply like the lie of the land in England, or you have still other reasons why you cannot or do not want to leave.

- Why should the first occupiers of the land be advantaged?

§37 Locke argues that the appropriation of land "does not lessen but increase the common stock of mankind." The investment of labor in land, then, has two consequences: (1) the laborer acquires right of property in the land worked, and (2) the land yields more than it would if left unworked. The latter consequence permits the support of a larger population and at a higher standard of living (§41). He makes another claim: He who labors on ten acres for his own consumption "may truly be said, to give society ninety acres to Mankind"—on the assumption that 100 acres of uncultivated land is needed to sustain one person.

- Has the appropriation of the ten acres reduced or enlarged the size of the common?

§40–43 In these paragraphs, as he had in §37, Locke seeks to calculate the contribution of labor to use-value. In §37, he puts that contribution at 9:1. It may be the case that the application of labor makes a plot of uncultivated land produce ten times what it did before (the increase might be greater or lesser depending on the fertility of the ground, the weather, and

THE *SECOND TREATISE*   167

other factors). That does not imply that labor contributes 90 percent of the value of the produce.

- If Locke's fountain (§29) quenches no thirst without labor, but quenches his thirst when he dips a pitcher into it and drinks from it, does the fountain contribute nothing to the use-value of the water in the pitcher?

§50 The same principles of appropriation would still hold were it not for the invention of money (§36). "Gold, Silver and Diamonds, are things, that Fancy or Agreement hath put the Value on, more than real Use, and the necessary Support of Life" (§46). Men consent, tacitly and voluntarily, to the use of money by accepting it in exchange for the "truly useful" (§47), and they have done so before the institution of civil society. Since money does not spoil, a man may without infringing on anyone else's rights (§46) enlarge his possession of land and sell for money the grain or cattle he raises upon it (§48). Therefore, Locke infers, men have agreed to economic inequality. He dismisses the idea that consent is necessary for the acquisition of property but adduces consent as justification for the "disproportionate and unequal Possession of the Earth."

The inequalities that result from different degrees of industry are not great before the introduction of money, and they confer no power over others on those who have more. After the introduction of money, the inequalities are great, and those who have more have considerable power over those with less. The product of the labor of Locke's servant is no longer his own (§28). The servant is dependent on Locke for the very opportunity to labor and the servant works on Locke's terms.

- What force do you give to the argument that, because men have consented to the use of money, they have consented to the economic inequality that money permits?
- Would economic inequality increase the probability of conflict among men?

Men, we are told, have consented to the use of money "out of the bounds of Societie." This would require the existence of a condition—no civil society and no government—in which men act "without a common Superior on Earth, with Authority to judge between them." Unless Locke can show the existence of such a condition, then must we not conclude

168   J. T. BOOKMAN

that the introduction of money and the consequent unequal distribution of property occurred under the auspices of government? In §107–108, he puts the establishment of government before the introduction of money (cf. "Labour" in Goldie, *Locke*, 329).

We should not read into Locke's views on property an intention to encourage the unlimited appropriation of property, although his views may well permit such appropriation. For Locke, God "sent [men] into the world by his order and about his business" (§6). He does not think that the accumulation of property is that business. Rather "Man's first care should be of his soul" (*A Letter Concerning Toleration* in Klibansky and Gough, *Epistola*, 131; cf. 123–125). And, in the same place, he singles out Christianity as "the religion which is most opposed to covetousness, ambition, discord, disputes, and worldly desires" (145).

§52 This whole chapter, comprising §52–76, is a reply to Filmer's patriarchialism, that is, his claim that God had provided for inequality among human beings: men over women, some men over other men, fathers over sons, masters over servants, and kings above all others. Locke contends that human beings are to be accounted as equals "unless the Lord and Master of them all, should by any manifest Declaration of his Will set one above another, and confer on him by an evident and clear appointment an undoubted Right to Dominion and Sovereignty" (§4). The *First Treatise* concludes, based upon scriptural interpretation, that God has made no such "manifest Declaration of his Will." This chapter of the *Second Treatise*, while referring here and there to Scripture, also brings the patriarchal case before the bar of reason.

§54 Locke emphatically rejects Plato's contention that reason justifies rule by the best, that is, those who live according to reason—the wise. "A man may owe *honour* and respect to an ancient, or wise Man," but that wisdom gives "no Authority" to the wise over him from whom that honor is owed (cf. §70). Men may be unequal in a number of respects, but he denies that any such inequality is ground for the exercise of "political power" without the consent of those subject to it (§95). "Political power," however, is not the only kind of authority; parental authority is another.

§55–58 Birth subjects us all, at least for a while, to the authority of parents, and this without our consent (cf. §63).

§57 Locke insists that the law, natural or civil (cf. §59 and 170), is not a limitation on but a condition for freedom. We might concede that one

THE *SECOND TREATISE* 169

restrained and attacked by others (§57) or subjected to the arbitrary will of another (§57) suffers a marked reduction in freedom. The law, however, imposes restraints not only upon others but upon each of us. On Locke's understanding, I am rightly forbidden by the law to take my neighbor's property and to take my own life, for example.

- However right he may be about this, do such prohibitions decrease my freedom? In this regard, see *Essay Concerning Human Understanding*, IV. iii. 18.

Locke conceives of freedom as the opportunity to dispose of oneself and one's possessions as one sees fit as permitted under the law (§57).

- Is freedom wholly a matter of what one may do under the law?
- Does freedom also have to do with participation in the making of the law?

§58 Unlike, say, Plato and Aristotle, Locke accords education no central place in his political philosophy. His brief remarks here and at §59–64 constitute the whole of his attention to the matter in the *Second Treatise*. He denies to the state a role in the formation of character. In "An Essay on Toleration" (Goldie, Locke, 135–136; cf. *A Letter on Toleration* in Klibansky and Gough, *Epistola*, 65–67), he confines the state's authority to the preservation of civic peace and the protection of property. It "hath nothing to do with moral virtues and vices, nor ought to enjoin the duties of the second table [the second half of the Ten Commandments] any otherwise than barely as they are subservient to the good and preservation of mankind under government" (Goldie, *Locke*, 144). Locke regards the state as the principal threat to that natural freedom with which God has endowed humankind. His great concern is the imposition of a religious orthodoxy, but the limitations that he imposes on the state extend well beyond making criminal the practice of a religion.

- Are there other agents in civil society in addition to government that threaten freedom?
- Does the Lockean state depend any less for its stability and longevity on the development of certain qualities in its citizens than the *polities* of Plato and Aristotle? Locke answers this question in the "Epistle Dedicatory" of his *Some Thoughts Concerning Education*.

170   J. T. BOOKMAN

§64 Parents bear primary responsibility for the education of their children (cf. §58). They are under a divine injunction to care for them (§60, 63, and 66), and children ought to honor their parents (§66–70). Honor is given during childhood in important part by obedience. Parents are well-fitted to discharge this obligation because they have "suitable inclinations of Tenderness and Concern" (cf. §63 and 67), and children are dependent upon them for food, shelter, and protection (*First Treatise*, §89–90). The desire of a child to inherit his father's estate also encourages obedience (§72–73). Finally, parents are more likely than anyone else to give their children the individual attention that effective education requires (*Some Thoughts*, §66 and 101–102).

The family home affords the most propitious circumstances for the education of the young. Locke opposes schools, which for him meant boarding schools like that he attended at Westminster. To parents, then, falls the task of producing citizens who will "be most useful to themselves and others." In this task, church will have a part, but it will be the church of the parents' choosing. *In Some Thoughts Concerning Education*, Locke says that "the great Principle and Foundation of all Vertue and Worth is placed in this, That a Man is able to *deny himself* his own Desires, cross his own Inclinations, and purely follow what Reason directs as best, tho' the Appetite lean the other way" (§33). Children are restrained in order that they learn to restrain themselves.

Some Thoughts describes an education aimed at the nurture of a person restrained by his own reason. It is an education for "a Gentleman's Son" and, indeed, for one lucky enough to have parents "so irregularly bold, that they dare venture to consult their own Reason [and Locke's recommendations], in the Education of their Children, rather than wholly to rely upon Old Custom" (§216). Such an education is beyond the means and understanding of most parents, who, along with their children, live in conditions of "horrid ignorance and brutality" ("Labour" in Goldie, *Locke*, 328). Nevertheless, the disadvantaged child, like the gentleman's son, becomes free of parental authority to dispose of himself and his possessions as he see fit "within the bounds of that law he is under" (§58–59). Upon attaining his majority, Locke says, "he might be suppos'd capable to know that Law" and "he is presumed to know how far that Law is to be his Guide" (§59).

THE *SECOND TREATISE*   171

§66 Locke opposes an "*Absolute Arbitrary Dominion of the Father*" (§64), but this opposition does not extend to the family itself as he makes clear here. The family is part of God's "great design."

§73 He who inherits the landed estate of his father must consent to the government under whose jurisdiction the land falls. Just as the prospect of a bequest encourages the child to obey his father, so possession of an estate encourages the heir to obey the government.

- Does the heir give express or tacit consent?
- How does the heir give express consent?

§74–76 These paragraphs give reason to doubt that there were ever historical instances of many people (Robinson Crusoe to the side) living in the state of nature "without a common Superior on Earth, with Authority to judge between them" (§19). "'Tis obvious," Locke says, "to conceive how easie it was in the first Ages of the World" for monarchy to develop out of a father's power. In keeping with his insistence that consent alone creates political power, he justifies the exercise of political power by a father over his children "by the express or tacit Consent of the Children, when they were grown up." The consent that Locke requires is not stringent: "'Twas easie, and almost natural for Children by a tacit and scarce avoidable consent to make way for the *Father's Authority and Government.*"

§77–87 In passages reminiscent of Aristotle's *Politics* (1252a1–29), Locke describes the development of political society from its beginnings in the "*first Society* ... between Man and Wife." Human beings are social creatures who associate with their fellows "under strong Obligations of Necessity, Convenience, and Inclination." They create many voluntary associations; Locke here calls them "societies." In part these societies may be founded on necessity as manifest in the dependence of children upon their parents, but inclination may figure much more prominently in others as in the association of man and woman. Human beings enjoy the company of one another. Locke, of course, has a very different conception of political society than does Aristotle. In particular, he denies to the state the very role in moral education to which Aristotle accords primary importance. Therefore, after the authority of parents ceases with the attainment of the age of discretion, moral education falls to all those with whom an individual associates

172   J. T. BOOKMAN

in the universal society informed by the law of nature. Among those associ-ates are family members, fellow-parishioners, friends, work companions, and the like. Most people "accomodate themselves to the opinions and rules of those with whom they converse." "Commendation and disgrace" are strong motives and "so they do that which keeps them in reputation with their company" (*Essay Concerning Human Understanding*, II. xxviii. 4–16).

§82 Locke speaks in the *Second Treatise* of "man" and "men." He means by these words to refer to all human beings. Thus when he claims for man or men an equal right to natural freedom (§54), a right to be subjected to political power only by his or their own consent (§95) and a right to rebel when deprived of his or their rights (§168), he makes these claims on behalf of both men and women, black and white, children—at any rate when they come of age—and their parents, and the propertied and the unpropertied. His understanding of equality, however, does not lead him to argue against many of the conventional inequalities of his day. He does not argue, for example, that all adults ought to have the franchise or that women ought to have the same property rights as men. Indeed, here he explicitly denies equal parental authority to mothers because the man is "abler and stronger." And, while in principle it would seem that a person, white or black, captured in a just war might be enslaved, Locke speaks only of black slavery (§§88–89). In entering civil society, men give up to the commonwealth their right to punish violations of the law of nature. In its execution of this power, the commonwealth may "imploy all the force of all the Members when there shall be need" (see also §3 and 136). Locke thereby invests the commonwealth with the authority to raise armies and *posse comitatus*. He does not tell us how this is to be done consistent with the respect due to the life, liberty, and estates of the citizen.

§95 Men may quit the state of nature and institute civil society only as they consent to do so. The choice, Locke implies, is between a condition in which men are "without a common Superior, with Authority to judge between them" and civil society and government. The required consent is individual. It must be voluntary, for any use of force in the state of nature except to punish violations of the law is force without right. And it must be deliberate, that is, in consenting a man must know that he is thereby "agreeing with other Men to joyn and unite into a Community." We shall need to be on the lookout for the answers to these questions:

THE *SECOND TREATISE*   173

- How is one's consent to be given?
- Just what does one consent to?

§96 Unanimous consent is necessary for the formation of civil society. Thereafter, "the *Majority* have a Right to act and conclude the rest" (§95). Majority rule, then, is to apply in the making of collective decisions, that is, decisions that all in the society are obligated to obey. Why did Locke adopt this decision-making rule? He rejects unanimity on the grounds that it would be impossible to attain (§98). He apparently does not think that the prospect of a return to the state of nature would be sufficient motivation to bring about the agreement of all (§98).

Locke's argument on behalf of majority rule is that "the Body should move that way whither the greater force carries it." His language—"the greater force"—suggests that the majority ought to be obeyed because it is stronger. Hobbes takes that position, and it is consistent with the rest of his teaching. For him, men in the state of nature are equal in strength and intelligence and, therefore, no one can be superior to another. Once men gather together to consider the institution of a sovereign, the majority rules because, on his assumptions about equality, in a knock-down, drag-out fight, the majority would win. The minority consents out of fear. Locke denies that agreements made under duress are valid (§176). Moreover, he might well deny that men are equal in the respects that Hobbes claims (§54). In any event, the equality that is important to him is moral: everyone has a right to dispose of himself and his possessions as he sees fit within the bounds of the law. And this moral equality creates a strong presumption in favor of majority rule.

- If some collective decisions must be made, why should the preferences of any individual be advantaged in making them?

Locke allows a decision-making rule that requires agreement among more than a simple majority but, presumably, among fewer than all. He does not argue for decision by extraordinary majorities, but he does not argue against it either.

- Does a rule that requires more than 50 percent plus one to make a decision confer an advantage on some?
- Why should they be advantaged?

174   J. T. BOOKMAN

The role of that group whose majority is to act and conclude the rest is twofold. It is to decide on the form of government (§132). The form chosen might be direct democracy, but Locke assumes that typically the majority will delegate authority to a smaller body, perhaps even to one man. The majority must also consent to taxation either directly or by deputies chosen by them (§138 and 140).

- Would any divisions among men along economic, religious, racial, or ethnic lines persuade many not to consent to civil society in which the majority rules?
- What sort of guarantees might be sought by an economic, religious, racial, or ethnic minority as a condition of their consent?

§105–112 Locke renews his attack on Filmer's patriarchialism.

§116 This paragraph should be read against my comments at §14 and 95. If Locke means to maintain that men have actually consented to civil society and government, then he requires a real state of nature for which men might opt. Here he comes close to conceding that men do not institute civil society and government by agreeing one with another. They are born in civil society and subject to government. He claims that this makes no difference (§100–101). To be sure, he does hold out alternatives to any man in a particular civil society and under a particular government. Such a man "is at liberty to go and incorporate himself into any other Commonwealth, or to agree with others to begin a new one, in *vacuis locis*, in any part of the World, they can find free and unpossessed" (§121). But this is to redefine the alternatives. Rather than a choice between the state of nature and civil society and government, men have a choice between this or that government. Men may not, of course, consent to just any government. "For a Man, not having the Power of his own life, *cannot*, by Compact or his own Consent, *enslave himself* to any one, nor put himself under the Absolute, Arbitrary Power of another" (§23). Furthermore, Locke says, to think that men would consent to a contract investing absolute power in any government "is to think that Men are so foolish that they take care to avoid what Mischiefs may be done them by *Pole-cats*, or *Foxes*, but are content, nay think it Safety, to be devoured by *Lions*" (§93).

This suggests that we might understand Locke's teaching in a different way. The consent that men give is hypothetical rather than actual: If men had the opportunity to found government anew or if they were asked,

THE *SECOND TREATISE* 175

they would consent to government with certain qualities. The question to be asked, then, in determining whether the individual has an obligation to obey is not "has he consented?" but "does the government possess the necessary qualities?" If the government has those qualities, then it is legitimate and the individual has an obligation to obey it. This shifts the stress of Locke's theory from the consent of the individual to the legitimacy of the government.

- What are the qualities of legitimate government?

To understand Locke's teaching in the way suggested has its attractions. It circumvents the difficulties of his doctrine of consent. The problem with such an understanding, however, is that it ignores his repeated insistence that only the consent of the individual creates an obligation to obey another human being (§22, 95, 96, 97, 106, 112, 117, 119 and *passim*). Thus, a government might satisfy the criteria of legitimate government and a person may withhold consent to that government. One has no obligation to join a political society.

§119 Locke does not indicate how express consent is to be given. Tacit consent is given easily, or should we say, is easily acquired by government. Anyone within the jurisdiction of a government has consented and is obliged to obey it. He introduces the idea of tacit consent because most people have not consented expressly. If consent had to be given expressly, most would not be obligated to obey. His conception of tacit consent is so broad, however, that everyone turns out to have consented and done so without even recognizing it.

- If everyone has consented, how can we distinguish between legitimate and illegitimate governments?

§120 Taking possession of land binds the possessor to the "Government and Dominion of that Commonwealth, as long as it hath a being." Since the only act that perpetually binds anyone to any community is express consent, taking possession of land involves the giving of express consent and makes the possessor a member of that community.

Locke identifies no other forms of express consent, but surely the oaths taken by public officials and military officers would seem to qualify and there may well be other forms as well.

176   J. T. BOOKMAN

§121–122 Tacit consent obligates one to obey the laws of a particular government only so long as one is within its jurisdiction. The heir to a landed estate gives only tacit consent until "he dwells upon, and enjoys that" estate. Therefore, that heir might "quit the said possession" and emigrate or remain in the commonwealth without land but subject to the government along with everyone else who enjoys its protection.

§122 Locke distinguishes members (those who have expressly consented) from non-members (those who have tacitly consented). He is clear about the significance of this distinction for men as subjects of the law. Both members and non-members are obligated to obey the government, but the member "is perpetually and indispensably obliged to be and remain unalterably a Subject to it" (§121), whereas the non-member may end his obligation to that government by leaving its jurisdiction. What he is not clear about is the significance of this distinction for men as participants in the making of the law.

- Do only members make up that body the majority of which is to decide upon the form of government and upon taxes?

§123–126 At §19, Locke described the extremes that life might take in the absence of government. Here and in §131 we learn that, while men have a guide to right conduct in the law of nature, "yet Men being biassed by their Interest, as well as ignorant for want of study of it, are not apt to allow of it as a Law binding to them in the application of it to their particular Cases." Thus, men with partiality interpret the law of nature, judge their own cases, and enforce the law; furthermore, enforcement is uncertain. It is these circumstances that Locke calls the "inconveniences" of the state of nature which impel men to institute civil society (§13). Because "the greater part [of humankind] are no strict Observers of Equity and Justice," the enjoyment of freedom in the state of nature is "very uncertain, and constantly exposed to the Invasion of others," "very unsafe, very insecure," "full of fear and continual dangers," and "unsafe and uneasie" (§131). With these circumstances in mind, Locke describes the motivation to leave the state of nature as "the mutual Preservation of their Lives, Liberties and Estates."

§129 By consenting to civil society and government, the individual gives up his right to dispose of himself and his possessions as he sees fit "so far forth as the preservation of himself, and the rest of that society shall

THE *SECOND TREATISE*   177

require," "as the good, prosperity, and safety of the Society shall require" (§130), and "as the good of the society shall require" (§131). Locke makes a special point of bringing property in the narrower sense under the authority of government (§120).

§131 He expresses the same idea as in §129, but here as a limit on the authority to make laws (what he calls the "legislative"). "The power of the Society, or *Legislative* constituted by them, *can never be suppos'd to extend farther than the common good.*"

- How severe a limitation does the "common good" impose upon government?

Locke does insist that government has the authority to regulate, not to confiscate (§138–139). With particular reference to property in the narrower sense, government must secure consent to any appropriation. Nevertheless, Lockean government has considerable discretion. He does not envision government exercising that discretion on behalf of ambitious redistributive programs as he makes clear in a *Letter Concerning Toleration* (Klibansky and Gough, 91): "The care, therefore, of every man's soul belongs to himself and is to be left to him. You will say: What if he neglects the care of his soul? I answer: What if he neglects the care of his health or of his estate, things which more nearly concern the government of the magistrate? Shall the magistrate provide by an express law against such a man becoming poor or sick? Laws endeavour, as far as possible, to protect the goods and health of subjects from violence of others, or from fraud, not from the negligence or prodigality of the owners themselves. No man against his will can be forced to be healthy or rich."

§132 The majority may adopt any form of government from direct democracy to hereditary monarchy. If the majority adopts monarchy, it would be necessary for the monarch to hold a referendum or call for the election of an assembly to consent to tax measures.

- If popular consent, direct or indirect, is required for the collection of taxes, why is it unnecessary for the adoption of other governmental measures?
- If the majority is to be the final judge of whether or not government has served the common good, what institutions are necessary to give expression and effect to majority sentiment?

§*134* Upon joining civil society, people acquire political obligations, namely, "*the preservation of the Society*, and (as far as will consist with the publick good) of every person in it." This passage should be laid alongside §6. Notice the shift in identity of the agent to whom one is first obligated. It is no longer oneself (the individual) but the society. Secondarily, obligation has shifted from all mankind to fellow members of one's society. Presumably, the priorities of §6 would remain in place with respect to all of those with whom we are in the state of nature.

§*135* Does a law serve the common or "publick good"? If it does not, then the legislative has exceeded its authority and exercised arbitrary power or, in language made familiar to us earlier, force without right.

§*138* Locke expresses a preference for a government "where the *Legislative* consists, wholly or in part, in Assemblies which are variable, whose Members upon the Dissolution of the Assembly, are Subjects under the common Laws of their Country, equally with the rest," and he says that in "well order'd Commonwealths" (§143) legislative and executive authority are separated, at least in part, and exercised by different bodies. He does not, however, include these qualities among the criteria of legitimate government.

§*142* This paragraph summarizes the criteria of legitimate government discussed in §134–141. To these we need to add several criteria discussed elsewhere: (1) In all disputes between individual or groups, the government is judge (§87–89, 150, and 212); (2) in disputes between individuals or groups and the government, heaven is the judge, that is, the former may rebel, and should the government be dissolved, the majority may institute a new government (§95–98, 149, 220, 226, and 242); and (3) any form of government may be established by the majority so long as its authority is limited (§74–75, 132, and 135).

§*143* This paragraph is a *locus classicus* for the doctrine of separation of powers. Locke suspects that "it may be too great a temptation to human frailty apt to grasp at Power" to invest one body or person with the authority to both make the laws and to execute them. If the legislators, he explains, were to possess executive authority, "they may exempt themselves from Obedience to the Laws they make." Such exemption would defeat institution of the rule of law—the very purpose for which men establish civil society. There is, of course, law in the state of nature, but, owing to the "inconveniences" of the state of nature, it "serves not, as it ought, to determine the Rights, and fence the Properties of those that live under it" (§136). It is to avoid that self-interested and passionate interpretation and execution of the law of nature that men establish government. The law ought to advance the "publick good" and not the legislators' "private advantage." If legislators "are themselves subject to the laws" they make, they are more likely to "make them for the publick good." Locke assumes that an executive independent of the legislature will subject legislators to the law.

- If legislative authority is exercised by representatives electorally responsible to the people, how likely is it that they will pursue interests "distinct … from the rest of the community"?

Notice that the danger about which Locke is concerned in recommending separation of powers is not that the legislature will seek to advance the interests of one part of the community at the expense of another but that it will seek to advance its members' fortunes at the expense of everybody else.

§154–156 The executive convenes and dismisses the legislature.

§157–158 A connection between consent, express or tacit, and the franchise is not made. Representation ought to be "fair and equal." It ought to have some, unspecified, relationship to numbers of people and wealth. Who gets to vote or run for office is not specified. The *Fundamental Constitutions of Carolina* (Goldie, *Locke*, 174–175) provide that "[n]o man shall be chosen a member of parliament who has less than five hundred acres of freehold within the precinct for which he is chosen; nor shall any have a vote in choosing the said members that has less than fifty acres of freehold within the said precinct."

§159–168 These paragraphs give the executive the authority to act "without the prescription of the Law, and sometimes even against it" (§160). This prerogative must be exercised for the "publick good" (§164), although Locke suggests that the people "are very seldom, or never scrupulous" about this (§161). It is enough if its use is "in any tolerable degree in the public good" and "not manifestly against it."

- What distinguishes Locke's executive from Hobbes's absolute monarch?

180   J. T. BOOKMAN

§160 Locke sets out what has been called the "efficiency" argument for separation of powers. On this argument, the efficient discharge of the several governmental functions requires different qualities in the agencies responsible for their performance. Locke stipulates that execution of the law requires "dispatch." A legislature "not always in being," "numerous," and "too slow" cannot act with dispatch and, therefore, is ill-fitted for execution of the law. The executive, on the other hand, can act with dispatch.

§168 Who shall be judge between the people and government? The people may "judge whether they have just Cause to make their Appeal to Heaven." Even "any single Man" deprived of his rights may rebel, although he is unlikely to secure vindication of his rights unless he is supported by a majority. This is so because the government is incomparably more powerful than any single man.

§201 Any form of government, he claims, might become tyrannical.

- How, on Locke's theory, could a direct democracy be determined to be tyrannical?

§208 Locke seeks here and in subsequent paragraphs (§209, 223–225, 228, and 230) to allay the fears of those who see in the right to rebel an invitation to anarchy. He argues that it is only when "the Body of the People," "the Majority of the People" (§209), "*the People generally*" (§224), "*the greater part*" (§230) feel themselves subjected to unlawful force that government is threatened. Furthermore, "*such Revolutions happen* not upon every little mismanagement in publick affairs" but only following "a long train of Abuses, Prevarications, and Artifices, all tending the same way" (§225).

As we have seen, in §168 and references there, Locke makes the people judge in disputes between the government and individuals. Now, if someone believes that the government has denied his rights, he may rebel. But, unless the majority comes to his defense, he will be crushed. Some rebels, the "raving mad Man, or heady Male-content" and the "busie head, or turbulent spirit" (§230) may well have an idiosyncratic understanding of their rights, and they will come, he says, to "their just ruine and perdition"

THE *SECOND TREATISE*   181

(§230). We can hardly say this, however, about all claims that the government has denied rights. Indeed, Locke assumes here and in §230 that some really have suffered oppression as the majority understands it.

§211 A society along with its government is dissolved by foreign conquest. On Locke's principles, men would then be returned to the state of nature to enjoy the liberty provided by the law of nature. In reality, they would be subjected to despotical rule whether the conqueror had waged a just or an unjust war. Government is dissolved whenever the legislature is altered (§212) or government acts contrary to the trust reposed in it (§221). Although Locke says that the government is dissolved, how is one to know unless the people rebel? We can count on the rulers who have committed injustice to remain in office until unseated and to maintain their innocence of any wrongdoing. And Locke seems to think so too (§218).

What Locke says about the consequences of the dissolution of government for the status of the individual is ambiguous. For example, he says that if the executive fails to administer the law, the government is dissolved and "the People become a confused Multitude, without Order or Connexion" (§219). More typically, he speaks of the consequences of the dissolution of government as the resumption of the right of the people to establish a new legislative (§212, 220, 222, and 226). This is to say men remain in civil society even after the dissolution of government. A group of men do not become a *people* until they have instituted a society (§89). The right that men recover is not a right to act "without asking leave, or depending upon the Will of any other Man," but a right to establish a new legislative. Moreover, Locke concludes the *Second Treatise* with the observation that "*the Power that every individual gave the Society, when he entered into it, can never revert to the Individuals again, as long as the Society lasts, but will always remain in the Community*" (§243).

§223 Government rests on opinion, upon the convictions people have about who ought to rule and about the ends for which power is exercised. That is Hobbes's position as well. Of course, Hobbes seeks to persuade us that it is both our obligation and in our interest to obey any government that is preserving peace and order and that those governments best fashioned to realize that end are absolute monarchies.

182   J. T. BOOKMAN

§224 Locke responds to Hobbes and all those who deny a right to rebel that if "*the People* [are] *generally* ill treated, and contrary to right," they will rebel even against governments that claim absolute authority. He can hardly deny, however, that Hobbes's principle—no right to rebel—as it gained acceptance, might affect the likelihood of rebellion. Did not Locke say that government rests on opinion? Were the people to believe that they ought not to rebel they might well not rebel.

§226 Locke claims that this principle—people have a right to rebel—will, as it gains acceptance, make a difference. It is, he says, "*the best fence against Rebellion.*" Rulers, conscious of the right of the people to rebel, will be less likely to give cause for rebellion by violating the law or otherwise abusing the people's trust. He calls wayward rulers the real rebels; their tyranny is the real rebellion.

- Is a right to rebel the best fence against tyranny?
- Must not things be far gone before tyranny would be challenged in this risky and costly way?
- Are there no other ways to reduce the risk of tyranny and to arrest its growth early on?

A BIBLIOGRAPHICAL ESSAY

In 1947 the Bodleian Library purchased a collection of Locke's papers from the Earl of Lovelace, a descendant of the first Lord King. It was to the latter, his young cousin Peter King, that Locke had bequeathed his papers and half of his library (the King barony became the Earldom of Lovelace in 1838). That bequest was unconsulted until 1829 when the seventh Lord King brought out a biography of his famous ancestor that included lengthy extracts from his papers. Apart from King's biography, this valuable source of information remained undisturbed for decades in the care of the Lovelace estate. During World War II the Earl transferred the papers to the Bodleian for safekeeping, where, on behalf of the Clarendon Press, Professor Wolfgang von Leyden of the University of Durham examined the collection, appraised its contents, and began work on what would become *Essays on the Law of Nature*. On the strength of von Leyden's appraisal, the Bodleian purchased the collection in 1947. Paul Mellon, the American philanthropist, purchased in 1951 the remaining manuscripts still in the possession of Lovelace as well as his part of

Locke's library. Mellon subsequently donated all this to the Bodleian where it has place alongside the 1947 acquisition in the Duke Humphrey reading room. Interested scholars now have available (mostly on microfilm) this marvelous resource, which continues to inspire publication down to the present day—including the Clarendon edition of Locke's complete works still in progress.

The most recent bibliography of Locke's works is that of Jean Yolton (9). She provides a printing history of all editions and translations from first publication to 1801. Each entry receives annotation regarding physical appearance and any emendations made to the text. Chapter 2 is devoted to printings of the *Two Treatises*. The chapter on spurious and doubtful attributions includes the *Fundamental Constitutions of Carolina*. For all but the most devoted bibliophile, Attig's bibliography (1) is probably the more useful. He covers all editions and translations including abridgements and selections in anthologies from first publication to 1985. He identifies reviews of significant editions. The *Fundamental Constitutions* does not appear on his list of spurious or doubtful works.

There is no recent, comprehensive bibliography of the secondary literature. Christopherson (2) is an extended bibliographical essay largely devoted to the various printings of Locke's works in major European languages and to contemporary criticism of those works. He gives full descriptions of the several editions and brief exposition of the criticism levied against Locke's works. Just 25 pages identify and describe the secondary literature that appeared in 1704–1930—much of it nineteenth century. Hall and Woolhouse (4) cover the years 1900–1980 in a work that cites books, articles, and dissertations in major languages. They organize by year the over 2000 entries. The annotations identify reviews, reprints, and discussions in other works for many entries. All aspects of Locke's philosophy receive attention. This is true as well for the Yoltons's bibliography (8), which comprehends the years 1689–1982. They identify some 1800 secondary works and provide a short abstract for each entry. Eccleshall and Kenny (3) are much more selective—165 entries for Locke. Their bibliography is somewhat more recent than those above, and it provides critical annotations for most entries. Hall (5 and 6) in the journal that he has long edited has kept Locke scholars current in the literature in his annual "Recent Publications on Locke."

Woolhouse has written the best, and most recent, life. He successfully treats Locke's intellectual life in a philosophically sophisticated way alongside an account of his other social and political activities. Woolhouse taps

184   J. T. BOOKMAN

resources unavailable to Cranston (16). The latter was the standard biography for decades. There was much to recommend it, but it did slight Locke's intellectual development. The earlier biographies by Lord King (29) and Fox Bourne (13) share a hagiographic view of their subject, but in other respects are quite different. Fox Bourne mounts a thorough, careful effort given the resources available. In particular, the only access he had to the documents comprising the Lovelace collection was provided by Lord King in his biography. Unfortunately, King inaccurately transcribed many of the documents and organized them in a haphazard fashion. Still earlier accounts of Locke's life are the subject of the volume compiled by Goldie and Soulard (23). They reproduce the memoirs of Pierre Coste, Jean LeClere, and Damaris Masham and other of Locke's contemporaries and near contemporaries.

Particular aspects of Locke's life are addressed by Dewhurst (19), who transcribes all of Locke's journal entries dealing with medicine, and by J. R. Milton (32), who describes Locke's career at Oxford. Lough (31) omits the entries on medicine, religion, and science in Locke's journal kept in France but transcribes the rest. A complete transcription of the journals in the Clarendon Press edition of the works is forthcoming from Shankula (34). De Beer (18) transcribes nearly the whole of Locke's extant correspondence in eight volumes; a ninth will be an index. Some 1000 of the letters, including unsent drafts, are from Locke; the balance of the 3650 entries are from his correspondents. He organizes them in a single chronological sequence and assigns each an index number now widely cited in the secondary literature. Goldie (22) has made a judicious selection from De Beer in one volume. Harrison and Laslett (26) reproduce Locke's master catalogue of his books as compiled in 1692–1704 and a catalogue of 1681 of his Oxford library. In an introduction, Laslett describes the development of Locke's library and the annotations that he made to his books. Anthony Ashley Cooper, Earl of Shaftesbury, who looms large in any account of Locke's life, is the subject of a modern biography by Haley (25). Sydenham and Boyle figured less prominently, but they too contributed much to his education, particularly on scientific matters. The leading biographies are by Dewhurst (20) on Sydenham and Hunter (27) on Boyle.

Garland Publishing brought out 16 volumes in 1984 under the general editorship of Peter Schouls. These volumes appear under separate title in this bibliography. Most are reprints of the works of Locke's contemporary opponents—Filmer, Proast, and Edwards among them. Sir Robert Filmer

THE *SECOND TREATISE*   185

against whom Locke inveighed in the *First Treatise* receives careful attention at the hands of Daly (17). Both Laslett (30) and Sommerville (35)
have published editions of Filmer's works. Wootton (38) has compiled a
selection of the political essays of Locke's seventeenth-century contemporaries and written an excellent introduction to their thinking. Appleby
(11), Clark (14), Kenyon (28), Wilson (36), and Wrightson (39) describe
the historical context in which Locke lived. Coffey (15) and Grell (24)
take up the religious controversies that so unsettled the times.

The Clarendon Press in 1975 undertook publication of a complete
works under the general editorship of Peter Nidditch, who has been followed by John Yolton and then M. A. Stewart. Individual volumes have
appeared sporadically under separate title. Some 19 volumes have been
published with a total of 34 projected. For the first time we now have the
complete correspondence and a critical edition of "An Essay on Toleration"
among other things. A complete edition of the journals—unavailable earlier—is in progress. At the end of this project students of Locke will have
a complete works that reflects modern scholarship and incorporates
manuscript material uncovered throughout the twentieth century and in
many countries. The individual editions will supplant in many instances
earlier editions of the same work and in total supersede altogether earlier
works like that brought out by Thomas Tegg (54) in 1823. The latter had
long been the standard.

There are many collections of one and another of Locke's works.
Gough (45) and Sherman (51) bring together the *Second Treatise* and *A
Letter Concerning Toleration*. Shapiro (50) provides both *Treatises* and the
Letter. Yolton (55) extracts passages from a wide range of Locke's works
and organizes them topically. He gives prominence to *An Essay Concerning
Human Understanding*. "Part III: The Science of Action" will be of par-
ticular interest to students of Locke's political thought. Sigmund (52) in a
Norton critical edition gives us the whole of the *Second Treatise* as well as
brief selections from the *First Treatise*, "Essays on the Law of Nature," *An
Essay Concerning Human Understanding*, and the *Reasonableness of
Christianity*. He includes as well passages from the works of Locke's
immediate predecessors and from modern commentators. Goldie (44)
assembles an excellent collection of materials heretofore scattered widely:
the full text of *Two Tracts on Government*, "Essays on the Law of Nature,"
"An Essay on Toleration," the *Fundamental Constitutions of Carolina*,
"An Essay on the Poor Law," and many minor pieces including Locke's
criticism of the Licensing Act and 15 others never before published.

186   J. T. BOOKMAN

Wootton (53) collects the major political works and relevant excerpts from Locke's journals. His introduction shows the debt Locke owed to James Tyrrell.

Nuovo (49) has the *Reasonableness of Christianity* and many of Locke's shorter essays on religion including the uncompleted, but projected, final chapter of *Human Understanding* entitled "Of Ethick in General." Axtell (43) supplants Adamson (41) as the source for *Some Thoughts Concerning Education* as well as Locke's lesser known writing on the subject. The Clarendon edition of "An Essay Concerning Toleration" is in J. R. Milton and Philip Milton (47). The editors describe in detail the four extant manuscripts of that essay. Locke's several drafts of *Human Understanding*, save for the final, fourth draft, and *Of the Conduct of the Understanding* can be found in Nidditch and Rogers (48). These volumes make it unnecessary to consult Aaron and Gibb (40). Anstey and Principe (42) have in preparation Locke's "Writings on Medicine and Natural Philosophy." Until that volume is published, one must turn to Dewhurst (19) and delve here and there in the 1823 edition (54) of Locke's works, particularly Volume 3, 301–330 and Volume 10, 328–356. Kelly (46) is the editor of the Clarendon edition of Locke's writings on economic matters. He includes several tables describing the English economy of the 1690s. In his introduction, Kelly shows the connections between Locke's early work on money and interest and his treatment of property in the *Second Treatise*.

The Clarendon works include editions of Locke's major works. All are introduced by learned essays. The editors decided early on to adopt von Leyden's *Essays on the Law of Nature* (61) and Laslett's *Two Treatises* (67) as part of the complete works and, thereby, set a high standard for the project. Klibansky and Gough (56) provide Locke's original Latin text and their own translation of *Epistola de Tolerantia* on facing pages. Their translation differs in insignificant ways from the widely reproduced translation done by William Popple in 1689. Fraser (58) was long the standard edition for *Human Understanding*. It has been displaced by Nidditch (60). Woolhouse (59) makes some emendations to the Nidditch edition. He has written a cogent analysis as introduction. Yolton's edition (57) is available in two volumes from Everyman's. Under the title *Questions Concerning the Law of Nature*, Horwitz, J. Clay and D. Clay (62) have brought out an "Essays on the Law of Nature" distinguished by an introductory essay taking Locke to task for his departures from the traditional natural law teaching as understood by Leo Strauss. Scholars have long been indebted to Abrams (65) for his edition of *Two Tracts on Government*. A Clarendon edition by Rose and Maxwell-Stuart is forthcoming. Higgins-Biddle (64) edited the Clarendon Press's *Reasonableness of Christianity*, and Nuovo (68), Locke's *Vindications*. Wainwright (63) edited the Clarendon Press's *Paraphrase and Notes on the Epistles of St. Paul*.

Anstey (69), Ashcraft (71), and Dunn and Harris (75) have collected many scholarly articles ranging across the whole Locke corpus. There is overlap among them. Anstey is the most recent. His four volumes number almost 2000 pages and reprint 70 articles. Ashcraft's earlier collection in the same series reprints over 100 articles published in 1904–1989. Dunn and Harris reprint 59 articles in the space of some 1200 pages. Chappell (73) edited the *Cambridge Companion to Locke*. He includes essays on Locke's thinking on religion, ethics, and politics and a useful bibliography. Chappell (74) has also edited a volume in a Garland series on early modern philosophers. Savonius-Wroth, Schuurman, and Walmaley (84) edited the *Continuum Companion to Locke*. This volume is well worth consulting for its brief accounts of the lives and ideas of Locke's important contemporaries, its analyses of significant concepts as used by Locke, synopses of his major works, and estimates of his influence in the eighteenth century—all written by prominent scholars in the field.

In 1932, upon the tricentenary of Locke's birth, Michael Oakeshott (in Dunn and Harris, v. 1: 72) declared Locke's political philosophy to be moribund. Locke's liberalism, he said, "appears likely ... to die of neglect." Within several decades Locke studies were flourishing. Many things contributed to this development. Certainly access to the Lovelace collection allowed scholars to enlarge and refine our understanding of Locke's philosophy. Macpherson (109) and Strauss (126) advanced new perspectives and provoked considerable controversy. The publication of Laslett's edition of the *Two Treatises* (67) placed that work in a new context and, thereby, raised new questions. Not to be overlooked either is John Rawls's *Theory of Justice*, which inspired a revival of interest not only in contract theory, including Locke's, but in political philosophy more generally.

Dunn (93), Mabbott (105), and Parry (115) have written the best, short introductions. Parry is the most thorough in addressing the views of others and in consulting the whole of the Lockean corpus. Mack (106) is a more recent effort. He casts Locke as a modern-day libertarian. Among the more comprehensive studies, Ashcraft (88), Dunn (94), and Harris (100) provide close textual analysis of the *Two Treatises* but differ significantly in emphasis. Ashcraft characterizes Locke as a radical for his moral egalitarianism, his investing of a right of revolution in all persons, and a

188   J. T. BOOKMAN

purported openness to an expanded franchise. Dunn finds the foundations of Locke's political philosophy in Calvinist theology. Harris seeks to place that philosophy more securely in the context of the whole body of his work.

Ashcraft and Dunn along with Skinner and Pocock have figured prominently on the contextualist side in the debate about how to discern the meaning of a text. They insist that a theorist cannot be understood outside the cultural context (social, economic, and political) in which he or she wrote. They make a still stronger claim: The cultural context limits the meaning that can be attached to the words of the theorist—no theorist writes for the ages. Ashcraft (118) urges that "we need to think of political theory in terms of its relationship to a *political movement.*" From this perspective, Locke, he maintains, is the ideologue of the Whig Party of late seventeenth-century England. In support of this view, Ashcraft (89) emphasizes the influence of Shaftesbury on the development of Locke's ideas and Locke's participation in Whig opposition to Charles II. Pocock (118) who shares Ashcraft's approach to the interpretation of texts reads the evidence differently and dismisses the idea of Locke as Whig spokesman as a myth. Dunn (94) concludes from his close study of the *Two Treatises* that Locke's thinking is so suffused by his religious beliefs as to be irrelevant in the modern, more secular, world. He more recently allowed (155) that significant elements of Locke's politics like natural rights, consent as the basis of political authority, and religious toleration do not require a religious foundation.

Textualists like Plamenatz (116) and Schochet (188) concede that Locke like other political theorists was a man of his times. They deny, however, that he is only a man of his times. Locke at the start of the *Second Treatise* puts to himself questions that recur perennially in the history of political thought, and he answers them in an abstract way. The cultural context in which Locke wrote informed his answers, but, so textualists claim, it does not affect the validity of his arguments. Locke may have something to teach us once we determine what he is saying. Both Grant (99) and Seliger (119) look to Locke for guidance in responding to the critics of modern liberalism who fault Locke's heirs for a failure to recognize the importance of community and for so limiting the authority of the state that it cannot respond to pressing problems. Simmons (122) emphasizes the "diversity of Locke's arguments" and, *pace* Dunn (94), finds in Locke arguments for rights independent of the theological foundations from which he began. Simmons reads Locke to develop a Lockean theory

THE SECOND TREATISE 189

of rights—"not Locke's own theory, as he presented it, but instead the *best version* of that theory." From the textualist perspective, then, Locke is worth reading for more than historical interest.

Laslett (67) in his 1960 edition of the *Two Treatises* laid out the results of his research on its date of composition. He was able to show that Locke wrote in the circumstances of the Exclusion Crisis and not, as long held, to justify the Glorious Revolution. This much of his thesis is now widely accepted. Laslett's effort, however, to fix more precisely the date and order of composition of the *Two Treatises* became controversial. Against Laslett's claim that Locke began, perhaps largely completed, the *Second Treatise* as early as 1679 and only then decided to write the *First Treatise*, Ashcraft (88, 89) argues for a slightly later date and for a different order of composition. Laslett (67) is unconvinced as his appendix to the 1988 student edition makes clear. Others have waded in on the matter. Wootton (53) sorts through the several claims and the evidence adduced on their behalf in his introduction and propounds a view of his own. No definitive chronology has been established as Milton (176) attests. For some of those who read Locke from the contextualist perspective, the question of just when the *Two Treatises* were written remains something more than a tempest in a teapot.

Property in the sense of material goods looms large in the *Second Treatise*. Day (153), Cohen (151), and Olivecrona (179, 180) provide close analysis of Locke's theory of property. Their essays are a good place to begin. Macpherson (109) provoked controversy by claiming to find the ideological origins of "possessive individualism" in the *Second Treatise*. He argues that Locke removes all moral constraint on the appropriation of property and that he excludes the propertyless from full membership in the community because they are wanting in reason. Both these contentions are subjected to attack by Berlin (147), Gough (98), Hampsher-Monk (161), Hundert (166), Laslett (171), and Ryan (184). The critics are able to show that Macpherson's claims are exaggerated. Most concede, however, that the implications of Locke's words are more far-reaching than what he would seem to have had in mind. Wood (134) is no less concerned than Macpherson about the plight of the powerless and the impoverished. He too places Locke among the apologists for a nascent capitalism, but that capitalism is agrarian rather than commercial. Hughes (164) faults Wood for his characterization of Locke as supporter of a property-based oligarchy.

190   J. T. BOOKMAN

Like Hughes, Tully (129) regards Locke as arguing for a kind of distributive justice: "According to Locke's argument, if men agreed to private property in land it would be purely conventional and it would be justified only if it were a prudential means of bringing about a just distribution of property in accordance with the natural right to the product of one's labour and the three claim rights [to life, liberty, and subsistence]." Hartogh (160), Mackie (174), and Waldron (198), all have a hard time squaring this with the text of the *Two Treatises*. Tully also resurrects an argument first made by Kendall (102) that by consenting to majority rule, the individual permits the government to determine rights. This majoritarian reading would allow the very redistributive policies that Tully believes are implied by Locke's principles. Macpherson (109) also concurs with Kendall's contention, but he seeks to reconcile Locke's majoritarianism with his justification of economic inequality by showing that the propertyless (would-be beneficiaries of redistributive policies) are excluded from political participation.

Assuming that contemporary inequalities—political, economic, and social—are to be preserved in Locke's community, would people consent to the Lockean contract? Cohen (152) and Ryan (184) argue that they would. They agree with many that Locke is conserving of socioeconomic inequalities and of a state dominated by the propertied. Nevertheless, the propertyless, as rational and free persons and with interests to advance, would consent because they too will enjoy benefits from political organization and because the alternatives are worse. Dissent from this view can be found in Ashcraft (89), Hughes (164), Kramer (103), and Tully (129) who reject Cohen's and Ryan's assumptions. They regard Locke as either favoring a significantly enlarged franchise or redistributive justice or both. Some associate Locke with the Levellers. Schochet (188) and Wootton (200) take Ashcraft to task on the first score. He replies (145, 146) to them and others. McNally (175) and Wood (201) maintain that Locke was no radical even by the standards of his day. Hughes (165) presses the radical reading in a reply to Wood.

The influence that Locke may have had on later generations and particularly in the United States is much debated. Hartz (101) makes the largest claims in this regard. He describes Americans as devoted in theory and practice to a Lockean creed. That creed as received includes egalitarianism, natural rights, limited government, and popular representation. Hartz is careful to distinguish the received creed from the ideas of the historic Locke. Indeed, the American attachment to Locke, he says, is

THE *SECOND TREATISE* 191

"irrational." Americans have never read Filmer; they have never heard his name. Lockean ideas have known no opposition in the United States and, consequently, those ideas have been accepted without critical examination, that is, as self-evident. Tarcov (127) also regards Locke as "our [Americans'] political philosopher." This view long dominated American historiography. Wills (132) advances an eccentric dissent in which he accords primary importance to the philosophers of the Scottish Enlightenment and particularly to Francis Hutcheson. Wills has few supporters but many detractors including Hamowy (159). A more formidable challenge to Locke's dominance comes from Pocock (117) who describes an "Atlantic" tradition of "civic republicanism." This tradition, sustained by seventeenth-century English country politicians and pamphleteers, emphasizes popular participation in deliberation about the common good and the importance of civic virtue. Dworetz (95) finds unconvincing both the liberal Lockean and civic republican interpretations on the grounds that their proponents have insufficient command of the classic texts and slight appreciation for how those texts might have been interpreted by American revolutionaries. Furthermore, he accuses the proponents of the civic republican view of severing Locke's liberalism from its theological moorings.

Pangle (114) denies that Locke's political philosophy has any such foundation and rues its influence on the American founders. Pangle's disclosure of the "still partly-hidden implications" of that philosophy reveals that Locke teaches that "there exists no moral law" and that ethical rules are no more than prudential principles for the attainment of happiness, defined as the enjoyment of pleasure and the absence of pain. On Pangle's reading, Locke has "a fundamental lack of piety and reverence." Bluhm (148), Horwitz (62), Kraynack (170), and Zuckert (140, 141) also allege that Locke is hostile to Christianity and to moral law. All these commentators get their inspiration from Strauss (126, 194) who accuses Locke of an elaborate deception aimed at concealing his Hobbesian convictions. Locke's professed belief in God and a duty-based ethics is a fraud. Cox (92) lends his support to the Straussian position. The importance Strauss and his followers attach to their interpretation of Locke can hardly be overstated. They regard Locke's theory as leading to nihilism and totalitarianism. Aarsleff (142), Colman (91), Dunn (154), and Yolton (204) criticize the Straussian approach for its sloppy scholarship and its esoteric reading, which, so Straussians claim, reveals Locke's real intentions. Colman and Yolton argue that passages in *An Essay Concerning Human*

Understanding and in "Essays on the Law of Nature" about the role of pleasure and pain in shaping human conduct are not an expression of a hedonistic ethics but observations about motivation. Simmons (190) rejects any reading that casts Locke as utilitarian because Locke's ethics rest on divine will and both revelation and natural law aim at the preservation of humankind rather than happiness or pleasure.

Controversy over Locke's political philosophy has several sources. In their attempt to fix Locke's place in the history of political thought, scholars have used such terms as "radical," "democrat," and "liberal" in different ways and ended up talking past one another. Locke himself contributed to misunderstanding by arguing in different ways and, thereby, encouraging different interpretations. He often advances, for example, both secular and religious arguments for the same conclusion. In part, too, interpretive approaches have fueled the fire among students of Locke—indeed, among students of the whole of political thought. Marxists, feminists, and Straussians, for example, have different points of view and their studies advance different interpretations.

A SELECT BIBLIOGRAPHY OF WORKS IN ENGLISH

1. Attig, John C., comp. *The Works of John Locke: A Comprehensive Bibliography from the Seventeenth Century to the Present.* Westport, CT: Greenwood Press, 1985.
2. Christophersen, H. O. *A Bibliographical Introduction to the Study of John Locke.* New York: Burt Franklin, 1968 [1930].
3. Eccleshall, Robert and Michael Kenny, comp. *Western Political Thought: A Bibliographical Guide to Post-War Research.* New York: Manchester University Press, 1995.
4. Hall, Roland and Roger Woolhouse, eds. *Eighty Years of Locke Scholarship: A Bibliographical Guide.* Edinburgh: Edinburgh University Press, 1983.
5. Hall, Roland. "Recent Publications on Locke." Locke Studies, vs. 1 – (2001 –).
6. ———. "Recent Publications on Locke." *The Locke Newsletter*, vs. 1–31 (1971–2000).
7. Long, Philip. *A Summary Catalogue of the Lovelace Collection of Papers of John Locke in the Bodleian Library.* Oxford: Oxford University Press, 1959.
8. Yolton, Jean S. and John W. Yolton. *John Locke, A Reference Guide.* Boston: G. K. Hall, 1985.

THE SECOND TREATISE   193

9. Yolton, Jean S. John Locke: *A Descriptive Bibliography*. Dulles, VA: Thoemmes Press, 1998.
10. Zuckert, Michael P. "The Recent Literature on Locke's Political Philosophy." *Political Science Reviewer*, 5 (Fall, 1975).

His Life and Times

11. Appleby, Joyce O. *Economic Thought and Ideology in Seventeenth Century England*. Princeton: Princeton University Press, 1978.
12. Bill, E. G. W. *Education at Christ Church Oxford (1660–1680)*. Oxford: Clarendon Press, 1988.
13. Bourne, H. R. Fox. *The Life of John Locke*. 2 vs. Aalen: Scientia Verlag, 1969 [1876].
14. Clark, J. C. D. *Revolution and Rebellion: State and Society in England in the Seventeenth and Eighteenth Centuries*. Cambridge: Cambridge University Press, 1986.
15. Coffey, John. *Persecution and Toleration in Protestant England 1558–1689*. New York: Longmans, 2000.
16. Cranston, Maurice. *John Locke: A Biography*. London: Longmans, 1957.
17. Daly, James. *Sir Robert Filmer and English Political Thought*. Toronto: University of Toronto Press, 1979.
18. De Beer, Esmond S., ed. *The Correspondence of John Locke*. 8 vs. Oxford: Clarendon Press, 1976–89.
19. Dewhurst, Kenneth. *John Locke (1632–1704), Physician and Philosopher: A Medical Biography*. London: Wellcome Historical Medical Library, 1963.
20. ———. *Thomas Sydenham (1624–1689): His Life and Original Writings*. London: Wellcome Historical Medical Library, 1966.
21. Edwards, John. *Some Thoughts concerning the several causes . . . of atheism . . . . With some Brief Reflections on Socianism: and on . . . the Reasonableness of Christianity, etc.* New York: Garland, 1984 [1695].
22. Goldie, Mark. John Locke: *Selected Correspondence from the Clarendon edition by E. S. De Beer*. New York: Oxford University Press, 2007.
23. ——— and Delphine Soulard, eds. *The Early Lives of John Locke*. Oxford: Clarendon Press, forthcoming.
24. Grell, O. P. et al., eds. *From Persecution to Toleration: The Glorious Revolution and Religion in England*. Oxford: Clarendon Press, 1991.

194   J. T. BOOKMAN

25. Haley, K. H. D. *The First Earl of Shaftesbury*. Oxford: Clarendon Press, 1968.
26. Harrison, J. R. and Peter Laslett. *The Library of John Locke*. 2d ed. Oxford: Clarendon Press, 1971.
27. Hunter, Michael. *Robert Boyle* (1627–91). Woodbridge: Boydell Press, 2000.
28. Kenyon, John P. *Revolution Principles: The Politics of Party, 1689–1720*. Cambridge: Cambridge University Press, 1977.
29. King, Lord Peter. *The Life and Letters of John Locke*. New York: Garland, 1984 [1829].
30. Laslett, Peter, ed. *Patriarcha and Other Political Writings by Sir Robert Filmer*. New York: Garland, 1984 [1949].
31. Lough, John, ed. *Locke's Travels in France, 1675–9*. Cambridge: Cambridge University Press, 1953.
32. Milton, J. R. "Locke at Oxford" in G. A. J. Rogers, ed. *Locke's Philosophy: Context and Content*. Oxford: Clarendon Press, 1994, 29–47.
33. Proast, Jonas. *The Argument of the Letter concerning Toleration*. New York: Garland, 1984 [1690].
34. Shankula, H. A. S., ed. *Journals* 1675–1704. 4 vs. Oxford: Clarendon Press, forthcoming.
35. Sommerville, J. P., ed. *Patriarcha and Other Writings* by Sir Robert Filmer. Cambridge: Cambridge University Press, 1991.
36. Wilson, Charles H. *England's Apprenticeship, 1603–1763*. Rev. ed. London: Longmans, 1985.
37. Woolhouse, Roger. *John Locke: A Biography*. Cambridge: Cambridge University Press, 2006.
38. Wootton, David, ed. *Divine Right and Democracy: An Anthology of Political Writing in Stuart England*. Harmondsworth: Penguin, 1986.
39. Wrightson, Keith. *English Society, 1580–1680*. London: Hutchinson, 1982.

COLLECTED WORKS

40. Aaron, Richard I. and Jocelyn Gibb, eds. *An Early Draft of Locke's Essay, Together with Excerpts from his Journals*. Oxford: Clarendon Press, 1936.
41. Adamson, John W., ed. *The Educational Writings of John Locke*. 2d ed. Cambridge: Cambridge University Press, 1922.

THE SECOND TREATISE   195

42. Anstey, Peter and Lawrence Principe, eds. *Writings on Medicine and Natural Philosophy.* Oxford: Clarendon Press, forthcoming.
43. Axtell, James L., ed. *The Educational Writings of John Locke: A Critical Edition.* London: Cambridge University Press, 1968.
44. Goldie, Mark, ed. *Locke: Political Essays.* Cambridge: Cambridge University Press, 1997.
45. Gough, J. W., ed. *The Second Treatise of Civil Government and A Letter concerning Toleration.* 3d ed. Oxford: Basil Blackwell, 1966.
46. Kelly, Patrick Hyde, ed. *Locke on Money.* 2 vs. Oxford: Clarendon Press, 1991.
47. Milton, J. R. and Philip Milton, eds. *An Essay concerning Toleration and Other Writings on Law and Politics, 1667–1683.* Oxford: Clarendon Press, 2006.
48. Nidditch, Peter H. and G. A. J. Rogers, eds. *Drafts for the Essay concerning Human Understanding and Other Philosophical Writings.* 3 vs. Oxford: Clarendon Press, 1990.
49. Nuovo, Victor, ed. *John Locke: Writings on Religion.* Oxford: Clarendon Press, 2002.
50. Shapiro, Ian, ed. *Two Treatises of Government and a Letter concerning Toleration.* New Haven, CT: Yale University Press, 2003.
51. Sherman, Charles L., ed. *Treatise of Civil Government and A Letter concerning Toleration.* New York: Appleton-Century, 1959.
52. Sigmund, Paul E., ed. *The Selected Political Writings of John Locke: Texts, Background Selections, Sources, Interpretations.* New York: Norton, 2005.
53. Wootton, David, ed. *Political Writings of John Locke.* Harmondsworth: Penguin, 1993.
54. *The Works of John Locke. A New Edition, corrected.* 10 vs. Aalen: Scientia Verlag, 1963 [1823].
55. Yolton, John W., ed. *The Locke Reader: Selections from the Works of John Locke.* New York: Cambridge University Press, 1977.

INDIVIDUAL WORKS

56. *Epistola de Tolerantia: A Letter on Toleration.* Raymond Klibansky and J. W. Gough, eds. Oxford: Clarendon Press, 1968.
57. *An Essay concerning Human Understanding.* John W. Yolton, ed. 2 vs. Rev. Ed. New York: Dutton (Everyman's), 1965.

58. ———. A. C. Fraser, ed., 2 vs. Oxford: Clarendon Press, 1894.
59. ———. Roger Woolhouse, ed. London: Penguin, 1997.
60. ———. Peter H. Nidditch, ed., Oxford: Clarendon Press, 1975.
61. *Essays on the Law of Nature*. W. von Leyden, ed. Oxford: Clarendon Press, 1954.
62. *Questions concerning the Law of Nature*. Robert Horwitz, Jenny Strauss Clay and Diskin Clay, eds. and trans. Ithaca: Cornell University Press, 1990.
63. *A Paraphrase and Notes on the Epistles of St. Paul*. Arthur W. Wainwright, ed. 2 vs. Oxford: Clarendon Press, 1987.
64. *The Reasonableness of Christianity: as delivered in the Scriptures*. John C. Higgins-Biddle, ed. Oxford: Clarendon Press, 1999.
65. *Two Tracts on Government*. Philip Abrams, ed. Cambridge: Cambridge University Press, 1967.
66. ———. Jacqueline Rose and Peter Maxwell-Stuart, eds. Oxford: Clarendon Press, forthcoming.
67. *Two Treatises of Government*. Peter Laslett, ed. Student ed. Cambridge: Cambridge University Press, 1988.
68. *Vindications of the Reasonableness of Christianity*. Victor Nuovo, ed. Oxford: Clarendon Press, 2012.

COMMENTARY: COLLECTIONS

69. Anstey, Peter, ed. *John Locke: Critical Assessments*, II. New York: Routledge, 2006.
70. ———, ed. *The Philosophy of John Locke: New Perspectives*. London: Routledge, 2003.
71. Ashcraft, Richard, ed. *John Locke: Critical Assessments*. 4 vs. London: Routledge, 1991.
72. Brandt, Richard, ed. *John Locke Symposium*, Wolfenbuttel. New York: Walter de Gruyter, 1981.
73. Chappell, Vere, ed. *The Cambridge Companion to Locke*. Cambridge: Cambridge University Press, 1994.
74. ———, ed. *John Locke: Political Philosophy*. New York: Garland, 1992.
75. Dunn, John and Ian Harris, eds. *Locke*. 2 vs. Lyme, NH: Edward Elgar, 1997.
76. Fuller, Gary, Robert Stecke, and John P. Wright, eds. *John Locke: An Essay concerning Human Understanding in Focus*. London: Routledge, 2000.

THE SECOND TREATISE   197

77. Goldie, Mark, ed. *The Reception of Locke's Politics*. 6 vs. London: Pickering & Chatto, 1999.
78. Harpham, Edward S., ed. *John Locke's Two Treatises of Government: New Interpretations*. Lawrence, KS: University of Kansas Press, 1992.
79. Hirschmann, Nancy J. and Kristie M. McClure, eds. *Feminist Interpretations of John Locke*. University Park, PA: Pennsylvania State University Press, 2007.
80. Horton, John and Susan Mendus, eds. *John Locke, a Letter concerning Toleration: In Focus*. London: Routledge, 1991.
81. Martin, Charles B. and D. M. Armstrong, eds. *Locke and Berkeley; a Collection of Critical Essays*. Garden City, NY: Anchor, 1968.
82. Rogers, G. A. J., ed. *Locke's Philosophy: Content and Context*. Oxford: Oxford University Press, 1994.
83. ———, ed. *Locke's Enlightenment: Aspects of the Origin, Nature and Impact of his Philosophy*. Hildesheim: G. Olms, 1998.
84. Savonius-Wroth, S.-J., Paul Schuurman, and Jonathan Walmaley, eds. *The Continuum Companion to Locke*. New York: Continuum, 2010.
85. Schochet, Gordon J., ed. *Life, Liberty and Property: Essays on Locke's Political Ideas*. Belmont, CA: Wadsworth, 1971.
86. Tipton, I. C., ed. *Locke on Human Understanding: Selected Essays*. New York: Oxford University Press, 1977.
87. Yolton, John W., ed. *John Locke: Problems and Perspectives; a Collection of New Essays*. London: Cambridge University Press, 1969.

COMMENTARY: BOOKS

88. Ashcraft, Richard. *Locke's Two Treatises of Government*. Boston: Allen & Unwin, 1987.
89. ———. *Revolutionary Politics and Locke's Two Treatises of Government*. Princeton: Princeton University Press, 1986.
90. Ayers, Michael. *Locke*. 2 vs. London: Routledge, 1991.
91. Colman, John. *John Locke's Moral Philosophy*. Edinburgh: Edinburgh University Press, 1983.
92. Cox, Richard H. *Locke on War and Peace*. Oxford: Clarendon Press, 1960.
93. Dunn, John. *Locke: A Very Short Introduction*. Rev. ed. Oxford: Oxford University Press, 2003,
94. ———. *The Political Thought of John Locke: An Historical Account of the Argument of the "Two Treatises of Government."* Cambridge: Cambridge University Press, 1969.

198   J. T. BOOKMAN

95. Dworetz, Steven. *The Unvarnished Doctrine: Locke, Liberalism and the American Revolution.* Durham: Duke University Press, 1990.
96. Forster, Greg. *John Locke's Politics of Moral Consensus.* New York: Cambridge University Press, 2005.
97. Franklin, Julian H. *John Locke and the Theory of Sovereignty: Mixed Monarchy and the Right of Resistance in the Political Thought of the English Revolution.* Cambridge: Cambridge University Press, 1978.
98. Gough, J. W. *John Locke's Political Philosophy: Eight Studies.* 2d ed. Oxford: Clarendon Press, 1973.
99. Grant, Ruth. *John Locke's Liberalism.* Chicago: University of Chicago Press, 1987.
100. Harris, Ian. *The Mind of John Locke: A Study of Political Theory in Its Intellectual Setting.* Cambridge: Cambridge University Press, 1994.
101. Hartz, Louis. *The Liberal Tradition in America: An Interpretation of American Political Thought Since the Revolution.* New York: Harcourt, Brace, 1955.
102. Kendall, Willmoore. *John Locke and the Doctrine of Majority Rule.* Urbana, IL: University of Illinois Press, 1944.
103. Kramer, Matthew H. *John Locke and the Origins of Private Property: Philosophical Explorations of Individualism, Community, and Equality.* Cambridge: Cambridge University Press, 1997.
104. Lutz, Donald. *The Origins of American Constitutionalism.* Baton Rouge, LA: Louisiana State University Press, 1988.
105. Mabbott, J. D. *John Locke.* London: Macmillan, 1973.
106. Mack, Eric. *John Locke.* New York: Continuum, 2009.
107. Mackie, John L. *Problems from Locke.* Oxford: Clarendon Press, 1976.
108. McClure, Kirstie. *Judging Rights: Lockean Politics and the Limits of Consent.* New York: Cornell University Press, 1996.
109. Macpherson, C. D. *The Political Theory of Possessive Individualism: Hobbes to Locke.* Oxford: Clarendon Press, 1962.
110. Marshall, John. *John Locke, Toleration and Early Enlightenment Culture: Religious Intolerance and Arguments for Religious Toleration in Early Modern and Early Enlightenment Europe.* Cambridge: Cambridge University Press, 2006.
111. ———. *John Locke: Resistance, Religion and Responsibility.* Cambridge: Cambridge University Press, 1994.
112. Murray, John Courtney, S. J. *We Hold These Truths.* New York: Sheed and Ward, 1960.
113. Nyquist, Mary. *Arbitrary Rule: Slavery, Tyranny, and the Power of Life and Death.* Chicago: University of Chicago Press, 2013.

THE SECOND TREATISE   199

114. Pangle, Thomas. *The Spirit of Modern Republicanism: The Moral Vision of the American Founders and the Philosophy of Locke.* Chicago: University of Chicago Press, 1988.
115. Parry, Geraint. *John Locke.* Boston: G. Allen & Unwin, 1978.
116. Plamenatz, John P. *Man and Society: Political and Social Theory: Machiavelli through Marx.* 2 vs. New York: McGraw-Hill, 1963. V: 1, Ch. 6.
117. Pocock, J. G. A. *The Machiavellian Moment: Florentine Political Thought and the Atlantic Republican Tradition.* Princeton, NJ: Princeton University Press, 1975.
118. Pocock, J. G. A. and Richard Ashcraft. *John Locke: Papers Read at a Clark Library Seminar.* Los Angeles, CA: William Andrew Clark Memorial Library, 1980.
119. Seliger, Martin. *The Liberal Politics of John Locke.* New York: Praeger, 1969.
120. Shapiro, Ian. *The Evolution of Rights in Liberal Theory.* Cambridge: Cambridge University Press, 1986.
121. Simmons, A. J. *On the Edge of Anarchy: Locke, Consent, and the Limits of Society.* Princeton: Princeton University Press, 1993.
122. ———. *The Lockean Theory of Rights.* Princeton: Princeton University Press, 1992.
123. Skinner, Quentin. *The Foundations of Modern Political Thought.* 2 vs. Cambridge: Cambridge University Press, 1978.
124. Spellman, W. M. *John Locke and the Problem of Depravity.* Oxford: Oxford University Press, 1988.
125. ———. *John Locke.* New York: St. Martin's, 1997.
126. Leo Strauss. *Natural Right and History.* Chicago: University of Chicago Press, 1953. Ch. V, B.
127. Tarcov, Nathan. *Locke's Education for Liberty.* Chicago: University of Chicago Press, 1984.
128. Tuck, Richard. *Natural Rights Theories: Their Origin and Development.* Cambridge: Cambridge University Press. 1979.
129. Tully, James. *A Discourse on Property: John Locke and His Adversaries.* Cambridge: Cambridge University Press, 1980.
130. ———. *An Approach to Political Philosophy: Locke in Contexts.* Cambridge: Cambridge University Press, 1993.
131. Waldron, Jeremy. *God, Locke, and Equality: Christian Foundations of John Locke's Political Thought.* Cambridge: Cambridge University Press, 2002.
132. Wills, Garry. *Inventing America: Jefferson's Declaration of Independence.* New York: Vintage, Press, 1979.

200   J. T. BOOKMAN

133. Wolin, Sheldon. *Politics and Vision: Continuity and Innovation in Western Political Thought.* Expanded ed. Princeton: Princeton University Press, 2004. Ch. 9.
134. Wood, Neal. *John Locke and Agrarian Capitalism.* Berkeley, CA: University of California Press, 1984.
135. ———. *The Politics of Locke's Philosophy: A Social Study of "An Essay concerning Human Understanding".* Berkeley, CA: University of California Press, 1983.
136. Yolton, John W. *John Locke and Education.* New York: Random House, 1971.
137. ———. *John Locke and the Way of Ideas.* Oxford: Clarendon Press, 1956.
138. ———. *John Locke: An Introduction.* Oxford: Basil Blackwell, 1985.
139. ———. *A Locke Dictionary.* Oxford: Basil Blackwell, 1993.
140. Zuckert, Michael. *Launching Liberalism: On Lockean Political Philosophy.* Lawrence, KS: University Press of Kansas, 2002.
141. ———. *Natural Rights and the New Republicanism.* Princeton: Princeton University Press, 1994.

COMMENTARY: ARTICLES

142. Aarsleff, Hans. "Some Observations on Recent Locke Scholarship" in John W. Yolton, ed. *John Locke: Problems and Perspectives.* Cambridge: Cambridge University Press, 1969, 262–71.
143. Armitage, David. "John Locke, Carolina, and the *Two Treatises of Government.*" *Political Theory,* 32 (Oct., 2004), 602–626 and in Anstey, v. 1, 278.
144. Ashcraft, Richard. "Locke's State of Nature: Historical Fact or Moral Fiction?" *American Political Science Review,* 57 (Sept., 1968), 898–915 and in Ashcraft, v. 3, 212.
145. ———. "The Radical Dimensions of Locke's Political Thought: A Dialogic Essay on Some Problems of Interpretation." *History of Political Thought,* 13 (1992), 703–772.
146. ———. "Simple Objections and Complex Reality: Theorizing Political Radicalism in Seventeenth-Century England." *Political Studies,* 40 (Mar., 1992), 99–115 and in Anstey, v. 1, 153 and Dunn and Harris, v. 2, 553.
147. Berlin, Isaiah. "Hobbes, Locke and Professor Macpherson." *Political Quarterly,* 35 (Oct.- Dec., 1964), 444–68.

148. Bluhm, W. T., N. Wintfeld, and S. Teger. "Locke's Idea of God: Rational Truth or Political Myth?" *Journal of Politics*, 42 (May, 1980), 414–38.

149. Butler, Melissa A. "Early Liberal Roots of Feminism: John Locke and the Attack on Patriarchy." *American Political Science Review*, 72 (Mar., 1978), 135–50.

150. Clark, Lorenne M. G. "Women and John Locke; or, Who Owns the Apples in the Garden of Eden? *Canadian Journal of Philosophy*, 7 (Dec., 1977), 699–724.

151. Cohen, G. A. "Marx and Locke on Land and Labour." *Proceedings of the British Academy*, 71 (1985), 357–88.

152. Cohen, Joshua G. A. "Structure, Choice and Legitimacy: John Locke's Theory of the State." *Philosophy and Public Affairs*, 15 (1986), 301–24 and in Dunn and Harris, v. 2, 139.

153. Day, J. P. "Locke and Property." *Philosophical Quarterly*, 16 (1966), 207–20.

154. Dunn, John. "Justice and the Interpretation of Locke's Political Theory." *Political Studies*, 16 (1968), 68–87 and in Ashcraft, v. 2, 43.

155. ———. "What is Living and What is Dead in the Political Theory of John Locke?" in John Dunn, *Interpreting Political Responsibility: Essays 1981–1989*, Princeton: Princeton University Press, 1990 and in Dunn and Harris, v. 2, 443.

156. Farr, James. "'So Vile and Miserable an Estate': The Problem of Slavery in Locke's Political Thought." *Political Theory*, 14 (May, 1986), 263–89 and in Ashcraft, v. 3, 666.

157. Glausser, Wayne. "Three Approaches to Locke and the Slave Trade." *Journal of the History of Ideas*, 51 (Apr., 1990), 199–216.

158. Goldie, Mark. "John Locke and Anglican Royalism." *Political Studies*, 31 (Mar., 1983), 61–85 and in Ashcraft, v. 1, 151.

159. Hamowy, Ronald. "Jefferson and the Scottish Enlightenment: A Critique of Garry Wills's *Inventing America: Jefferson's Declaration of Independence*." William and Mary Quarterly, 3rd ser., no. 4 (Oct., 1979), 502–523.

160. Hartogh, G. den. "Tully's Locke." *Political Theory*, 18 (1990), 656–72.

161. Hampsher-Monk, Ian W. "The Political Theory of the Levellers: Putney, Property and Professor Macpherson." *Political Studies*, 24 (Dec., 1976), 397–422.

162. Henry, John F. "John Locke, Property Rights, and Economic Theory." *Journal of Economic Issues*, 33 (Sept., 1999), 609–24.

202   J. T. BOOKMAN

163. Hinshelwood, Brad. "The Carolinian Context of John Locke's Theory of Slavery." *Political Theory*, 41 (Aug., 2013), 562–90.
164. Hughes, M. "Locke on Taxation and Suffrage." *History of Political Thought*, 11 (1990), 423–43.
165. ———. "Locke, Taxation, and Reform: A Reply to Wood." *History of Political Thought*, 13 (1992), 691–702.
166. Hundert, E. J. "Market Society and Meaning in Locke's Political Philosophy." *Journal of the History of Philosophy*, 15 (Jan., 1977), 33–44 and in Dunn and Harris, v. 1, 349 and Ashcraft, v. 3, 457.
167. ———. "The Making of Homo Faber: John Locke between Ideology and History." *Journal of the History of Ideas*, 33 (Jan., 1972), 3–22 and in Dunn and Harris, v. 1, 294 and Ashcraft, v.3, 438.
168. Jacob, James R. "Locke's *Two Treatises* and the Revolution of 1688–1689: The State of the Argument." *Annals of Scholarship*, 5 (1987–88), 311–33.
169. Kelly, Patrick Hyde. "All Things Richly to Enjoy: Economics and Politics in Locke's Two Treatises of Government." *Political Studies*, 36 (1988), 273–93 and in Dunn and Harris, v. 2, 215 and Anstey, v. 1, 421.
170. Kraynack, Robert. "John Locke from Absolutism to Toleration." *American Political Science Review*, 74 (Mar., 1980), 53–69.
171. Laslett, Peter. "Market Economy and Political Theory." *Historical Journal*, 7 (Mar., 1964), 150–54.
172. ———. "Introduction" in his *John Locke: Two Treatises of Government*. Student ed. Cambridge: Cambridge University Press, 1988, 3–126.
173. Leyden, Wolfgang von. "John Locke and Natural Law." *Philosophy*, 31 (Jan., 1956), 23–35 and in Ashcraft, v. 2, 3 and Dunn and Harris, v. 1, 115.
174. Mackie, J. L. "Review of James Tully: A Discourse on Property: John Locke and His Adversaries." *Philosophical Quarterly*, 32 (Jan., 1982), 91–94 and in Dunn and Harris, V. 1, 555.
175. McNally, David. "Locke, Levellers and Liberty: Property and Democracy in the Thought of the First Whigs." *History of Political Thought*, 10 (1989), 17–40.
176. Milton, J. R. *"Dating Locke's Second Treatise,"* History of Political Thought, 16 (Aut, 1995), 356–90.
177. ———. "John Locke and the Fundamental Constitutions of Carolina." *Locke Newsletter*, 21 (1990), 111–33 and in Dunn and Harris, v. 2, 463.

178. Monson, Charles H. "Locke and His Interpreters." *Political Studies*, 6 (June, 1958), 120–33 and in Ashcraft, v. 3, 13.
179. Olivecrona, Karl. "Appropriation in the State of Nature: Locke on the Origin of Property." *Journal of the History of Ideas*, 35 (1974), 211–30 and in Ashcraft, v. 3, 308.
180. ———. "Locke's Theory of Appropriation." *Philosophical Quarterly*, 24 (July, 1974), 220–34 and in Ashcraft, v. 3, 327 and Dunn and Harris, v. 1, 334.
181. Parry, G. "Individuality, Politics and the Critique of Paternalism in John Locke." *Political Studies*, 12 (June, 1964), 163–77 and in Ashcraft, v. 3, 27.
182. Pitkin, Hanna Fenichel. "Obligation and Consent." *American Political Science Review*, 59 (Dec., 1965), 39–52.
183. Riley, Patrick. "On Finding an Equilibrium between Consent and Natural Law in Locke's Political Philosophy." *Political Studies*, 22 (Dec., 1974), 432–52 and in Ashcraft, v. 3, 557.
184. Ryan, Alan. "Locke and the Dictatorship of the Bourgeoisie." *Political Studies*, 13 (June, 1965), 219–30 and in Ashcraft, v. 3, 419.
185. Russell, Paul. "Locke on Express and Tacit Consent: Misinterpretations and Inconsistencies." *Political Theory*, 14 (May, 1986), 291–306.
186. Schaar, John H. "John Locke's Liberalism." *American Political Science Review*, 84 (Sept., 1990), 966.
187. Schochet, Gordon J. "The Family and the Origins of the State in Locke's Political Philosophy" in John W. Yolton, ed., *John Locke: Problems and Perspectives*, Cambridge: Cambridge University Press, 1969, 81–98.
188. ———. "Radical Politics and Ashcraft's Treatise on Locke." *Journal of the History of Ideas*, 50 (July, 1989), 491–510 and in Dunn and Harris, v. 2, 375.
189. Shapiro, Ian. "John Locke's Democratic Theory" in Ian Shapiro, ed., *Two Treatises and A Letter Concerning Toleration*, New Haven, CT: Yale University Press, 2003, 309–340.
190. Simmons, A. J. "Locke's State of Nature." *Political Theory*, 17 (Aug., 1989), 449–70 and in Dunn and Harris, v. 2, 417.
191. Skinner, Quentin. "Meaning and Understanding in the History of Ideas" in James Tully, ed. *Meaning and Context: Quentin Skinner and His Critics*, Princeton: Princeton University Press, 1988, 29–67.

204   J. T. BOOKMAN

192. Stanton, T. "Hobbes and Locke on Natural Law and Jesus Christ." *History of Political Thought*, 29 (2008), 65–88.
193. Stoner, James R. "Was Leo Strauss Wrong about John Locke?" *Review of Politics*, 66 (Oct., 2004), 553–63.
194. Strauss, Leo. "Locke's Doctrine of Natural Law." *American Political Science Review*, 52 (June, 1958), 490–502 and in Ashcraft, v. 3, 161 and Dunn and Harris, v. 1, 128.
195. Sevanson, S. G. "The Medieval Foundations of John Locke's Political Thought." *History of Political Thought*, 28 (1997), 399–459.
196. Thompson, Martyn P. "Significant Silences in Locke's *Two Treatises of Government*: Constitutional History, Contract and Law." *Historical Journal*, 31 (1988), 275–94 and in Dunn and Harris, v. 2, 269.
197. Tuckness, Alex. "The Coherence of a Mind: John Locke and the Law of Nature." *Journal of the History of Philosophy*, 37 (Jan., 1999), 73–90.
198. Waldron, Jeremy. "John Locke: Social Contract versus Political Anthropology." *Review of Politics*, 51 (Jan., 1989), 2–28 and in Dunn and Harris, v. 2, 417.
199. ———. "Locke: Toleration and the Rationality of Persecution" in Susan Mendus, ed., *Justifying Toleration: Conceptual and Historical Perspectives*, Cambridge: Cambridge University Press, 1988, 61–86 and in Dunn and Harris, v. 2, 349.
200. ———. "Locke, Tully and the Regulation of Property." *Political Studies*, 32 (Mar., 1984), 98–106.
201. Wood, Ellen M. "Locke against Democracy: Consent, Representation and Suffrage in the *Two Treatises*." *History of Political Thought*, 13 (Wint., 1992), 657–89 and in Dunn and Harris, v. 2, 570.
202. Wootton, David. "John Locke: Socinian or Natural Law Theorist?" in James Crimmens, ed., *Religion, Secularization and Political Thought*, London: Routledge, 1989, 39–67.
203. ——— "John Locke and Richard Ashcraft's *Revolutionary Politics*." *Political Studies*, 40 (Mar., 1992), 79–98 and in Anstey, v. 1, 129.
204. Yolton, John W. "Locke on the Law of Nature." *Philosophical Review*, 67 (Oct., 1958), 477–98 and in Ashcraft, v. 2, 16 and Dunn and Harris, v. 1, 140.

CHAPTER 5

A Critique

The Prince, Leviathan, and the *Second Treatise* are works that mark a significant turning point in thinking about politics. Machiavelli, Hobbes, and Locke ignore the questions that so engaged their ancient and medieval predecessors. They are not concerned with human excellence. They do not make the best way of life a part of their philosophical enterprise. For them, the preservation of life itself is the more pressing problem. If life is to be preserved, people need strong, stable government. And there can be no strong, stable government without the obedience of those subject to it. Thus the problem of political obligation displaces the quest for human excellence: Why is one ever obligated to obey any government? What are the limits, if any, of an obligation to obey? What (or whom) is one obligated to obey? What is the difference between authority—the legitimate exercise of power—and mere coercion? This is not the only respect in which they differ from their predecessors. Contrary to the ancient Greeks, they do not think that the purpose of the state is to promote certain ways of life, wants, or sensibilities. They reject as well the Christian teaching that the state is ordained by God to restrain men from falling into graver sin or, at its best, to act as steward of natural law. For them, the state is a human contrivance created to serve temporal ends, and those ends are the interests and rights of individuals.

In his consideration of the problem of political obligation, Machiavelli takes the view described in the preface to *The Prince* as "high atop the

© The Author(s) 2019
J. T. Bookman, *A Reader's Companion*
to The Prince, Leviathan, *and the* Second Treatise,
https://doi.org/10.1007/978-3-030-02880-0_5

205

mountains," that is, the vantage point of a prince. From this perspective, the problem is an empirical one: How can the citizenry be brought to obey the law? He discounts the efficacy of love and persuasion in securing law-abidingness. A new prince, in particular, in departing from custom must rely on coercion. But no state can preserve itself without the use of force. The interests and recalcitrance of the ruled—rich and poor, the powerful and the weak, the ambitious and the apathetic—constantly tug at the fetters of the law in even settled states. Force and the threat of force can secure the acquiescence of many, particularly among the general citizenry. Acquiescence contributes to the maintenance of domestic order and to keeping a ruler in power. Christianity with its emphasis on salvation, obedience to the powers that be, and humility has a like effect. Machiavelli does recognize that not everyone can be forced to obey and that the Christian teaching is often ignored—in part, he believes, because of the evil example of the Roman Church. Some must obey voluntarily if a ruler is to stay in power.

A prince must cultivate support for his rule by serving interests. The ruled have a common interest in domestic order and external security. Machiavelli does not argue, however, that, if the ruled enjoy peace and order, they ought to obey the law. He does think that the provision of those interests will increase obedience to law. The ruled have other interests that pit one section of the society against another. Where can the prince win the support he needs to realize common interests and to settle disputes over parochial interests? The nobility and other grandees are a possible foundation upon which to build. They, however, pose a challenge to state authority. They regard themselves as the equal of the ruler, and their demands are not easily satisfied. They wish to oppress and dominate the people. The people are more easily satisfied. They demand only respect for their property and women. Compared to the nobility, the favor of the people can be more easily won by satisfaction of their modest demands, and they can more readily be brought to obey by the threat of force.

The people are relatively tractable. But more is necessary than a citizen who abstains from assaulting his neighbor, stealing a chicken at the market, giving underweight to the buyers of his bread, or setting fire to the prince's *palazzo*. Passivity does not permit the pursuit of ends that require the active participation of the citizenry. Nowhere is this more evident than in defending the state against its enemies, foreign and domestic. Something more is needed than coercion and the satisfaction of interests to develop the necessary civic-mindedness. Religion,

A CRITIQUE   207

Machiavelli contends, can inspire fellow-feeling and a willingness to put the interests of the community before one's own. He is full of praise for pagan religion for performing this function. Something like it must be found. Christianity might have functioned in this way, it once did he believes, but it now fosters piety and humility at the expense of secular interests. And, in its institutional form it competes with the state for the loyalty of citizens. Neither Florentines nor Italians generally were about to forsake Christianity for paganism. Christianity, however, is a poor candidate for a civil religion. Its ideals and institutions are international, not national. Its focus is on eternal, not temporal, ends. It is doctrinaire, and doctrinaire religions tend to divide not unify. Hobbes and Locke sought to reduce the divisive force of Christianity by greatly simplifying doctrine. The fundamental tenet of Christianity, they argue, is that Jesus Christ is the messiah. Machiavelli adopts a different course. He attempts to arouse a sense of Italian nationalism but in vain. Elsewhere the development of national feeling contributed to the formation of states better able to elicit the obedience and loyalty of their subjects. And, it should be added, states able to subject the church to their authority.

Machiavelli on the problem of political obligation is not a moralist. He is very much the moralist in considering acts that a prince might have to take to acquire or maintain his rule. There is no obfuscation about what might be necessary, at least in the unsettled politics of sixteenth-century Italy: committing murder, telling lies, taking what is not yours, and so on. These are wrong acts according to a deontological ethics like that set out in the Second Tablet of the Ten Commandments and on the traditional understanding of natural law. Machiavelli acknowledges that such acts are wrong. Were he arguing that the good of the prince justifies violation of these prohibitions, we could dismiss his teaching as childish and harmful—as many have. Childish because no one doubts that in some circumstances such acts can be effective in obtaining or preserving power. It is to state the obvious. Harmful because it eliminates any moral restraint on conduct if one is pursuing political power. This is nihilism and would promote a struggle for power from which all, combatants and non-combatants alike, would suffer. Such a reading has inspired some to conclude that *The Prince* is satire.[1]

---

[1] See, for example, Garrett Mattingly, "Machiavelli's *Prince:* Political Science or Political Satire?" *American Scholar*, 27 (1957–1958), 482–491.

208   J. T. BOOKMAN

There are passages in *The Prince* that suggest another understanding of his position—one worthy of serious reflection. On this understanding, the good is not satisfaction of the prince's desire for power but the provision of external security and domestic order for the community. Strong, stable government is necessary if the community is to enjoy external security and domestic order. In order to institute and maintain such a government, political leaders might have to commit wrong acts. For this reason, Machiavelli asserts the paradoxical principle: It is right to do wrong. Now, had he adopted a consequentialist ethics like utilitarianism that defines the right by reference to the good, he could have avoided paradox. Thus, if he had defined the good as external security and domestic order, then those acts that advance realization of the good are right. He does not proceed in this way. Like most of us, he assumes that generosity, mercy, and honesty are right acts, that those who are generous, merciful, and honest are morally good persons, and that murder, lying, and theft are wrong. The nature of politics, however, will require the commission of wrong acts if external security and domestic order are to be realized. It is these suppositions that create the paradox and lead to his maxim that rulers must learn how to be not good.

One might question Machiavelli's implicit assumption that political actors are often incapacitated by a deontological ethics. This is not to impugn the character of politicians in general. It is to say that politicians are disposed to put aside, as they sometimes must, the prohibitions and prescriptions of such an ethics in order to pursue many desirable ends. One might also doubt his contention that the domestic order and external security concomitant with princely power and reputation are desirable. It may be that no prince can be powerful and highly esteemed unless his state has domestic order and external security, but domestic order and external security can take pernicious form. Nevertheless, Machiavelli is on to something important. The moral dilemma that confronted his sixteenth-century prince confronts all political actors.

In order to realize the ends that politics serves, many—often innocent of any wrongdoing—must be made to suffer. Political actors have undertaken grand projects like national independence, national unification, and the institution of democratic government. They have pursued those ends at the cost of many lives and, incidentally, by jeopardizing external security and disrupting domestic order. A failure to act by the champions of such ends might have had consequences even more harmful to the lives and liberties of those living under the existing circumstances. Had Lincoln failed to respond to Southern secession with force, more generations of black Americans would have lived in slavery. Lincoln knew well the probable consequences of his decision. Had the leaders of the civil rights movement not taken to the streets and, thereby, provoked the violence of white supremacists in the police and the public, segregation would have remained in place. Martin Luther King anticipated that lives would be lost, including his own. Whenever political actors contemplate action that will imperil life, we can only hope that their moral sensibilities, including an aversion to the taking of life, inspire long and sober reflection about the possible consequences. Such reflection ought not to be confined to actions that imperil life. All politics involves choice among alternatives, including doing nothing, that will affect the lives, liberties, and livelihoods of many. The alternative chosen will enlarge opportunities and resources for some and reduce opportunities and resources for others to pursue their goals. Environmental regulations adopted to improve air and water quality and to combat climate change hasten the demise of the coal industry in Appalachia. Coal miners lose their jobs. Many of them cannot readily be trained for jobs in the private sector in the communities where they live. Alternative employment when it is provided, public service jobs, for example, might not pay so well. Those who cannot find jobs and become wards of the state experience a loss of dignity. Against those undesirable consequences must be weighed the baleful effects of polluted air and water and the potentially disastrous effects of climate change.

The moral dilemma that attends all political action is central to Machiavelli's larger view of the political. In that view, violence is a defining characteristic of politics. Force and the threat of force are necessary to realize the ends for which the state exists. In the pursuit of those ends, consequences are the measure of right. The motives of the politically ambitious are irrelevant. We can assume that there are no selfless persons among them, and that in some, the desire for power, reputation, and gain is greater than in others. And, the ruled cannot know the motives of their rulers. Rulers attempt to deceive the ruled about their motives, and, as students of Freud, we assume that rulers deceive themselves to some extent. It is to the consequences of action that we must look in evaluating the performance of rulers. Furthermore, it is not enough that rulers intend the good; they must realize it. Perfection, of course, is not to be had. The availability of resources and opportunities imposes limits on what even the most competent, well-intentioned actors can accomplish. And, there are always unintended consequences. As democrats, we insist that the ruled ought to decide in popular elections whether rulers have satisfied popular standards. *The Prince* allows no such accountability. The *Discourses* prescribes some, albeit limited, accountability of rulers to ruled.

Machiavelli contributes much to a depiction of the political terrain. His rendering of some landmarks, however, is opaque, and he omits other features altogether. Domestic order and external security are important public goods. A strong, stable government is a necessary condition for their realization. Neither anarchy nor subjection to a foreign power has much appeal to anyone. Taking up a position described in his preface as "low on the plain," we may concede all this and still insist that domestic order is not the unqualified good that Machiavelli assumes. These regimes have provided domestic order: the police state of communist East Germany, the segregated society of post-Reconstruction America, and Saudi Arabia under Sharia law. Historical circumstances, of course, reduce the range of possibilities open to any people. Nevertheless, the domestic order enforced by some regimes deserves condemnation, not approbation. The same can be said of external security. Ancient Sparta instituted a warfare state in pursuit of external security, Machiavelli's Florence commanded tribute from its less powerful neighbors, and imperial Japan ravaged East Asia. Any regime that adopts such policies corrupts its own people and destroys the lives and livelihoods of many. External security can be acquired at less cost.

Machiavelli's conception of the public good is confined to domestic order and external security. These are goods from which all might benefit and most obviously the prince. He recognizes that economic inequality is a major source of conflict, but he recommends no policies to reduce the gap between rich and poor or to ameliorate the suffering of the poor. The prince, he advises, must handle the rich and poor differently. Welfare in many of its forms—food, shelter, health, and education—has no place on his governmental agenda. Yet from the point of view of a prince, the provision of welfare could win the support of his subjects and create stronger, healthier recruits for a citizen army. This is not to fault Machiavelli because he is not a New Deal Democrat. Governments have long provided welfare in one form or another. The Roman republic in 123 BC under the Gracchi began monthly distribution of grain at subsidized prices to the poor. This program before long gave away grain to those satisfying a means test. Public health measures like removal of the dead, the disposal of waste, and the supply of water were common government services. The city council of Siena maintained a famous hospital for pilgrims and the poor, *Santa*

A CRITIQUE   211

Maria della Scala, first established in the eleventh century. Government also provided food and shelter to widows and orphans in many states. The Florentine republic established the university, the *Studium Generale*, in 1321. The universities at Padua and Bologna were instituted even earlier. Welfare is not a modern idea. For someone who places interests in the foreground, their pursuit and realization and resolution of conflicts over interests, the omission of welfare leaves a large hole. It might be objected that safety is a part of welfare and that without safety the enjoyment of other aspects of welfare is uncertain and fleeting. Machiavelli's focus, then, on domestic order and external security to the exclusion of other aspects of welfare comprehends the really important features of political life. From this perspective, the pursuit of power overshadows everything else. He does encourage us to see politics in this way in his observation that the prince "must have no other object or thought, nor take any thing as his art save warfare and its institutions and training."[2] If that is all the prince knows, he will neglect that which order and security permit, namely, the pursuit of justice.

Machiavelli excuses the commission of wrong acts when necessary to secure domestic order and external security. What constitutes a threat to domestic order or external security? How imminent and grave must a threat be to excuse wrong acts? *The Prince* has little to offer in response to these questions. Machiavelli grants to his authoritarian prince unlimited discretion in his pursuit of domestic order and external security. He advises only that cruelty be well used. This license permits the very abuses that earned for him his evil reputation. Political actors have long invoked threats to domestic order and external security, real and purported, to justify the suppression of their opponents and the imposition of a repressive regime upon all. No one doubts that domestic order and external security can be of great benefit. When they are realized (it is always a matter of more or less) under a regime that respects life and liberty, they are among the conditions that permit people to go about their lives as they see fit. Machiavelli admires people who strive to live after their own lights, who are assertive and independent, but it was his successors who advanced the concept of individual rights to protect assertion and independence and to provide a criterion for the evaluation of political action.

---

[2] *The Prince*, William J. Connell, ed. and trans. (Boston: Bedford/St. Martin's, 2005), 84 (Ch. 14).

212   J. T. BOOKMAN

Hobbes and Locke did not create the concept of rights. They did think of rights in ways significantly different from their Roman and medieval predecessors. They claim that human beings have equally at least some rights as individuals and not as possessors of a certain status, a peer of the realm, say, or as members of a corporate community like a guild or university, or as a citizen, a Roman, for example. Unlike these customary or legal rights, their "natural" rights inhere in the individual; they are not the creation of society or government. Hobbes's right is grounded in nature. God bestows Lockean rights.

Hobbes's right of nature is a right to preserve oneself by whatever means one believes necessary including first-strike violence on the merest suspicion that another is one's enemy. This is much more than a right of self-defense. It imposes no correlative duty on others to not impede exercise of the right. It is not a moral concept. It prescribes no rule whose observance deserves approbation and whose violation deserves condemnation. It prescribes no rule that, if observed, orders social relations in ways that protect life, liberty, and property. On the contrary, given the "natural inclinations" of mankind as Hobbes sees them, namely, unremitting desire for power, reputation, and gain, exercise of the right of nature in the absence of government greatly reduces the prospects for everyone to enjoy life, liberty, and property. Part of the right of nature can be alienated—the right to use pre-emptive violence. One can never alienate the right to defend oneself. The right to use pre-emptive violence must be alienated if there is to be peace and if people are to enjoy the considerable benefits of civil society. Motivated by fear and counseled by reason which suggests the laws of nature, men and women consent to the contract creating civil society including government. Parenthetically, "civil society" is today often used to name non-governmental organizations to distinguish them from governmental agencies. These non-governmental organizations do not, in common usage, include families, friendship groups, work colleagues, or fellow-parishioners for example. I use the term "civil society," as Hobbes and Locke did, to comprehend all the groups above and government.

Once civil society is established, government creates all rights whose violation is unjust. Thus government does no injustice in ignoring the right of nature when it enforces the law. It may impose fines, imprisonment, and even death in its pursuit of order and security. A citizen's claim to protection by government in how he or she lives is confined to that liberty afforded by the silence of the law. Hobbes's lawgiver is not silent about fundamental matters. With respect to religion, it requires observance of a common doctrine and ritual. People do not have a right to practice religion

A CRITIQUE   213

of their own choosing. Government also determines the conditions upon which property is held. A citizen's right to property runs against his fellows but not against government. Hobbes's conception of rights, then, provides no basis for the evaluation of government on moral grounds. It is not a criterion for determining legitimacy. It does provide a test of the effectiveness of government. One is relieved of the obligation to obey if government is unable to provide any greater protection than might be had in the absence of government. That judgment is an exercise of the right of nature.

The right of nature subverts the power of the sovereign. The authority of the sovereign is, of course, unlimited, and the sovereign can do no injustice. Furthermore, the right of nature provides no basis for a claim against the sovereign. The sovereign, in addition to authority, also requires power to realize the ends for which civil society is instituted. That power must come from the willing obedience of the citizenry. Citizens must join the *posse comitatus* when called upon to do so. They must participate in the execution of the law in other ways as well: reporting offenses, giving testimony, and serving on juries. They must enlist in the armed forces and stay on the battlefield as necessary to protect the nation's borders. They are obligated to do these things; they have consented to the social contract. The right of nature, however, gives great discretion to the individual to decide how best to preserve life. It is in the long-term interests of everyone to support the government in its enforcement of the law against everyone else. Nevertheless, it strains credulity to think that Hobbesian men and women motivated by a desire for power, reputation, and gain or, probably more frequently, seized by fear would jeopardize their lives by joining the *posse comitatus* or the armed forces.

Locke's conception of rights is, at first blush, more promising than that of Hobbes. It identifies rules that could order human interactions in ways that protect life, liberty, and property. Everyone, Locke claims, has by nature an equal right to dispose of oneself and one's possessions as one sees fit. In the exercise of this right, one must observe the law of nature which commands that one preserve oneself and, if it is not too dangerous, preserve the rest of mankind. The law of nature is an expression of God's will and obligatory for that reason. The duty it imposes requires not only that one not impede another in exercise of his rights but that one come to another's assistance if a third party seeks to impede an exercise of rights. Locke's rights have correlative duties.[3]

---

[3] W. N. Hohfeld, *Fundamental Legal Conceptions* (Westport, Ct: Greenwood Press, 1978 [1919]), 35–64, provides a succinct analysis of rights.

214   J. T. BOOKMAN

Locke's natural right to dispose of oneself and one's possessions as one sees fit is a generalized right to freedom. Its usefulness as a criterion for the evaluation of conduct suffers for that very reason. Particular rights to play the mandolin, drink beer, and ride a horse are no doubt worth having. Threats to other particular rights are far more likely and, therefore, are more in need of protection. Many have thought specification of these rights to be desirable and necessary. Americans of the founding generation, suspicious of a remote national government, demanded a bill of rights specifying the freedoms of speech, press, and assembly, the free exercise of religion, a right to due process of law, and so on. The French followed a similar course a few years later and, more recently, constituent bodies the world over have done the same.[4] Where such lists of rights have the support of the politically active, they have proved to be effective devices for the protection of life, liberty, and property. Locke himself in *A Letter Concerning Toleration* singles out the free exercise of religion as in need of protection. The Clarendon Code imposed criminal penalties on the practice of religion by non-Anglicans. He accords the greatest importance among all rights to the free exercise of religion, because salvation of one's soul ought to be one's principal care and one must find one's own way to salvation. He is concerned not at all with what Americans call "establishment of religion." He also regards the right to private property as sufficiently important and threatened to mount a defense against its opponents. Apart from these two particular rights, Lockean natural rights are indeterminate.

Even a more detailed list of rights than Locke specifies would leave unaddressed the problem of limitations. All rights are necessarily limited. An exercise of speech can slander another's reputation. Even a peaceful assembly of citizens can infringe the property rights of a farmer. Property rights themselves can often conflict: A farmer applies pesticide to his crop. A breeze carries the pesticide onto his neighbor's bee hives causing the death of the colonies. A limb of the neighbor's apple tree hangs over my driveway. Falling apples damage the roof of my car. Lines must be drawn between competing claims to rights.

Conflicts between an individual right and the common good must also be resolved. Such conflict occurs in starkest form when government

---

[4] Richard Dagger, "Rights" in Terence Ball, J. Farr, and R. L. Hanson, eds., *Political Innovation and Conceptual Change* (Cambridge: Cambridge University Press, 1989), 292–308, traces the development of the concept of rights.

A CRITIQUE   215

conscripts an armed force for defense of the country. It occurs as well when government takes property in the form of taxes to pay for public projects. The Lockean limit on the exercise of the individual right to freedom is given by the law of nature which requires preservation of oneself and preservation of the rest of humankind. He tells us little about the implications of this law. It forbids suicide, it requires that assistance be given to those whose rights are threatened, and, we are told in the *First Treatise*, it requires that the propertied give enough of their excess to preserve the lives of the needy.[5] Beyond this, Locke leaves to government the task of drawing lines between competing claims to rights and between an individual right and the common good. Indeed, given the general nature of the individual right to freedom, government must also, except for a right to private property and a right to free exercise of religion, specify all other rights. The natural right to freedom is subject to the "inconveniences" of the state of nature. A government of limited authority is the remedy for those inconveniences. It can protect the individual against interference by other individuals. Government is, of course, incomparably more powerful than the individuals who are subject to it. And government might deny (they often have denied) freedom.

Locke's measures for mitigating the threat to freedom from government are inadequate. We need first take notice that the criterion for evaluating conduct undergoes significant change. Before the institution of government the law of nature commands everyone to preserve himself and to preserve the rest of mankind when his own is not in competition.[6] After the institution of government, that law—an "Eternal Rule to all Men, *Legislators* as well as others"—acquires new meaning.[7] Locke now understands the law of nature to command "*the preservation of the society*, and (as far as will consist with the publick good) of every person in it."[8] In this revised version, the public good supplants respect for individual rights as the criterion for evaluating conduct and, more particularly, governmental conduct. The exercise of individual rights might promote the public good on this criterion, but the burden of showing that to be so falls upon the individual. And, it would seem, such a showing would have to be

[5] *First Treatise*, §42.
[6] *Second Treatise*, §6.
[7] *Ibid.*, §135.
[8] *Ibid.*, §134.

216   J. T. BOOKMAN

made upon each exercise of an individual right were the holder of the right to be challenged. The recognition and institution of rights is intended to obviate such a showing. If certain conduct is recognized as a right, then it is assumed to be in the public good.[9] The freedoms of speech, press, and assembly, for example, promote the discovery of truth—a public good. Freedom of religion, free exercise and establishment, much reduces sectarian conflict—a public good. Locke's revised law of nature makes these assumptions problematic.

The public good is the criterion by which the conduct of government ought to be evaluated. In what does the public good consist? Do individual rights like rights of political participation, equal protection of the law, and a right to a fair trial, among others, promote the public good? He is indefinite about this. A government that observes his revised law of nature can be expected to emphasize utility and to be illiberal in its specification of individual rights and in its resolution of conflicts between a right and the public good. Locke himself denies free exercise of religion to Catholics and atheists on the grounds that they threaten the public good.

Locke fails to devise institutions that could support the exercise of rights. Let us assume along with Locke that the people believe that the individual ought to be able to conduct himself or herself in certain ways that deserve protection against other individuals and against the government, that is, the individual has rights. According to Locke, it is in order to secure rights against their infringement by other individuals that government is instituted. How is the performance of government in this regard to be evaluated and by whom? Government itself can infringe rights. How is the conduct of government to be controlled? Locke does insist that the legitimate exercise of governmental power is limited, its authority extending no further than the public good and that the people are the ultimate judge of governmental conduct. He also expresses a preference for representative assemblies and the separation of executive and legislative authority. Neither of these preferences, however, appears among his criteria of legitimate government. Nor does he recognize the suffrage as an individual right. The right to vote is a consequence of a collective decision. It is not a natural right; it can be held only in civil society and civil society may deny that right with one exception. Legitimate governments—

---

[9] David Braybrooke, *Three Tests for Democracy* (New York: Random House, 1968), 38–43, on this point.

Locke counts hereditary monarchy among them—need not be electorally accountable to the people for their exercise of power. Locke is not a democrat. He is a majoritarian with respect to two important decisions. The majority should prevail in that group which, in a constituent capacity, determines the form of government, and it should prevail among those people who must consent to taxation. He distinguishes between those who consent expressly to civil society—typically by possession of landed property—and those who consent tacitly. Both groups are obligated to obey but obligated only if government observes the law of nature. The significance of the distinction between tacit and express consent for people as participants in the constituent assembly or in consenting to taxation is unclear. Locke does regard only those who give express consent as members of the community. Those who give tacit consent are non-members as are foreign travelers. This suggests that the group whose majority must consent to taxation is a minority of the general populace.

The *Second Treatise* does not explore the possible use of consent to taxation to encourage government to respect and protect individual rights. For Locke, consent to taxation is necessary because the imposition of taxes would be to use force without right. A hereditary monarch, consistent with this requirement, could hold a referendum on the matter. In order for consent to taxation to be used to hold government accountable on rights would require institutions that provide access to information about governmental conduct, permit the expression of popular views about rights and the organization of groups to aggregate those views, and provide for popular election of decision-making bodies. Locke does not insist on such institutions. Instead, he relies on a right to revolt to keep the government within the bounds of the law of nature. As Locke acknowledges, such a costly, hazardous enterprise will be undertaken only upon persistent and severe deprivation of rights suffered by many.

Locke gives special emphasis in his theory to the right to private property. He includes that right among the natural rights that inhere in the individual. A person acquires a right to a particular thing to use as he or she thinks fit by expending labor. God gave the world in common to humankind, but by picking apples from a tree or netting fish from the sea, for example, a person may appropriate things. Land, too, can be taken out of the common by the investment of labor. You dig out the rocks, clear the brambles, till the field, and erect a fence; the land is yours. There are limits on what may be acquired in this way. First, there must be enough and as good left for others, and, secondly, there must be no spoilage or waste.

218   J. T. BOOKMAN

Private property acquired in this way and within those limits, Locke argues, would provoke little conflict. Domestic peace would still be disturbed by some who violate the law of nature. And, in discharging their duty to enforce the law of nature, people would, with partiality, interpret the law, judge their own cases, and enforce the law. Furthermore, enforcement would be uncertain. These are the circumstances that Locke calls the "inconveniences" of the state of nature and for which government is the remedy. Government is a condition for freedom. It can far more effectively (and equitably) protect people in the exercise of their rights than they as individuals can protect themselves. Government, however, is a "lion" incomparably more powerful than the "polecats" and "foxes" who would disturb the peace in the state of nature. It poses a great threat to freedom, and its authority must, therefore, be limited.

This model of civil society proved to be immensely attractive to many Americans.[10] Many in the revolutionary generation saw it as applicable to their own society. Among those Americans was Thomas Jefferson, who found in the *Second Treatise* a prescription for freedom. Although neither a necessary nor sufficient condition for freedom, economic independence certainly supports freedom. Self-sufficient farmers, not dependent on the will of any other person, would be free to exercise their rights if government were limited to the punishment of force and fraud and if government itself respected rights.[11] Jefferson regarded the Louisiana Purchase as creating an opportunity to perpetuate a society that already had a substantial number of self-sufficient farmers. He proposed to secure the people against government misconduct by specifying rights and by making government closely accountable to the people by means of frequent elections, short terms for office-holders, and separation of powers and checks and balances.[12]

Unlike Jefferson, Locke does not insist, as we have seen, on the electoral accountability of government to the people. Although, like Jefferson, he advocates a limited government, the limitations that he imposes are so vague as to permit government broad discretion. He also makes a heedless

[10] *Ibid.*, 48–58, reconstructs the "simplified version" of Locke's doctrine of private property to which I refer here.

[11] For his agrarianism, see Query XIX in "Notes on the State of Virginia" and pp. 574–575 in Adrienne Koch and William Peden, eds., *The Life and Selected Writings of Thomas Jefferson* (New York: Modern Library, 1944).

[12] *Ibid.*, the "First Inaugural," 321–325.

A CRITIQUE 219

move from a society in which there are no significant economic inequalities to a society in which all the land is appropriated. Most become dependent on others for the opportunity to earn a livelihood. Locke explains this development as a consequence of the adoption of money—to which all have consented. This removes the limits on appropriation. He ignores the implications of this development for those who do not own wealth-producing property. He persists in seeing government as the only agent in civil society that threatens freedom—apart from the "polecats" and "foxes." Only government can lawfully use force, but there are other sanctions available to non-governmental agents. Those who own wealth-producing property decide who is to be hired, fired, and promoted and what are to be the conditions of work, that is, who, and under what conditions, is to have the opportunity to acquire the necessities of life. This dependence creates vulnerability to which the self-sufficient farmer is not exposed.

Left out of all this is the matter of who is to enjoy rights, who ought to be free in civil society. Slaves are absent from Jefferson's agrarian theory. Unlike Locke, he does not attempt to justify black slavery. He is well aware how ill black slavery comports with his ideas about human equality and freedom. His theory demands abolition and the distribution of home-steads to freed slaves. Neither takes much notice of women. In principle, their "man" and "men" comprehend men and women alike. It takes more than lexicographical inclusion to extend Lockean or Jeffersonian rights to women. The people who live in Lockean society and in Jefferson's society of self-sufficient farmers live in households dominated by men who are, Locke says, "abler and stronger."[13] Until women acquired political rights and economic independence, their freedom was contingent on the sufferance of husbands. More generally, neither Hobbes nor Locke (or, for that matter, Machiavelli) is much concerned with justice. The problem of political obligation crowds out in their thinking questions about the just distribution of goods, including individual rights, in civil society.

Like Machiavelli, Hobbes and Locke see that government rests on opinion—the opinions of the ruled about the performance of government and about its legitimacy. No government is strong enough to compel obedience from all its subjects. Not all opinions are equal, of course, in determining the stability of government. The opinions of the politically active

---

[13] *Second Treatise*, §82. 14.

and of those who command resources count for more than those of the weak and apathetic. However great the inequalities in these regards, many must obey voluntarily if the state is to be able to provide order and security and the other benefits of civil society. Hobbes and Locke introduce the idea of the state of nature in part to reveal in sharp contrast the benefits of civil society. In the absence of the restraints of civil society, men and women would be, they believe, fearful and suspicious of their fellows and even more selfish and ruthless than they are when restrained by law and custom. As a consequence, in Hobbes's famous aphorism, life would be "poor, solitary, nasty, brutish, and short." Locke's state of nature, after the introduction of money, would also often be a state of war.

The state of nature serves another function in their theories. It reveals the existence and nature of natural rights. In the absence of civil society, Hobbes contends, everyone must decide for himself or herself how best to advance his or her interests and, more particularly, how best to preserve his or her life. It is a natural right. This right is held by individuals among whom there are no significant inequalities in strength or intellect by which to preserve their lives. Locke's state of nature defines a moral situation. God has bestowed on no one person or group of persons authority to rule over others. On God's authority people are subject to the law of nature which commands that one preserve oneself and the rest of humankind. Within those limits, people are free to live as they see fit. It is their natural right. The circumstances of the state of nature require that people consent to civil society. For Hobbes, the requirement is a physical necessity. There is no one strong or clever enough to compel obedience. Therefore, people must consent to obey. For Locke, the requirement is moral. People have a natural right to dispose of themselves and their possessions as they see fit within the bounds of the law of nature. Government can acquire authority in no other way than by the consent of the people.

On this understanding, civil society is a voluntary association. It is not. Their conception of the individual shorn of all ties to others and indistinguishable by race, ethnicity, language, religion, and gender, among many other things, defies experience. At birth we become members unwittingly of a civil society and subject to the authority of our parents and ultimately that of the government. Our very lives depend on the protection and nurture provided by our parents in infancy and childhood. The character of our parents and those with whom we associate in friendship, educational, religious, and work groups shapes our moral and intellectual development. It is as members of those groups that we learn restraint, if we learn

A CRITIQUE 221

it at all and even if it is only the restraint of prudence. It is there that we learn that others have wants and aspirations of their own that must be taken into account. We may even learn to sympathize with others in their efforts to make their way in the world. The culture of our parents and those with whom we associate shapes our very identity. Someone who speaks French, drinks pastis, programs computers, cheers on a soccer team, wears Versace, and reads Camus has learned from others those capacities and tastes. These qualities, of course, do not uniquely describe any one person. A great deal of elaboration would be necessary to do that. Those qualities do distinguish perhaps hundreds from the billions of others in the world. Many of the distinguishing qualities in a more complete description would also be effects of cultural socialization. It is only as an adult that consent figures in any significant way in social relations. Far before the age of consent has the largely unformed infant been transformed into an individual. Human beings are social through and through. Aristotle was right in characterizing man as a "political animal."

The influence of the state on these socializing groups varies greatly from regime to regime. Totalitarian regimes seek to control groups in every way. Those it cannot bring under its thumb, it prohibits. In the absence of a widely shared conception of the best way of life, governments in liberal democracies permit a profusion of groups that express the many interests present in a modern society. Their influence over these groups is far less than in totalitarian regimes, but it is not negligible. In the United States, the most liberal of all, parents must see that their children receive an education. Government establishes the curriculum wholly in the case of public schools and in large part for sectarian and charter schools and for the homeschooled. Government now supports inter-racial and gay marriage. It forbids polygamy and forced marriage. With few and limited exceptions, government denies the use of force to non-governmental groups including religious groups. It also prohibits employers from discriminating on the basis of race or gender. Socrates characterized the *polis* as a parent. Liberal democracies are permissive parents, but like Athens, and for the same reason, they are owed obedience by their citizens.

Hobbes and Locke regard consent as necessary to create an obligation to obey. No one, however, consents to the institution of civil society. Locke dismisses this objection as insignificant.[14] People can leave the jurisdiction of a government and join with others in the institution of another

---

[14] *Ibid.*, §100–101.

222   J. T. BOOKMAN

civil society elsewhere. The state of nature gets lost in this response. It is only as the state of nature exists as an alternative that an individual could decide to join or not join civil society. Furthermore, relatively few consent to a particular regime. Among them are public officials, members of the armed services, and naturalized citizens; they take oaths of obedience. Locke mentions only property-holders as expressly consenting to government. All others tacitly consent. His definition of tacit consent is so broad that only revolution would expose the absence of consent to a government. In Hobbes's view, people consent even when their consent is exacted by the conqueror's sword. In both theories, almost everyone consents tacitly, and consent is given unknowingly. Hobbes robs consent of its obligatory character by approving consent under duress. Locke trivializes consent by defining it so broadly as to include traveling on the highway. There is little novelty in this criticism. David Hume made much of it many years ago.[15] Despite the difficulties in their theories, Hobbes and Locke contributed much to a conception of humankind and of the human condition that has currency even today: individualism, the serving of interests and the protection of rights as the ends of politics, the state as necessary constraint on human desire, and the fragility of civil society manifest in the state of nature.

How then do people acquire an obligation to obey and what does distinguish legitimate from illegitimate government? What follows is more of a sketch of an answer than the well-developed theory the questions deserve. It begs important questions, among them the nature of justice—understood as the right ordering of civil society. This is a book about Machiavelli, Hobbes, and Locke, however, and not about my understanding of these matters. Nevertheless, I owe them at least that much after taking them to task in these last pages.

People acquire an obligation to obey government because they are beneficiaries of public goods. Fortunate are those who are born in a civil society whose government provides domestic order, external security, and welfare. They are beneficiaries of goods that number among the conditions for the development of one's talents and the pursuit of one's interests. Still more fortunate are those who reside in a civil society whose government also respects individual rights. They are beneficiaries of goods

---

[15] "Of the Original Contract" in Knud Kaakonssen, ed., *Hume: Political Essays* (Cambridge: Cambridge University Press, 1994), 186–201.

A CRITIQUE 223

that number among the conditions for the development of one's talents and for the pursuit of one's interests. The most fortunate of all are those who enjoy in addition the right to participate in politics.

The obligation that people acquire as beneficiaries of public goods is a *prima facie* obligation that can be disregarded in the face of manifest injustice. No one was obligated to obey the Nazi law that required the reporting of Jews in hiding or the antebellum American law that required the return of runaway slaves. We are children of civil society, but civil society teaches several lessons. The Germans and Americans who disobeyed those laws acted to preserve life and liberty and in defiance of governments that excluded from participation substantial parts of their populations and, in Nazi Germany, coerced participation from others. Black slaves and European Jews to whom all public goods were denied had no obligation to obey. The obligation to obey is greatest under governments that provide opportunity for all their subjects to right injustices within the law. This is the criterion of legitimacy.

Legitimate government has a greater claim on the obedience of its citizens than illegitimate government. Legitimacy does not define a dichotomous classification but a continuum ranging at one end from regimes that deny any opportunity to their citizens to influence policy to, at the other end, regimes that respect, protect, and promote all those participant rights definitive of democracy.[16] On this continuum, autocracy exemplifies the regime that confines policy-making to a one or a few, and direct democracy exemplifies the regime in which all participate in making policy. Today's representative democracies occupy places (they are different places) at the "afford greater opportunity for righting injustice" end of the continuum. The more legitimate the regime, the greater the burden of justification for disobedience and the stronger the prohibition on violence. No regime, however, even the most democratic, can ensure that no one will suffer injustice. Political obligation, therefore, even under legitimate regimes, is not absolute, although it ought to take the form of civil disobedience.

Under regimes in which channels for making change are few or absent altogether, the obligation to obey is less exacting. Confronted by injustices persistent and profound, people may revolt. Such a course ought to

---

[16] See Robert A. Dahl, *Democracy and Its Critics* (New Haven: Yale University Press, 1989), Ch. 8.

be undertaken only with circumspection. How widely shared is the view that the government is unjust? How hostile is the government to reform? How likely is the revolution to be successful, not only in overthrowing the existing regime but in instituting a better one? How costly in shattered lives will the revolution be? Hard questions to answer, particularly under non-democratic governments, but worthy of consideration nevertheless. These questions remind us again of the moral dilemma that attends political action.[17]

[17] These questions are demanded by the "ethic of responsibility" advocated by Max Weber in his "Politics as a Vocation" in *From Max Weber: Essays in Sociology*, H. H. Gerth and C. Wright Mills, eds. (New York: Oxford University Press, 1958 [1946]), 117–128.